M000316067

*Welcome to Capitol Hill*

# Welcome to Capitol Hill

## 50 YEARS OF SCANDAL
★ ★ ★ IN ★ ★ ★
## TENNESSEE POLITICS

**Joel Ebert and Erik Schelzig**

Vanderbilt University Press

Nashville, Tennessee

Copyright 2023 by Joel Ebert and Erik Schelzig
Published 2023 by Vanderbilt University Press
All rights reserved
First printing 2023

Photographs not otherwise credited are by Erik Schelzig.

Cover images: Gov. Ray Blanton (Bob Ray, *Nashville Banner*, image courtesy of Nashville Public Library, Special Collections); Tom Hensley (Dean Dixon, *Nashville Banner*, image courtesy of Nashville Public Library, Special Collections); Marie Ragghianti (*Nashville Banner*, image courtesy of Nashville Public Library, Special Collections); Jake Butcher (Owen Cartwright, *Nashville Banner*, image courtesy of Nashville Public Library, Special Collections); John Ford (Larry McCormack, *Nashville Banner*, image courtesy of Nashville Public Library, Special Collections); Glen Casada (Erik Schelzig)

Library of Congress Cataloging-in-Publication Data

Names: Ebert, Joel, 1984 - author. | Schelzig, Erik, 1975 - author.
Title: Welcome to Capitol Hill : 50 years of scandal in Tennessee politics
    / Joel Ebert and Erik Schelzig.
Description: Nashville, Tennessee : Vanderbilt University Press, 2023. |
    Includes bibliographical references
Identifiers: LCCN 2023008559 (print) | LCCN 2023008560 (ebook) | ISBN
    9780826505859 (paperback) | ISBN 9780826505866 (epub) | ISBN
    9780826505873 (adobe pdf)
Subjects: LCSH: Political corruption --Tennessee. | Politics and
    government --Tennessee --History.
Classification: LCC JK5245 .E24 2023  (print) | LCC JK5245  (ebook) | DDC
    364.1/32309768--dc23/eng/20230501
LC record available at https://lccn.loc.gov/2023008559
LC ebook record available at https://lccn.loc.gov/2023008560

# CONTENTS

# ACKNOWLEDGMENTS

THE IDEA FOR THIS book emerged when Joel was working on a retrospective of the Rocky Top public corruption probe of the late 1980s. In searching for contemporary sources, it soon became clear that details of the scandal were quickly being lost to the march of time. Retirements of longtime statehouse reporters and the thinning of the Capitol press corps had led to an overall loss of institutional memory that we hope to combat by committing these events to print.

Our reporting has been informed by scores of interviews, public records, digitized newspaper records, and our own recollections from covering some of the more recent events as reporters. But we've also benefited from the osmotic effect of hearing firsthand accounts of major news events from longtime statehouse reporters like Rick Locker of the *Memphis Commercial Appeal*, Tom Humphrey of the *Knoxville News-Sentinel*, and Andy Sher of the *Chattanooga Times Free Press*.

We leaned on our friend Dave Boucher, a fellow former political reporter for the *Tennessean* who had a major hand in breaking news about then state representative Jeremy Durham, for writing large portions of the chapter on the ousted lawmaker's troubles. Former political blogger and current "flack" Adam Kleinheider, former *Nashville Banner* managing editor Tony Kessler, and Dave Eiznhamer provided invaluable feedback on early drafts of the book.

When we came up with the idea for the book—a first for both of us—we didn't know what to expect. But with boundless enthusiasm for the project, Betsy Phillips at Vanderbilt University Press helped us navigate through this complex but ultimately very rewarding process.

Finally, we'd like to extend our eternal thanks for the feedback, patience, and support of our spouses, Elaina and Tricia.

# FOREWORD

GOVERNOR BILL HASLAM

IT MIGHT SEEM STRANGE TO YOU that a former politician is writing the foreword for a book written by two journalists who used to cover that politician. To be honest, it seems a little strange to me, too. The relationship between journalists and politicians is rarely a mutual admiration society. Erik Schelzig and Joel Ebert had a job to do in covering Tennessee state government for their publications. Stories about problems are typically more interesting than stories about things that are working well. The state of Tennessee has about forty thousand employees and a budget of around $40 billion per year. It was my job to help lead the state of Tennessee in the best way I could. So, often their job was to write about how I was performing my job. It would be fair to say that we didn't always agree on how they were doing their jobs of critiquing how I was doing my job!

But this book had an interest to me for several reasons. First, I love history. I have always been fascinated by our ability to look back and trace the journey that led us to this point. We have to know the people, decisions, and events that have led us to where we are today. Today's elected officials did not just get dropped into their positions in the opening act of today's challenges. Democracy is like a long relay race with one set of elected officials handing the baton to the next. And just like in a track meet, sometimes you get the baton in an advantageous position, and sometimes you don't. I love Tennessee and I am immensely proud of our state. I loved having the chance to lead the state that has been my home for my entire life. However, just like every other state, we have some not-so-great moments in our past. It is important that we know and remember those events as well as our good times.

Second, there is nothing like a book about things that have gone wrong to remind us how important it is to elect the right people. Our political world has become incredibly polarized and partisan. We are tempted to only look at an election through the lens of which candidate agrees with our views. But, having served fifteen years as a mayor and governor, I am more convinced than ever that we have to elect people of competence and character, and not just focus on whether or not they agree with everything we believe politically. At its heart, good government is about solving problems—and we all know that we have plenty of problems that need to be addressed by today's leaders. It really does matter who we elect.

Leading in the public square has never been easy, but I honestly think that today's public square might be the most difficult environment that we have seen. Social media and cable news have made for a bitter atmosphere. Too many people just want to make a point rather than making a difference. Yet the issues are only becoming more complex. We will make a bad mistake if we don't pay full attention to the character of our leaders. This book is filled with good examples of what happens when we make bad choices.

Finally, while I might not have always liked everything that Erik and Joel wrote as journalists covering state government, I always knew how important it is to make certain that we have good journalists covering government, particularly state and local government. The rise of social media and cable television has changed the ways that all of us consume news. Because we have so many options, we now have the ability to choose the news that we want to see. No matter where we are on the political spectrum, there is social media commentary and a cable news channel that will fit our preference. One of the unfortunate byproducts of this is that, increasingly, people primarily look to national sources for their news.

When I first ran for Knoxville mayor in 2003, and when I ran for governor in 2010, most people still read their local newspaper and watched local television news. Today, more and more people get their news through social media or cable TV. This means that fewer and fewer people know what is happening in city councils, school board meetings, and state legislatures. So many decisions that impact our daily lives are made on the state and local level, but fewer of us are paying attention to those decisions. This is bad for our communities, our states, and our country.

Many of the scandals covered in this book were first unearthed by journalists from those local newspapers and TV stations. Maybe this book can be a reminder of how important it is for all of us to stay involved, not just in the national debate, but also in what is happening in our own backyard. Scandals can have a lot of results. I hope this book can be a reminder that good government matters and that good government starts with politicians who are more concerned about the people they serve than serving their own political ends.

# CAST OF CHARACTERS

David Alexander,
state representative

Lamar Alexander,
governor

James Allen,
Blanton administration aide

Charles Anderson,
US attorney

Joe Armstrong,
state representative

Victor Ashe,
state senator

Ben Atchley,
state representative

Tom Atwood,
WKRN-TV reporter

Howard Baker Jr.,
US senator

Jackson Baker,
*Memphis Flyer* reporter

Scott Bascue,
Johnson Controls staffer

Dewey Batson,
murderer

Mae Beavers,
state senator

Charles Benson,
Blanton aide

Larkin Bibbs,
murderer

Marsha Blackburn, state senator,
congresswoman, US senator

Ray Blanton,
governor

William Blount,
US senator

Kathryn Bowers,
state representative

Phil Bredesen,
governor

Rob Briley,
state representative

Bill Brock,
US senator

Bailey Brown,
federal judge

Gordon Browning,
governor

Amanda Bunning,
American Conservative Union

Tommy Burks,
state senator

Tommy Burnett,
state representative

C. H. Butcher Jr.,
businessman

**Jake Butcher,**
gubernatorial candidate, businessman

**David Byrd,**
state representative

**Kent Calfee,**
state representative

**Edward Ward Carmack,**
*Tennessean* editor, US senator

**Joseph Carroll,**
a.k.a. Joe Carson, FBI agent

**Mike Carter,**
state representative

**Glen Casada,**
state House Speaker

**Brian Christie,**
songwriter, TV weatherman

**E. N. Clabo,**
state senator

**Sandra Clark,**
state representative

**Bob Clement,**
congressman

**Frank Clement,**
governor

**Mike Cody,**
attorney general

**Steve Cohen,**
state senator, congressman

**Hayes Cooney,**
attorney

**Bob Corker,**
US senator

**Cade Cothren,**
legislative staffer

**Gentry Crowell,**
secretary of state

**E. H. Crump,**
Memphis political boss

**Ward Crutchfield,**
state senator

**Riley Darnell,**
state representative

**Larry Daughtrey,**
*Tennessean* reporter

**David Davis,**
congressman

**Ralph Davis,**
state House Speaker

**John DeBerry,**
state representative

**Lois DeBerry,**
state representative

**Eddie Dallas Denton,**
murderer

**Don Dills,**
state representative

**Roscoe Dixon,**
former state representative

**Bill Dunn,**
state representative

**Winfield Dunn,**
governor

**Jeremy Durham,**
state representative

**Buford Ellington,**
governor

**Henry Clay Evans,**
gubernatorial candidate, congressman

**Hickman Ewing,**
US attorney

**Jeremy Faison,**
state representative

**William Fallin,**
FBI agent

**Roger Farley,** Tennessee Bureau
of Investigation (TBI) agent

**Andrew Farmer,**
state representative

**Hank Fincher,**
Tennessee Registry of Election
Finance member

**Robert Fisher,**
state representative

**Chuck Fleischmann,**
US congressman

**Harold Ford Jr.,**
congressman

**Harold Ford Sr.,**
congressman

**Joe Ford,**
Shelby County commissioner

**John Ford,**
state senator

**Nathan Bedford Forrest,** Confederate
general, early Ku Klux Klan leader

**O. H. "Shorty" Freeland,**
Blanton administration official

**Rachel Freeman,**
Nashville Sexual Assault Center

**Sydney Friedopfer,**
treasurer of shadowy PAC

**Bill Frist,**
US senator

**Richard Fulton,**
Nashville mayor

**Johnny Garrett,**
state representative

**John Gill,**
US attorney

**Ed Gillock,**
state senator

**Scott Gilmer,**
legislative staffer

**Martin Grusin,**
attorney

**Milton Hamilton,**
state senator

**Franklin Haney,**
gubernatorial candidate

**Bill Harbison,**
attorney

**Hal Hardin,**
US attorney

**Mike Harrison,**
state representative

**Beth Harwell,**
state House Speaker

**Bill Haslam,**
governor

**Ryan Haynes,**
state Republican Party chair

**Patsy Hazlewood,**
state representative

**C. Murray Henderson,**
state correction commissioner

**Douglas Henry,**
state senator

**Jim Henry,**
state representative

**Joe Henry,** Tennessee
Supreme Court chief justice

**Tom "Golden Goose" Hensley,**
liquor lobbyist

**W. C. Herndon Jr.,**
state representative

**Matthew Hill,**
state representative

**Timothy Hill,** state representative

**Hank Hillin,** FBI agent

**Andy Holt,** state representative

**Clyde Edd Hood,** Blanton
administration official

**John Jay Hooker,** gubernatorial candidate

**Henry Horton,** governor

**John Roger Humphreys,** murderer

**Julius Hurst,** Tennessee
Republican Party chair

**Tom Jensen,** state representative

**Andrew Johnson,**
governor, vice president

**Gloria Johnson,** state representative

**Jack Johnson,** state senator

**Justin Jones,** state representative

**Estes Kefauver,** US senator

**Brian Kelsey,** state senator,
congressional candidate

**Mike Kernell,**
state representative

**Bill Ketron,** state senator

**Nelson Kieffer,**
truck driver

**S. J. King,**
Alcoholic Beverage Commission

**Richard Knudsen,**
FBI agent

**Bill Koch,**
attorney

**Carl Koella,**
state senator

**Rosalind Kurita,**
state senator

**David Kustoff,** Shelby County
Republican Party chair, congressman

**Dan Kuykendall,**
congressman

**William Lamberth,**
state representative

**Tom Lawless,** Tennessee
Registry of Election Finance

**David "Peabody" Ledford,**
lobbyist

**Bill Lee,**
governor

**William Leech,**
attorney general

**Jim Lewis,** state senator

**Robert Lillard,**
Blanton legal counsel

**Mary Littleton,**
state representative

**Rick Locker,**
*Commercial Appeal* reporter

**Jim Long,**
bingo lobbyist

**Byron "Low Tax" Looper,**
state Senate candidate, murderer

**Michael Lotfi,**
political consultant

**Charles Love,**
bagman

**Mark Lovell,**
state representative

**Jack Lowery,**
attorney

**Mary Mancini,**
state Democratic Party chair

**Carol Marin,**
WSM-TV reporter

**Connie Mathews,**
county clerk employee

**William McBee,**
bingo hall financier

**Gerald McCormick,**
state House majority leader

**Randy McNally,** lieutenant governor
and state Senate Speaker

**L. C. McNeil,**
cover identity for FBI agent

**Ned Ray McWherter,**
state House Speaker, governor

**Andy Miller,**
campaign donor

**Ted Ray Miller,**
state representative

**Tamara Mitchell-Ford,**
ex-wife of John Ford

**Ken Moore,**
Franklin mayor

**Jason Mumpower,**
state representative

**Ira Murphy,**
general sessions court judge

**Tom Murray,**
congressman

**John Paul Murrell,**
Blanton advisor

**Barry Myers,**
bagman

**Jimmy Naifeh,**
state House Speaker

**Oney Naifeh,**
father of House Speaker Jimmy Naifeh

**James Neal,** attorney

**Joseph Todd Neill,**
admitted rapist

**Chris Newton,**
state representative

**Jim O'Hara,**
*Tennessean* reporter

**Don Palmer,**
US senate candidate

**Larry Parrish,**
assistant US attorney

**Malcolm Patterson,**
governor

**Justin Pearson,**
state representative

**William Peeler,**
attorney

**Russell Perkins,**
Nashville judge

**Marc Perrusquia,**
*Commercial Appeal* reporter

**Curtis Person,**
state senator

**Samuel Pettyjohn,**
slain Chattanooga beer store owner

**Neal Pinkston,**
district attorney

**Tommy Powell,**
state election commissioner

**Dale Quillen,**
attorney

**Marie Ragghianti,**
Pardons and Paroles Board

**J. B. Ragon Jr.,** state representative

**Ron Ramsey,** lieutenant governor
and state Senate Speaker

**Drew Rawlins,**
state campaign finance watchdog

**Connie Ridley,**
legislative staffer

**Jim Roberson,** former Tennessee
secretary of state's office employee

**C. B. Robinson,**
state representative

**Katrina Robinson,**
state senator

**Courtney Rogers,**
state representative

**Ben Rose,**
attorney

**Jim Rout,**
Memphis mayoral candidate

**Tim Rudd,**
state representative

**Chip Saltsman,**
political consultant

**Jack Sammons,**
Memphis mayoral candidate

**Charles Sargent,**
state representative

**Jim Sasser,**
US senator

**John Seigenthaler,**
publisher of the *Tennessean*

**John Sevier,**
governor

**Cameron Sexton,**
state House Speaker

**Jerry Sexton,**
state representative

**Paul Sherrell,**
state representative

**John Simmonds,**
campaign donor

**Eddie Sisk,**
Blanton administration official

**Herbert Slatery,**
attorney general

**Dana Smith,**
clerk's office employee

**Josh Smith,**
owner of The Standard Club

**M. Lee Smith,**
publisher of the *Tennessee Journal*

**Robin Smith,**
state representative

**Stan Snodgrass,**
gubernatorial candidate

**Billy Spivey,**
state representative

**Jacque Srouji,**
*Tennessean* reporter

**Paul Stanley,**
state senator

**Rick Staples,**
state representative

**Harold Sterling,**
state representative

**Mike Stewart,**
state representative

**Peter Strianse,**
attorney

**Don Sundquist,**
governor

**Gabe Talarico,**
state senator

**John Tanner,**
US congressman

**Charles Frederick Taylor,**
Blanton bodyguard

**Kyle Testerman,**
Knoxville mayor

**Fate Thomas,**
former Nashville sheriff

**Fred Thompson,**
lawyer, actor, US senator

**William Aubrey Thompson,**
a.k.a. Bob Roundtree, bagman

**Rick Tillis,**
state representative

**Peter Turney,**
governor

**Donnie Walker,**
bingo regulator

**Ken Walsh,** a.k.a. Ken Wilson,
undercover FBI agent

**Todd Warner,**
state representative

**Terri Lynn Weaver,**
state representative

**Keith Westmoreland,**
state representative

**Michael Whitaker,**
district attorney general

**Ken Whitehouse,**
political operative

**Sam Whitson,**
state representative

**Shep Wilbun,**
Shelby County Juvenile Court clerk

**Leigh Wilburn,**
state representative

**John Wilder,** lieutenant governor
and state Senate Speaker

**John Williams,**
congressional candidate

**Kent Williams,**
state House Speaker

**Phil Williams,**
*Tennessean* and WTVF reporter

**Tim Willis,**
political operative, lobbyist

**John Mark Windle,**
state representative

**Nat Winston,**
gubernatorial candidate

**Thomas Wiseman,** state treasurer,
gubernatorial candidate

**Andy Womack,**
state senator

**Rick Womick,**
state representative

**Jack Woodall,**
congressional candidate, attorney

**Ed Yarbrough,**
US attorney, defense lawyer

State senator Ed Gillock (D-Memphis) speaks on the Senate floor in Nashville on February 20, 1980 (Dean Dixon, *Nashville Banner*, image courtesy of Nashville Public Library, Special Collections)

# Introduction

ED GILLOCK WAS IN TROUBLE with the law. The Democratic state senator from Memphis had been indicted in 1976 on federal charges for accepting a bribe "under the color of official right" and engaging in racketeering. The lawmaker was accused of using his position as a senator to prevent the extradition of a man facing charges in Illinois and taking payments to introduce legislation on behalf of four men looking to obtain master electrician's licenses.

Gillock, himself a criminal defense attorney, recognized the gravity of the situation and soon began soliciting contributions from lobbyists for his legal defense fund. He hired prominent Nashville attorney James F. Neal, a former Watergate prosecutor who would go on to successfully defend Ford Motor Company against reckless homicide charges over deaths in its subcompact Pinto car.[1]

Neal argued the "speech and debate" clause of the US Constitution, which protects members of Congress from being sued over anything they say in the course of their legislative activities, extended to Tennessee lawmakers. Therefore, Neal argued, none of Gillock's statements or actions as a member of the Tennessee General Assembly should be admitted as evidence in the case.

To the horror of federal prosecutors, US district judge Bailey Brown agreed.

"To the extent that venal legislators might go unconvicted because of the government's being barred from proving legislative acts and motives, this is the price that the Founding Fathers believed we should pay for legislative independence," Brown wrote.

Assistant US attorney Larry Parrish said the judge had "created a monster" by finding evidence couldn't be presented to the jury about lawmakers' misdeeds.

"This now makes black bag legislation legal," Parrish lamented.[2]

The case worked its way through the appeals process, with the Sixth Circuit agreeing that lawmakers' activities were privileged. But conflicting rulings in other circuits led the matter to be taken up by the US Supreme Court, which ultimately found in a 7–2 decision in 1980 that state lawmakers cannot claim immunity from federal prosecution for actions conducted while in office.

"We believe that recognition of an evidentiary privilege for state legislators for their legislative acts would impair the legitimate interest of the Federal Government in enforcing its criminal statutes with only speculative benefit to the state legislative process," Chief Justice Warren Burger wrote for the majority.[3]

The decision removed any doubt of the authority of federal law enforcement officials to prosecute state-level public corruption. Without it, many subsequent probes into illicit activity by state lawmakers in Tennessee and around the nation may have become more difficult—or even impossible.

Even as things stand, public officials have many advantages when it comes to fending off probes into alleged misdeeds. Lawmakers often circle the wagons around their colleagues, no matter how ugly—or believable—the allegations. State law enforcement officials tend to be tepid in their pursuit of public corruption probes, knowing they depend on the government for large portions of their funding.

Every state in America has its own roster of elected officials gone bad. Though some are worse than others, no matter how many bad actors or lengthy the list of misdeeds, there's one through line: the undeniable authority that comes with entering the hallowed and historic halls of the state Capitol.

Republican, Democrat, or independent, the stature that goes with joining the loyal club of public officials who call the Capitol their workplace has a way of attracting both those seeking to do right by their fellow citizens and those who try to exploit the system for their own gain.

For the latter, the dynamics at play are almost irresistible: power and privilege, politics and influence, temptation and excess, all in the name of governance. For the average person, it's a delectable cocktail that will never be tasted. But for some of those with keys to the doors of government, it can be all that matters.

From its early days to its modern era, Tennessee has been home to its own infamous miscreants: a duly elected governor who to this day stands out for his transgressions; an almost-governor with deep political connections whose loose banking practices led to a historic collapse; a host of corrupt officials who engaged in a wide-ranging gambling scheme at a time when betting was illegal; a prominent lawmaker who flouted ethical norms and took bribes from undercover agents posing as lobbyists; a serial sexual harasser who joined rare company after his colleagues' rebuke; and a haughty legislative leader whose pursuit of pure power led to his downfall.

While they weren't the first to face public fervor, federal charges, or falls from grace, history instructs they won't be the last. Tales of corruption by government officials in Tennessee are as old as the state itself.

In 1797—one year after statehood was granted—US senator William Blount, a founding father of the country, faced allegations of leading a plot to help the British seize land west of the Mississippi River that the senator owned. When the plan was discovered, Blount became the first federal government official to be subject to the impeachment and expulsion process in the US Senate. Despite a severe national backlash, Blount was warmly welcomed when he returned to Tennessee. He later became Speaker of the state Senate.

Records detail a host of other tales of corruption or questionable activities by Tennessee's elected officials.

"It was common talk about Nashville that lobbyists were trading upon the votes of their friends, and that members of the two houses, and employees, were guilty of accepting bribes on various occasions," the *Journal and Tribune* of Knoxville reported in 1887. The newspaper outlined a host of bills that were approved with bribes, including measures related to taxing sleeping cars and another to defeat a proposed amendment to the Tennessee Constitution.[4]

In 1895, both Democrats and Republicans in the legislature alleged that bribes had been offered to lawmakers in connection with the gubernatorial election between Peter Turney and Henry Clay Evans the year before. When the election results were contested, the legislature was tasked with deciding the outcome of the race, and Turney, who was the incumbent Democratic governor, was named the victor after thousands of votes for Evans were thrown out by the Democratic-controlled General Assembly.[5]

In 1910, Gov. Malcolm Patterson pardoned Col. Duncan B. Cooper and his son, who had been convicted of the 1908 murder of *Tennessean* editor

Edward Ward Carmack in a shootout on the street outside the state Capitol. Cooper, who was publisher of the *Nashville American*, was a friend of the governor. Carmack, a prohibitionist who lost to Patterson in the 1908 Democratic primary, had criticized the governor in editorials for supporting the sale and manufacturing of liquor. One day, Cooper and his son exchanged "heated words" with Carmack when he was walking home, and the confrontation escalated to the point where Carmack was shot three times and killed. Patterson pardoned the Coopers, saying they had not been given a fair and impartial trial. The *Pittsburgh (PA) Gazette* said Patterson's action was "high-handed and outrageous," adding he was "not fitted to be the executive of a great state." The *Richmond Virginian* called the pardon "treason to the state."[6]

In 1911, the *Nashville Tennessean and American* published a story on the first day of the legislature's return to Nashville that said two Republican lawmakers had been offered money the night before in exchange for voting for a candidate for House Speaker.[7]

In 1921, state senator E. N. Clabo was charged with accepting a $300 bribe—or the equivalent of nearly $4,750 in 2023—in exchange for his vote on a bill related to taxes.[8] He was later acquitted.[9]

"Almost always when the Tennessee Legislature is in session there are rumors of corrupt practices, and at times there have been evidences of the truth of the rumors," the *Bristol Herald Courier* reported days after Clabo was arrested.[10]

During the Great Depression, the collapse of several banks and the related loss of $6.6 million in state deposits (about $125 million in 2023) nearly led to the impeachment of Gov. Henry Horton. Memphis political boss E. H. Crump—a rival to Horton's Middle Tennessee backers—personally lobbied senators inside the chamber on the creation of a hand-picked committee to launch a formal investigation into the governor's activities. The *Chattanooga News* pronounced Crump the "New Czar of Tennessee Politics."[11]

A gleeful Crump told reporters about his approach to the deal: "First: observe, remember, compare. Second: read, listen, and ask. Third: plan your work and work your plan."[12]

As the investigation proceeded, Horton appeared headed for an ouster. But several lawmakers who had previously been critical of the governor were offered jobs with the administration, fielded offers to buy their land, or received proposals for contracts to do business with the state. The governor also announced he would move the 105th Aero Squadron back to

Liquor lobbyist Tom Hensley watches House proceedings from the gallery in April 1979 (Dean Dixon, *Nashville Banner*, image courtesy of Nashville Public Library, Special Collections)

Nashville after previously basing it in Memphis in what had been widely perceived as a deal with Crump.

With Crump's hold on the impeachment effort crumbling, Horton went on the offensive in a number of public appearances. He denounced Crump as "a man who struts like a peacock with a cane on his arm and crows like a bantam rooster."[13] In what was increasingly being cast as a Crump versus Horton battle, public opinion turned against the political boss and in favor of the embattled governor. The impeachment effort ultimately fizzled as a coalition of rural Democrats and East Tennessee Republicans turned against the ouster in 1932. Crump had failed, but he still came out on top in the following year's election when his chosen candidate, Hill McAlister, was elected governor.[14]

In 1937, Rep. J. B. Ragon Jr. said he was offered insurance business valued at $1,200, or the equivalent of more than $25,000 in 2023, if he voted for a bill related to county government.[15]

A reporter for the *Chattanooga Daily Times* said in 1946 it was "very clear to me" when a naturopathy bill was considered by the legislature a few years before that "money had been used" to offer lawmakers bribes.[16]

In 1975, Tom Hensley, a powerful liquor lobbyist known as the "Golden

Goose," testified in a legislative committee that he provided free bottles of whiskey to any member of the General Assembly who wanted one. The revelation came as little surprise to insiders, but the brazen confirmation of free booze flowing to lawmakers shocked the public. Hensley's testimony came after Lt. Gov. John Wilder formed a three-member committee to look into allegations that two state senators had been offered bribes in exchange for voting in favor of a liquor price-fixing law.[17]

During a 1987 debate on a bill that sought to give lawmakers a pay raise, Rep. C. B. Robinson, a Chattanooga Democrat, said he had seen a lot of money pass "under the table" during his time in the legislature.[18]

And then there was Gillock, the senator whose efforts to beat federal bribery charges ended with the US Supreme Court decision establishing once and for all that state lawmakers aren't immune from facing charges for their actions in office.

Gillock was known for his arrogant attitude while serving in the state House and Senate, often asserting that lawmakers should be given priority when riding Capitol elevators, standing in line in the cafeteria, or parking their cars. He also engaged in a "voter exchange program" with fellow Memphis Democrat Gabe Talarico, an ad hoc redistricting scheme in which predominantly Black voting precincts were moved back and forth between their neighboring districts to ensure neither white incumbent could be defeated by a Black Democratic primary challenger or a Republican general election opponent. A federal court blocked the practice in 1976, finding the moves were made "for no reason based on a rational state policy."[19]

"No one wins them all," Gillock's attorney James Neal said of the 1980 Supreme Court decision. "This was just a little round in the Gillock case. The only battle worth winning is the last one."[20]

The attorney's words turned out to be prophetic. Gillock's ensuing trial ended in a hung jury (he was elected to his fourth Senate term while the case was underway) and again in a retrial the following year. But that's when his luck ran out.

While waiting for the cases to go to trial, federal investigators received a tip that Gillock had been given a pickup truck by a Millington businessman. The gift led agents to evidence that executives with Honeywell had engaged Gillock to help land computer contracts worth $2.5 million with the Tennessee Department of Employment Security and $2 million with Shelby County. At his 1982 federal fraud trial, Gillock testified he was working as a consultant for the company, not as a lawmaker. He also showed disdain for federal prosecutors.

"You haven't convicted me in two other trials, and you're not going to convict me now," Gillock sneered from the witness stand.[21]

The jury thought otherwise, finding him guilty of using his elected office to obtain $130,365 in payments (about $400,000 in today's money) from the company. Gillock was sentenced to seven years in prison. He emerged from incarceration as a minister. Senate Speaker John Wilder, who had declined to remove Gillock from the chamber or his committee positions when he was first indicted in 1976, invited the former lawmaker to return to the Senate as chaplain of the day in 2000.

"He's found the Lord," Wilder said in introducing his former colleague from the well of the chamber. "I wish I had what he's got. I don't have an 800 number. I have to go through an operator."[22]

The following chapters are cautionary tales of corruption and wrong-doing in Tennessee. While most of the officials who are the subject of this book were charged with crimes, this by no means suggests that all public officials are dirty or looking for their next grift. Lessons can be learned from each of these characters, including the dangers of acting on tempta-tion, or the risk of letting pure power become a driving force that overrides the initial motivation that led someone to run for public office.

The cases written about here are far from an exhaustive exploration of unscrupulousness. Rather, the highlighted examples offer opportunities to make sense of the modern era of government and politics in Tennessee in a different way. Newspapers and history books are replete with partisan politicians' rehearsed speeches and talking points, and the daily twists and turns of government. This compendium of corruption contains lesser-explored stories about the inner workings of the political system, albeit ones that are equally necessary to understanding the process.

Without the scandals in the ensuing chapters, much would be different today. The state's campaign finance and ethics watchdogs exist because of malfeasance. Publicly known wrongdoing has led to many law, policy, and rule changes as well. Perhaps most importantly, without the ire that each official faced, the halls of the Capitol might still be reserved for those with privileged access. But much work remains.

While nothing can ultimately stop a decidedly corrupt or morally bankrupt public official from crossing the line, the stories featured in this book—and the consequences each person faced—should make those in elected office think twice before they act.

Gov. Ray Blanton addresses lawmakers in the House chamber in Nashville on January 10, 1979 (Bob Ray, *Nashville Banner*, image courtesy of Nashville Public Library, Special Collections)

# ONE

★ ★ ★

# From "Miracle Man" to "Pardon Me Ray"

A LOOK AT THE POLITICAL LANDSCAPE in Tennessee today shows a state of one-party dominance.

Republicans maintain control of the state's two US Senate seats, eight of the state's nine Congressional districts, the governor's office, both legislative chambers, the judiciary, including the state Supreme Court, and a plethora of mayors and county-elected offices. Further, when Donald Trump was on the presidential ballot in 2016 and 2020, he received more than 60 percent of the vote and won all but three of the state's ninety-five counties.

Long before Republicans took over, Democrats had a similarly dominant grip on power that lasted more than a century. Between 1871 and 1969, Tennessee had twenty-eight governors, all but three of whom were members of the Democratic Party. Likewise, both chambers of the General Assembly were controlled by Democrats for all but two years between Reconstruction and the early 2000s.

Despite the Democrats' success, Tennesseans have long been steered by and rooted in conservative values. Politicians from both major political parties have been rewarded by voters for maintaining a strong influence of religion and morality in lawmaking, as indicated by an official ban on gambling that lasted two centuries and a prohibition on alcohol sales that endures in some areas today (most famously in the county where Jack Daniel's whiskey is produced).

Tennessee's conservativism is so well established that much has been enshrined in the state constitution. In 1931, when lawmakers considered adding an income tax to the state, the Tennessee Supreme Court ruled it violated the constitution. Following a renewed effort in 2001 by a Republican governor, voters approved new language in the constitution explicitly banning the tax. Lawmakers and Tennessee voters have also amended the constitution to ban same-sex marriage (the amendment was voided after the 2015 landmark Supreme Court case), allow limits on abortion rights, and guarantee hunting and fishing as a personal right.

In many ways, the modern Republican tilt that currently defines Tennessee was long in the making.

Since 1968, a Republican presidential candidate has won the state every four years, with the exceptions of Bill Clinton and Jimmy Carter, who were both southern Democrats, much to the chagrin of Vice President Al Gore, a Tennessean who famously lost his home state in the 2000 presidential race. In 1968, 38 percent of the vote in Tennessee went to Richard Nixon while segregationist George Wallace received 34 percent. Democrat Hubert Humphrey finished third with 28 percent. Wallace's strong performance in the state offered a signal of the changing political landscape in the decades that followed.

When voters sent Howard Baker Jr. to the US Senate in 1966, he became the first Republican in Tennessee history to head to the upper chamber by popular vote. Since then, the state has sent seven Republicans to the Senate, compared with just three Democrats (the last one to win a Senate race being Al Gore in 1990, when he carried every county).[1]

Four years after Baker's election, Winfield Dunn, a West Tennessee dentist, became the state's first Republican governor since 1920. At the time, Dunn's election was largely seen as an aberration. It didn't help that the GOP's two-year stint in charge of the state House ended in the same election.[2]

In 2004, Republicans were given their first elected majority in the state Senate since Reconstruction. Even though Republicans had numerical control of the chamber, they voted to keep Democrat John Wilder as Senate Speaker until 2007.[3] Similarly, by 2008 voters had elected more Republicans to the state House, though parliamentary shenanigans gave Democrats two more years of partial control. Since then, Republicans have bolstered their numbers to the present supermajority status in both chambers of the Tennessee General Assembly.[4]

The past fifty years of Tennessee politics is a story of how the fault lines have shifted from one party to another, in part due to the scurrilous actions of a man who divided his own party and helped encourage voters to move from a fluke election of a Republican governor to a full embrace of the Grand Old Party.

## A MAN WHO KNEW TOO MUCH

The final nail in Ray Blanton's coffin came more than twenty-five years after the death of the former Democratic governor of the state of Tennessee.

Once described as a highly partisan, vindictive Democrat who was fiercely loyal to those who were devoted to him, Blanton was a governor who ruled with a winner-take-all approach and showed little sign of remorse or regret during his tumultuous four years in office. He and others in his administration were also seemingly unafraid to cross the line of legal limits.[5]

Speaking at a news conference in Chattanooga in 2021, Hamilton County district attorney Neal Pinkston made a shocking revelation about the governor who was one of the more infamous elected officials in Tennessee history.

Pinkston said Blanton's administration was implicated in the 1979 fatal shooting of Samuel Pettyjohn, a Chattanooga-based liquor store owner and friend of union boss Jimmy Hoffa, who had appeared before a grand jury looking into the governor.

"Essentially, Mr. Pettyjohn cooperated with authorities and knew too much about what was going on locally, as well as the state level, and individuals didn't like that and so individuals hired someone to murder him," Pinkston said.[6]

Pettyjohn's murder was one in a long list of sins and crimes chalked up to the Blanton administration.

## ADMIRING HOOVER

Born in Hardin County, Tennessee, in 1930, Leonard Ray Blanton grew up in rural McNairy County, the second of three children to Leonard and Ova Blanton, a poor sharecropping family. Blanton later recalled his childhood as one in which he roamed around barefoot on dusty roads, chopped cotton, harvested crops, and lifted the boards on his front porch to get eggs from the family's hen.[7]

After graduating from high school, Blanton attended college at the

University of Tennessee, where he obtained a bachelor's degree in chemistry and agriculture. After graduating, he briefly taught at a school in Mooresville, Indiana. Upon his return to Tennessee, he was hospitalized with polio.[8]

In 1954, Blanton's father and brother formed B&B Construction, a road-building company that operated in West Tennessee and North Mississippi. Blanton joined the family business, working as a foreman in the early days before learning to fly an airplane as the company expanded its territory. Eventually the construction company employed more than one hundred workers.[9]

During the 1960s, the Blanton family moved beyond business, entering the world of politics. Blanton's father became mayor of Adamsville, and by 1964, Ray Blanton had launched a bid for the Tennessee House. He won and was elected to represent Chester and McNairy counties. While in the General Assembly, Blanton was known for his support of the state's minimum wage law and of abolishing capital punishment.[10]

After just one term, Blanton set his sights on Congress, this time challenging twenty-four-year incumbent US representative Tom Murray, a conservative Democrat from West Tennessee. Although it took three days to find out the results, Blanton defeated the seventy-two-year-old Murray in the Democratic primary by 309 votes. He had a similarly narrow victory over Julius Hurst, a former state Republican Party chairman, in the 1966 general election. Blanton was heralded as the "Miracle Man" for Tennessee Democrats, who maintained a 5–4 advantage in the state's congressional delegation thanks to his win.[11]

Eight days after he was sworn into Congress, Blanton talked to an FBI agent who was part of a program to meet with newly elected members. According to an FBI memo summarizing the encounter, Blanton was "most friendly" and expressed an admiration for FBI director J. Edgar Hoover.[12]

"He stated that he was determined to provide the people of his district in Tennessee with outstanding service and he would certainly call on the FBI if we could assist him in any matter," the memo said. "He also said that he would be most pleased to cooperate with the Bureau in any way possible and asked that we not hesitate to request his assistance whenever it might be needed."

In August 1967, Blanton wrote a letter to Hoover, inviting him to join his weekly radio broadcast. Blanton said his constituents were concerned about the "subversive elements connected with the riots in urban areas, as well as subversive elements connected with the 'peace movement.'"

In what was later known as the "long, hot summer" of 1967, nearly 160 race-related riots erupted in US cities, ultimately resulting in the deaths of 83 people, 2,800 injuries, and 17,000 arrests. The death toll associated with the 1967 unrest was higher than what would occur the next year, when riots broke out throughout the nation after the assassination of Dr. Martin Luther King Jr. in Memphis.[13]

Writing back a few days later, Hoover declined Blanton's invitation, citing "heavy pressure" on his schedule, adding that he shared the concerns over the riots. "Again, thank you for thinking of me in this connection and for your understanding of the situation which prevents my acceptance," Hoover wrote to Blanton.[14]

Within a matter of years, the FBI would have a much less amiable relationship with Blanton.

## A DIFFERENT KIND OF DEMOCRAT

Facing a challenge from a member of his own party in the 1968 congressional primary, Blanton handily defeated his opponent, attorney Jack Woodall. While in office that year, Blanton frequently bucked the Democratic Party while further embracing his conservative tendencies—his favorite political figures were presidents Andrew Jackson and Harry Truman.[15]

In March, he endorsed President Lyndon Johnson as the Democratic Party's presidential nominee, criticizing US senator Robert Kennedy, who Blanton said represented "pure symbolism" and lacked concrete methods for ending the Vietnam War. By August, Blanton was blasting Johnson for vetoing a bill intended to limit US imports of cotton.[16]

Blanton later refused to attend the Democratic National Convention in Chicago and made an early departure from a meeting with two hundred Democratic congressmen who were set to be visited by Vice President Hubert Humphrey.[17]

With Republican John Williams, a former US marshal and insurance broker, hoping to unseat him in the 1968 congressional general election, Blanton expressed strong opposition to forced busing, a practice aimed at making public schools more racially balanced.[18]

In the days leading up to the general election, Blanton did his best to curry favor with supporters of American Independent Party candidate George Wallace. The Shelby County headquarters for the Tennessee Democratic congressman shared a driveway with the Wallace campaign. A newspaper account at the time noted how Blanton "knows better than

US senator Howard Baker (R-Huntsville) makes a television studio appearance in Nashville on February 7, 1978 (Jack Gunter *Nashville Banner*, image courtesy of Nashville Public Library, Special Collections)

anyone else that the Seventh District is jammed with supporters of the third-party presidential candidate. A hard word, a slip of the tongue and Democrat Blanton would be in trouble faster than you can say 'Hubert Horatio Humphrey.'"[19]

During October debates with his Republican opponent, Blanton was similarly measured when asked about the presidential race. Blanton said he would "abide by the convictions of my constituents," if the election had to be decided by the House. Pressed on whether that meant he would support Wallace if the presidential candidate carried his congressional district, Blanton affirmed he would vote for the candidate chosen by his home area.[20]

While Nixon ultimately won Tennessee and the presidency in 1968, Wallace performed quite well, especially in the western part of the state, where Blanton's district was located. Blanton handily won re-election.[21]

## AN UPHILL BATTLE FOR THE SENATE

In 1972, Blanton decided not to seek re-election to Congress and to instead challenge incumbent US senator Howard Baker. First elected to the Senate in 1966, Baker had become the first Republican senator to represent Tennessee since Reconstruction. Later known in his political career as the "Great Conciliator," Baker was elected to the Senate two years after he lost to a liberal Democrat in his effort to fill the seat left open due to the death of US senator Estes Kefauver, a Democrat. Although a Republican, Baker bucked his party throughout his career at times, voting in favor of the Civil Rights Act of 1968 and the confirmation of Thurgood Marshall to the US Supreme Court. After both Blanton and Baker won their party's nominations in the 1972 race, the duo squared off in a campaign that frequently put Baker on the defensive.[22]

During one debate, Blanton criticized Baker for trying to "buy his re-election" by planning to spend $850,000 on the race. Blanton accused Baker of using his position to promote himself to become Senate minority leader or vice president while blasting the Republican senator's voting record and for holding a $1,000-a-plate fundraiser. Blanton argued Baker was taking advantage of campaign finance laws to avoid revealing all of his donors.[23]

Although much of the mudslinging during the 1972 Senate race came from Blanton, one of his Democratic primary opponents, Maryville attorney Don Palmer, accused the congressman of having a "campaign slush fund" that included large contributions from out-of-state donors. Up until that point in his political career, Blanton had managed to avoid any major scandals or scrutiny.[24]

One of the few times he had faced ire during the early years of his career came in 1971, when a Washington newspaper reported his nineteen-year-old daughter was a paid intern with a congressional committee. At the time, the House had an anti-nepotism rule that prohibited members of Congress from hiring or advocating for the hiring of a relative. Blanton denied using his influence to get his daughter the internship.[25]

During the early stages of the 1972 general election, Baker largely ignored Blanton while touting Nixon as having done "a spectacularly good job" during his first term. But in the final weeks of the race, Baker criticized his opponent for distorting the senator's voting record while attempting to tie Blanton to Democratic presidential nominee George McGovern.[26]

Toward the end of the race, Blanton's campaign touted what it called an endorsement from George Wallace, the former Alabama governor and 1968 presidential candidate. Writing to Blanton in a telegram, Wallace said, "Please accept my grateful appreciation for your efforts on behalf of my candidacy in past elections and as your campaign for the US Senate in the state of Tennessee draws to a close, I take this opportunity of wishing you well. I know you have worked hard during this campaign, and I feel confident that your talents as well as the strong stand you have taken for those things in which we all believe will be recognized by the voters on Nov. 7."[27]

As the campaign came to a close, Baker launched a four-day "whistle stop" steam engine train ride through twenty-eight cities. While Baker was on the train tour, Blanton accused him of offering bribes to Black leaders in Memphis in an effort to secure their support, an allegation Baker and the Black leaders denied.[28]

Baker, who spent $1.1 million on his re-election campaign, ended up winning by a 61–38 margin, delivering Blanton his first electoral defeat. Blanton spent $233,000. The election was the eighth most expensive Senate race in the nation that year.[29]

## A SECOND STATEWIDE RACE

After holding no elected office for the first time in nearly a decade, Blanton spent much of 1973 out of the public eye. There was speculation that he was considering running for his old congressional seat, which was now represented by a Republican. For decades the Naifeh Coon Supper in Covington was the year's top political gathering in West Tennessee. Started by Oney Naifeh in 1945, the tradition would continue under his son Jimmy, who would go on to become the powerful Speaker of the Tennessee House. Blanton made a splash at the raccoon barbecue event by declaring he would be running again in 1974—although he declined to say which seat he was eyeing. "Don't get yourselves committed," he urged the gathered politicos.[30]

When he finally launched a campaign for governor in May 1974—less than three months before the primary—Blanton took an airplane to hold a series of news conferences throughout the state. He called for all candidates in the race to completely disclose their campaign finances, which at the time was not required by law. He also advocated for creating an open government law.[31]

Other ideas Blanton touted included a gubernatorial primary runoff law, the popular election of the lieutenant governor, and limiting campaign spending to what he called the "political season." He argued restrictions on campaign cash would prevent candidates from being "packaged and sold like a bar of soap."[32]

The Democratic primary was a cordial affair, with little in-fighting, in part because of a unity pledge signed by fifteen potential candidates,

Republican gubernatorial candidate Winfield Dunn makes a campaign appearance on September 15, 1970 (Vic Cooley, *Nashville Banner*, image courtesy of Nashville Public Library, Special Collections)

including Blanton, in 1973. The signatories vowed to avoid a "bloodletting," citing how bitterness in previous gubernatorial primary races had carried into the general election. The anti-bloodletting pledge did not, however, extend into the general election.[33]

As the governor's race heated up throughout 1974, Blanton faced more scrutiny than he had during his bid for the US Senate. After he disclosed his campaign donors, Blanton reported receiving money from several corporations, which was prohibited.[34] Blanton initially refused to return the donations but said if they were deemed improper, he would change his approach.

Eventually the field of Democrats ballooned to twelve candidates, including Knoxville banker Jake Butcher, state treasurer Thomas Wiseman, and Chattanooga real estate developer Franklin Haney. Blanton ultimately earned the party's nomination with a 22 percent plurality, just 2 percentage points more than second-place finisher Butcher.[35]

On the Republican side, Lamar Alexander, whose resume included working for Republican US senator Howard Baker and President Richard Nixon's administration, handily beat three other candidates, including Nat Winston, the former state health commissioner who was once viewed as the frontrunner.[36]

While running against Alexander, Blanton zeroed in on Nixon's Watergate scandal and the policies of Republican governor Winfield Dunn, who was term-limited from running for re-election. Blanton said voters needed to know whether Alexander, who had worked as a staff assistant for the White House from 1969 to 1970, had a role in "bringing disgrace" to the Republican Party. In addition to working as the national director of planning for United Citizens for Nixon-Agnew in 1968, Alexander had served as Dunn's campaign manager during the 1970 election, which saw the Nixon campaign send $1 million into the races for Tennessee governor and US Senate.[37]

Although Blanton said he would not engage in "mudslinging" during the election, two days later, Nixon resigned from the presidency, adding fuel to the Democrat's campaign rhetoric. Dunn, who said he was "emotionally drained" by Nixon's resignation, predicted it would help Alexander. Likewise, Alexander thought the president's resignation eliminated the possibility for the election to serve as a referendum on Nixon.[38]

Their predictions could not have been more wrong.

## CRITICISM FROM A "VENGEFUL MIND"

As the race unfolded, Blanton was viewed as the underdog, even among some Democrats, including former Democratic gubernatorial nominee John Jay Hooker.[39]

Among the state-related issues brought up during the general election race was Dunn's use of the state plane. The state initially bought a plane in 1973 for $685,000 to allow the governor and economic development officials to use it for official business. By September 1973, Dunn was under fire after the *Tennessean* reported his office had used $4,300 in taxpayer money in recent years to make thirty-four political trips via state airplanes. Blanton blasted Dunn's use of the newly purchased state airplane, saying the governor was using it to campaign for gubernatorial candidates in other states. The criticism came mere months after Blanton, while seeking the Democratic nomination, said he didn't fault Dunn for buying the aircraft.[40]

In the final stretch of the general election, Blanton faced his most serious allegations to date: that he enlisted "dirty tricks" in his 1972 bid for the Senate, including accepting illegal donations, attempting to sabotage Baker's campaign train, purposefully reporting wrong contributions, and failing to report certain expenditures. Behind the allegations was a former campaign aide to Blanton, who had filed an affidavit with the secretary of the Senate while seeking an investigation. Blanton denied the charges, which he called ridiculous, while Alexander's campaign said the allegations were provided to them but could not be verified. Blanton called for an investigation into the allegations and sent his own affidavit to the Senate denying the charges as the product of a "vengeful mind."[41]

Another issue raised during the final days of the 1974 race against Alexander was a $3,000 contribution Blanton received from the political arm of the Associated Milk Producers. Alexander had turned down a donation from the group, which had been at the center of the July 1974 indictment of former Nixon administration treasury secretary and former Texas governor John Connally, who was charged with perjury, obstruction of justice, and bribery. He was later acquitted.[42]

Like Baker's 1972 campaign, Alexander outlined his positions on issues while occasionally highlighting Blanton's record. Days before the election, Alexander said Blanton didn't deserve full-fledged support from Black voters because the congressman had opposed the Supreme Court nomination of Thurgood Marshall, the high court's first African American justice.[43]

Even while leading much of the charged campaign rhetoric, Blanton proved to be relatively popular throughout the state as he promised to be the "people's lobbyist." Dottie West, who was best known for her 1964 hit "Here Comes My Baby," wrote and recorded a tune that became Blanton's official campaign song, "We Need a Ray of Blanton Sunshine."[44]

Aside from the few controversies that arose during the campaign, Alexander and Blanton headed into the general election both predicting victory by a margin of more than one hundred thousand votes.[45]

In the end, Blanton coasted to victory over Alexander, netting 55 percent of the vote.[46]

## NO MORE HONEYMOON

When he officially took over as the forty-fourth governor of Tennessee in 1975 from Dunn, who had been the state's first Republican governor in half a century, Blanton and the state of Tennessee faced myriad problems. Tax collections were down, and inflation and a national energy shortage were wreaking havoc on the economy.

During his inaugural speech, Blanton acknowledged the difficulties. "I humbly confess a degree of fear and trembling as I approach this job," he told the audience inside Nashville's War Memorial Auditorium. "These are grievous times. This state and this nation face serious problems."

To overcome the challenges facing the state, Blanton said it was necessary to "build a new relationship of trust and cooperation between the people and their government and between government and business." He closed out his speech by calling for Tennesseans to support him and the state. "While coping with today's problems and today's challenges, let us keep the vision of tomorrow," he said. "Let us trust in the integrity of our state government. Let us work together with unshakable faith that we will overcome the problems of today and preserve for our children the benefits of a better tomorrow."[47]

While most newly elected officials often enjoy a certain grace period when they enter office, the honeymoon for the first-time governor was short-lived.

Before Blanton took office, he said he was considering asking the legislature to repeal a law that provided automatic pay increases to him and other state officials. The salary for the governor was set to go from $30,000 a year to $50,000 once Blanton entered office. "My opinion now is that it should be set aside for this year," Blanton told reporters before his inauguration while discussing the planned pay raises for state officials. "We in government should start with ourselves when we start talking about austerity."[48]

His views would shift significantly over time.

Dunn encouraged Blanton to accept the pay raise, which would increase by an additional $6,000 after Blanton was in office for six months because the new salary was being tied to federal cost of living increases. Three Knox County Republicans—Sen. Victor Ashe, House Minority Leader Tom Jensen and Rep. Ben Atchley—said it would be unfair for Blanton to accept the pay increase while talking about eliminating raises for teachers and other state employees. Blanton quietly accepted the raise but later asked the state attorney general to rule on whether the legislature could legally set aside previously approved pay raises for the state officials.[49]

Days after Blanton took his oath of office, he faced criticism from state representative Sandra Clark, a Knoxville Republican who ripped the governor for his use of the state plane. Clark said she had recently learned that Blanton allowed Jim Allen, one of his political operatives, to take the plane to Washington before the governor had even taken office. The next day it was revealed that two Blanton appointees could be challenged because they were approved in board meetings that did not comply with the recently enacted state sunshine law, which requires all meetings of state government bodies to be open and publicly announced before the meeting occurs.[50]

In March, it was revealed that Allen, who had previously worked as a car dealer before becoming the governor's campaign manager, was being paid $21,600 for a six-month consulting job in the administration. Before the disclosure was made, Allen had been introduced as the governor's unpaid administrative assistant. Rep. Harold Sterling, a Memphis Republican, said Allen's contract set a bad precedent that underscored the need for ethics laws on the state level.[51]

Later that month, when a Senate committee considered the governor's proposed budget for the year, the panel nearly rejected it while criticizing aspects of the spending plan, including money to cover an economic development trip Blanton planned to the Middle East.[52]

When the new governor addressed the legislature about his priorities, he said he was introducing a "bare-bones" budget that relied on no "gimmicks" but was necessary in order to put the state on solid financial footing. "I bring this message to you with deep concern," he said. "But I want to assure you that there is much cause for optimism in the outlook for the future."[53]

A few weeks later, Blanton's positive disposition would be challenged by a twenty-five-year-old University of Tennessee at Chattanooga student and Vietnam veteran who had asked his girlfriend to bake him a lemon meringue pie. While Blanton was visiting Chattanooga, the student hit Blanton in the face with the pie, calling him the "top stuffed shirt in the state." Blanton declined to press charges, showing remarkable restraint for a man who was famously quick to blast the media or his opponents.[54]

That same month, April 1975, unbeknownst to Blanton, the FBI launched an investigation into his 1972 Senate campaign. According to documents released through a Freedom of Information Act request, the probe came after the secretary of the US Senate provided the attorney general a report of "apparent violations of law" that were discovered during an audit of Blanton's unsuccessful Senate bid.

An April 2, 1975, FBI memo said "in as many as 35 cases, the Blanton for Senate Campaign Committee apparently altered its records and reported contributions from individuals other than those persons or corporations who had actually made the donations; that one person listed as having contributed in excess of $500 to the Blanton Campaign in public reports denied ever having made such a contribution; that the Blanton Committee failed to maintain proper records as to persons making contributions in excess of $100 as required by law; and that members of the Blanton committee made plans to derail and/or delay US senator Howard Baker's campaign train."

The allegations largely stemmed from an affidavit from a former Blanton campaign worker, who said the proposed plans to slow or stall Baker's train included separating the tracks, putting Crisco on the rails, or placing an "exploding warning device" on the tracks to alert train engineers of danger ahead. The campaign worker even alleged money was paid to dilute the train's diesel fuel with water.[55]

The FBI inquiry was picked up by the Washington correspondent for the *Commercial Appeal* newspaper, who reported in late April that the federal law enforcement agency was looking into "alleged dirty tricks" by Blanton's campaign workers during the 1972 race. At that point, Blanton faced a flurry of scrutinizing media reports and criticism. There were allegations that he and his aides once discussed offering US senator Bill Brock, a Republican, little re-election opposition if he could stop the FBI's probe of the 1972 race. Another report focused on the thousands of dollars that Blanton received in campaign contributions from the trucking industry just before his inauguration, all while the governor was considering legislation to increase truck weight limits. A Republican legislator accused Blanton of trying to build a political empire as he pushed for an election-related bill.[56]

The Builders Transportation Corp. of Memphis later pleaded guilty to federal charges of making illegal campaign contributions to Blanton's 1972 campaign. When the federal investigation into Blanton's Senate campaign heated up by the fall of 1975, the governor was called before the grand jury. An indictment of Blanton was drafted by the US attorney alleging federal election law violations, but the charges against Builders Transportation were the only indictment a grand jury would hand down related to the federal investigation, which closed in January 1976.[57]

## CRACKS IN THE SURFACE

Another problem Blanton faced during his first year in office were reports of state contracts and work being awarded to B&B Construction, which Blanton used to run with his father and brother.

B&B Construction equipment was seen on a state highway building project, raising questions about the Blanton family business. Although Ray Blanton no longer had a financial interest in the company, his family had a presence in his administration. His brother, Gene, who served on his gubernatorial transition team, had an office in the Capitol, despite not being paid by the state.[58]

Blanton's problems escalated further when more information about B&B Construction began to appear in newspapers. The company was paid $3,300 to pave a tennis court at a state park. The project was done through an emergency purchase order rather than through competitive bidding. When the governor was confronted about reports in the *Nashville Banner*, the city's conservative-leaning afternoon newspaper, that Blanton's family was profiting from state business, he called it "yellow journalism." Blanton said when he was campaigning for governor, he had made a promise that, while he was in office, B&B Construction would not bid on any state highway projects. "They have not, are not and will not," he said.[59]

Despite Blanton's assurance that everything was on the level with his family's construction company, Rep. Riley Darnell, a Clarksville Democrat, announced the legislature's fiscal review committee would look into allegations of state purchasing irregularities involving B&B Construction. The state Conservation Department launched an audit to investigate the tennis-court-paving project, which determined B&B Construction, as well as two other companies, had bid on the job, with the Blanton family business offering the best price. Although Blanton tried to save face by halting emergency purchasing procedures—the practice used for the paving project—days later, it was revealed Blanton's father, brother, and uncle were associated with each of the three companies to bid on the work. As a result, the commissioner of the Conservation Department ordered an investigation into whether there was possible collusion in the bidding for the tennis-court-paving project.[60]

Despite Blanton's rocky first year in office as governor, residents from his hometown of Adamsville stood by him, instead blaming the media for treating him unfairly.[61]

But not everyone was happy with Blanton. Michael Whitaker, the district attorney general for Lauderdale County, which is located in West Tennessee and north of Memphis, had a much more critical view of Blanton. Whitaker, who had been investigating issues with the state park tennis court project and a West Tennessee state prison, said Blanton and his supporters were a "disgrace" to the state.[62] Whitaker called for Blanton to "either get his house in order" or resign. "He and his buccaneer supporting staff have disgraced this state," he said.

Republican lawmakers, who had not been shy of criticizing Blanton throughout the year, drafted a resolution calling for an investigation to determine whether certain "activities" by Blanton would constitute grounds for impeachment. The effort ultimately didn't advance.

## "NOT A CROOK"

Blanton's first year in office had been a tumultuous one. During his first one hundred days in office, only four of the governor's thirty-three major legislative proposals were approved by the legislature. Several of Blanton's election-related bills were rejected by the General Assembly. Lawmakers, including many West Tennessee Democrats—Blanton's home base—pushed back on his call to pass a one-cent increase on gasoline taxes to fill the state's budget hole. The legislature similarly rejected Blanton's attempt to raise taxes on minerals and the sales tax on commercial property.[63]

The pushback on Blanton came after Democrats improved their numbers in the House during the 1974 election. Heading into the 89th General Assembly, Democrats controlled 63 of the House's 99 seats, up from the party's previous 51–48 edge. In the Senate, Democrats represented 20 of the chamber's 33 seats. Despite Democrats' comfortable majorities, the party showed independence from the new governor by overriding three of Blanton's vetoes. A West Tennessee Democrat declared it the "most independent legislature" in the state's history.[64]

By year's end, it became clear Blanton's legislative counterparts didn't hold a very high view of him. A United Press International survey of the General Assembly found that 37 percent of the Democrats who responded had a negative view of the governor. A sentiment they shared was that they were "just a plain Democrat, not a Blanton Democrat."[65]

As 1975 came to a close, Blanton reflected on the year, saying the allegations about his family's construction company would not drive him away from office.[66]

"It doesn't always make me feel so good to have to explain to my nine-year-old son about once a week that his father is not a crook," Blanton said, paraphrasing President Richard Nixon's famous denial. "But I can tell you this—you are not going to find Ray Blanton with mistletoe tied to his coattail leaving this job."

## CRISES BEGIN TO MOUNT

Blanton's term as governor was marred by other controversies.

After his election, he established county patronage committees to reward key supporters throughout the state with government jobs. The committees reported to the administration, a system that left fellow Democrats who ran the General Assembly upset about their inability to influence hiring decisions for their friends. Republicans who had benefited from the system under former governor Winfield Dunn were also left out in the cold.

For example, Kent Williams remembered being fired from his job as an engineer's aide in the state Transportation Department shortly after Blanton was elected. Williams, a Republican who would later rise to become Speaker of the state House, remembered refusing "to kiss every politician's behind in the county for an about minimum-wage job."[67] The patronage system overseen by Blanton aide O. H. "Shorty" Freeland came under increasing fire as being contrary to good government principles, and calls for nonpartisan civil service protections became more pronounced.[68]

In 1976, Blanton's administration faced scrutiny after he replaced members of the state Alcoholic Beverage Commission with political allies, who later awarded new liquor store licenses in the Nashville area to recipients who were political friends and contributors to the governor.[69]

Another controversy was over Blanton's frequent use of the state plane for economic development efforts, as well as for personal purposes. In 1977, he flew to Jamaica, along with his bodyguard, personal physician, and a member of the Alcoholic Beverage Commission who owned the company that had pleaded guilty in the case involving Blanton's 1972 US Senate campaign. Blanton said the trip was a mix of pleasure and work—a trade mission to explore the possibility of exporting soybeans to Jamaica. The trip was widely panned, including by the *Tennessean*, which until then had only written one critical editorial about Blanton during his nearly three years in office in part because the newspaper's owner, Amon Carter Evans, had a political and social friendship with the governor.[70]

When Blanton and his administration officials were on out-of-state travel, they often lived lavishly, using taxpayer money to cover the costs of massages, liquor, limousines, and stays at high-priced hotels. A *Commercial Appeal* analysis of flight logs found that, in the first eight months of 1977, Blanton had flown on a state airplane nearly every other working day. Eventually Blanton and members of his administration reimbursed the state for some of their personal use of the state airplane.[71]

Additionally, Blanton refused to answer questions about records that showed thirty-two phone calls from Blanton's office, the state plane, and a hotel room he had in Tokyo to a thirty-two-year-old woman working at an agency in Washington, DC, at the request of the governor's office.[72]

Blanton's administration was further blemished by what became known as the surplus car scandal.

Although it never touched Blanton directly, in early 1976 reports began to surface of a widespread practice of officials in the administration selling the state's surplus cars and pocketing the profits. Blanton's transportation commissioner, the director of the state surplus property division, and the head of the state motor pool, in addition to a state trooper, were all indicted.[73]

Another administration official who worked as the executive director of the Tennessee Real Estate Commission was indicted in 1976 for selling the questions and answers to the real estate license examination to people who had failed the test.[74]

When Blanton's biggest scandal began to unfold in late 1976, he would be unable to control the damage.

## THE RAIDS BEGIN

In October 1976, FBI agents seized records from the offices of Eddie Sisk, Blanton's former campaign manager turned gubernatorial legal counsel; the state corrections department; and the Pardon and Paroles Board. The agents were searching for any records dealing with executive clemency, pardons, and commutations since 1975.[75]

As the agents investigated, some of the cases that drew attention involved Larkin Bibbs and Dewey Batson, who were both convicted of murder. Bibbs was granted clemency by Blanton in December 1975, after serving just three months of his fifteen-year sentence, and Batson, who had been sentenced to a ninety-nine-year term in 1966, was released in 1976. The *Nashville Banner* reported that Batson was released on commutation after a $250 donation was made to a preacher in Memphis.[76]

The FBI was looking into the possibility that payoffs were involved in exchange for clemency, commutations, or paroles of state prisoners. Sisk denied ever being involved or even having any knowledge of payoffs. The denial from Sisk came more than a year after his name arose in a separate matter in which bribery allegations had surfaced. In April 1975, officials at the Nashville Bar Association said they had a tape-recorded conversation featuring an attorney who talked about the ability to bribe or influence Sisk in exchange for the early release of an inmate.[77]

The FBI agent in charge of the investigation later revealed the October 1976 raid had been ordered because Sisk and other potential targets of the federal probe had become aware of it and as a result were cleaning their offices.[78]

Blanton, who was in Washington when agents entered Sisk's office in 1976, asked US attorney general Edward Levi to investigate whether Republican US senator Bill Brock was using his connections with federal prosecutors to bolster his re-election campaign. Blanton—who once

Marie Ragghianti walks out of the federal courthouse in Nashville on July 6, 1977 (*Nashville Banner*, image courtesy of Nashville Public Library, Special Collections)

heralded the FBI when he was in Congress—said the pardons and parole subpoenas led him to believe that US Attorney Charles Anderson, who was appointed to head the Middle Tennessee office during the Nixon administration, and the FBI were being used to "further partisan political interests."[79]

Anderson, who was longtime friends with Brock, said he had nothing to do with the timing of the raids and denied discussing the investigation with Brock and his staff. He even revealed that "responsible" Democratic state officials had been behind the request for an FBI investigation.[80]

One of the officials to raise concerns about the Blanton administration's use of pardons was Jack Lowery, an attorney and the mayor of Lebanon, Tennessee. Lowery said in May 1976 a man walked into his law office, identified himself as Bob Roundtree, and offered to sell a pardon for a state prisoner who was Lowery's client. Lowery summarized the interaction in a written statement, which he sent to Sisk and Marie Ragghianti, the head of the state's Pardon and Paroles Board. Lowery's report would eventually make its way to the FBI and the US attorney's office.[81]

As the 1976 federal investigation continued for several months, additional revelations surfaced. Secretary of State Gentry Crowell said an assistant to his office was offered a bribe by a Blanton aide. The discussion was captured on a tape recorder at the request of the FBI. The Blanton aide, Charles Benson, who was in charge of extraditions, was suspended as the governor called for a state investigation to make sure the FBI probe was fair and not part of the "FBI vendetta" against him.[82]

During a TV appearance that month, Blanton questioned how the FBI could conduct a fair investigation and said the agency's Public Integrity Department on Crime was "set up to go after people on the enemies list, which I have been privileged to be on and I'm proud of it."[83]

Asked if he felt like he was being targeted, Blanton noted he had been facing "continuous" federal investigations for nearly two and a half years, with developments breaking ahead of elections. "The Pardons and Paroles Board came up 12 days before last November's election," he said. "The investigation of my 1972 Senate campaign came up four weeks before my election as governor. Now how else could you read it. A two-year-old child can understand that."[84]

Blanton's allegations put the FBI on the defensive, forcing a response. A memo from the Memphis division to the director's office said the agency would respond to inquiries with a simple statement: "We are aware of the comments of Governor Blanton concerning the FBI and the Justice Department. Of course there is no FBI vendetta against the governor. His comments have been furnished to Washington and any further statement will have to come from the Justice Department."[85]

In addition to ordering the state investigation into the FBI probe, Blanton took away the authority of state extradition hearings from the secretary of state.[86]

## A DOUBLE MURDERER AND A "FINE YOUNG MAN"

The pardon scandal entered new territory in August 1977, when M. Lee Smith, the publisher of the *Tennessee Journal*, a political newsletter he started in 1975 after leaving his position as chief legal counsel to Republican governor Winfield Dunn, was interviewing House Speaker Ned Ray McWherter. During the interview, a state photographer entered the office to take a passport photo of McWherter. Smith recognized the man as Roger Humphreys, a fellow Johnson City native.

Humphreys, the son of a local Blanton patronage committee member, had been found guilty of the 1973 murder of his ex-wife and her lover by firing eighteen bullets at them with a two-shot Derringer, reloading the pistol eight times.[87]

"I almost fell out of my chair," Smith recalled later.[88] While Humphreys

Convicted murderer Roger Humphreys, left, on November 1, 1978 (*Nashville Banner*, image courtesy of Nashville Public Library, Special Collections)

had been sentenced to twenty to forty years in prison, he was able to travel around Tennessee during the day in a state-owned vehicle without supervision to work as a photographer. At night, Humphreys was required to return to prison. The *Tennessee Journal* later noted Humphreys was given a "country club treatment" that allowed him to stay out on weekends, drink alcoholic beverages, and visit the apartment of the ex-wife that he murdered.[89]

When the *Tennessee Journal* ran a blurb about Humphreys' unusual work release arrangement in early September 1977, it set off a political firestorm.[90]

State corrections commissioner C. Murray Henderson later told a legislative committee Humphreys was put in the work release program as a photographer because of "direct orders" from the governor.[91]

As lawmakers looked into Humphreys' arrangement, Blanton took his usual approach of turning the table on his critics. He called a reporter stupid for asking about Humphreys and blamed a local TV station for its biased reporting.[92]

During a combative one-on-one interview with journalist Carol Marin on WSM-TV, Blanton dropped another bombshell: he planned to pardon Humphreys before he left office. He called the double murderer who shot his victims eighteen times a "fine young man." Perhaps most unusually,

Blanton said, unprovoked, "I haven't sold a single pardon, a single parole."[93]

Blanton's promise to pardon Humphreys created a media blitz and was widely criticized, including by the family of Humphreys' ex-wife, Republicans, and McWherter. Alexander—the Republican gubernatorial candidate who lost to Blanton in the 1974 election but was running again in the 1978 race—later encouraged Democrats who were eyeing a bid for governor to denounce the Blanton administration.[94]

Although Blanton later admitted he was "brash and possibly arrogant" in the way he announced his plans to pardon Humphreys, he defended his decision while expressing regret for criticizing the media.[95]

Blanton would soon change his tune and firmly stand his ground with both his media criticism and the public scrutiny he faced, showing little sign of regret.

## NO MORE NEGATIVE QUESTIONS

As Blanton entered the final year of his four-year term, the governor dug in his heels.

In December 1977, Blanton announced he would no longer answer "negative" questions from reporters without them first asking about the "positive" side of an issue. The sudden shift came after a reporter asked Blanton to answer allegations that he spent excessively during his overseas travels. When a reporter asked Blanton if he was suggesting they would need to write something positive before he'd respond, the governor said, "You got the message. That's exactly what I mean."[96]

Blanton's rejection of negative questions gained national attention.

Shortly thereafter, the governor took an ad out in the Tennessee Press Association's newspaper directory that reminded the media of the need to provide balanced news coverage.[97]

In January 1978, Blanton, while appearing before a crowd of 1,300 state Democrats, said he was like a "plowshare . . . sharpened by forge and hammer." "The more you hit, the harder you beat . . . the harder I get," he boasted. "Now, I can stand the heat."[98]

While addressing a journalism class at Peabody College, Blanton said the press had reached a "new low," giving an example of media inaccuracy when a TV station reported he was recently confined to bed with a kidney stone on a day he was in his office. Blanton estimated 82 percent of the media in Tennessee was controlled by Republicans.[99]

To take his message directly to Tennesseans, Blanton scheduled public events where he planned to highlight how his out-of-state travel had attracted millions of dollars in new investments in the state while also lowering the unemployment rate.[100]

By fall 1978, Blanton's relationship with the media was so frayed he alleged a reporter purposely tripped him at a press conference, leaving the governor injured and forced to wear a knee brace. "I never like to appear in public with mental incompetents," Blanton said. "And I never knowingly do except when I have a press conference."[101]

## A TEARY-EYED DECISION

Two and a half years into Blanton's term, Tennessee was in the midst of holding a convention to weigh more than a dozen changes to the state constitution, including whether to give the incumbent governor the chance to seek a consecutive four-year term.[102]

Up until then, governors could not serve consecutive terms but they could seek another term in office if they were elected after another governor held office, as was the case with seven Tennessee governors, including John Sevier, Andrew Johnson, Frank Clement, and Buford Ellington. As proposed, the constitutional amendment would have applied to Blanton and allowed him to seek a second term if he wanted.[103]

As the measure was being discussed in political circles, Blanton said it was a "very remote" possibility that he'd run for re-election if the amendment were ultimately approved by Tennessee voters. Instead, the governor said he planned to retire from public office when his term ended.[104]

The change to the constitution was approved by voters in March 1978, with 56 percent of the votes in favor. Blanton, who supported the amendment, said the results were an endorsement of his administration.[105]

Despite his earlier comments, Blanton kept his options open in the spring of 1978, with qualifying petitions being circulated throughout the state. With the Democratic field of gubernatorial candidates coming together, Blanton said he would make a final decision on the race before the June 3 qualifying deadline. As he weighed his decision, a University of Tennessee poll, which found 66 percent of respondents said Blanton's performance as governor was poor, was withheld from publication for fear of a backlash the university could face. Undaunted by the poll results, Blanton believed he could win a second term if he wanted to pursue one.[106]

Then in late May, while joined by more than two thousand Democrats who had gathered on the front lawn of the governor's residence, Blanton announced he would not seek re-election. "Home holds no terror for Ray Blanton," the governor said in an emotional speech. "This decision is probably the toughest I've ever made in my life because of you."[107]

With his time in office coming to a close, Blanton was unapologetic about the way he governed. "You that are here today have the distinction of being accused, of being reprimanded, of being part of the Blanton administration," he said. "And I want to say that we have the finest people at the grassroots level. You've been tested, tried, investigated, intimidated, and interrogated. But I worship all of you, because you've stood through thick and thin, and I know you will again."[108]

## ON SECOND THOUGHT

As Blanton was weighing his decision on whether to seek a second term, he received a bit of good news in April 1978, when, after seventeen months, the federal grand jury looking into his administration's pardon and parole practices appeared to conclude its work. The investigation, which focused on Blanton's aides, Eddie Sisk and Charles Benson, came to a close without anyone being indicted. Blanton had once again managed to escape major damage from another FBI investigation.[109]

The relief for the administration, however, would only prove temporary.

In late June, Marie Ragghianti, who had served as the administration's head of the state Pardons and Paroles Board for thirteen months until she was fired, testified during a trial over a lawsuit she brought against the state. She said that the governor's office had deliberately altered her agency's decisions regarding pardons.[110]

Ragghianti alleged the governor's office used "political favoritism" while granting clemencies. "Too many times I saw a man serve 10 years for something like auto theft, and someone else would serve a few months for a second degree murder conviction," she said.[111]

Ragghianti also revealed details about alleged bribery efforts in exchange for clemency and said Sisk was upset with her when she told Blanton directly about a bribery attempt. As the trial unfolded, Blanton was deposed by Ragghianti's lawyer, Fred Thompson, about the governor's reasons for firing her. A jury sided with Ragghianti, who was given back her old job.[112]

Ragghianti's story would later be adapted into a Hollywood movie,

Attorney Fred Thompson speaks to reporters in January 1979 (Dean Dixon, *Nashville Banner*, image courtesy of Nashville Public Library, Special Collections)

*Marie*, starring Thompson—who later represented the state in the US Senate—as himself, Jeff Daniels as Sisk, and Sissy Spacek in the title role.

With the FBI inquiry and Ragghianti's lawsuit complete, Blanton once again reiterated his intention to pardon Roger Humphreys, the convicted double murderer. With the governor's race whittled down to Democrat Jake Butcher and Republican Lamar Alexander—who had lost to Blanton in the 1974 primary and general elections, respectively—the candidates criticized the governor's pardon plans.[113]

Alexander, former Republican governor Winfield Dunn, and former 1970 Democratic gubernatorial nominee John Jay Hooker quickly announced an effort to collect one million signatures urging Blanton to not pardon Humphreys.[114]

Blanton, who said he would "weigh heavily" a request from Butcher to not move forward with the pardon, ended up changing his mind. On Oct. 31, one week before the general election, Blanton issued a statement, saying after "prayerful consideration," he had decided he would not pardon Humphreys after all.[115]

It was a rare reversal for Blanton, who was often a man who stuck to his convictions even while facing criticism and opposition. The decision, which was welcomed by many, was so unusual that some Tennesseans were skeptical. "Since it happened on Halloween, it's like some sort of

Politician and businessman John Jay Hooker, right, shares a laugh with boxer Muhammad Ali on August 24, 1980 (*Nashville Banner*, image courtesy of Nashville Public Library, Special Collections)

Gov. Lamar Alexander speaks to reporters after being sworn into office three days early on January 17, 1979 (Jack Gunter, *Nashville Banner*, image courtesy of Nashville Public Library, Special Collections)

'Trick or Treat' prank," said the father of John Scholl, one of Humphreys's victims.[116]

Scholl's skepticism would soon prove prescient.

## CRITICS FROM ALL SIDES

Four years after losing to Blanton in his first bid for public office, Alexander emerged from the 1978 general election victorious, beating Butcher in a landslide thanks in part to support from traditionally Democratic Middle Tennessee.[117]

The Republican's election was a rebuke to Tennessee Democrats—he picked up more votes in Nashville than Butcher—with Alexander chalking up his victory to voters who wanted a clean break from the Blanton years. After the election, Democrats privately laid blame on Blanton for Alexander's victory.[118]

Alexander would bring a notably different style and personality to the office compared with Blanton.[119]

The product of the East Tennessee town of Maryville, the thirty-eight-year-old Alexander spent months campaigning for governor by walking across the state wearing a red and black flannel shirt and khakis. Once describing him as a boyish lawyer who spoke with the fire of a small-town minister, Alexander's observers noted he had remarkable self-control and a cool manner, so much so that while campaigning during the 1978 race he calmly handled an incident when he was hit by a pickup truck after stepping off a curb. Struck on the shoulder, Alexander went over the top of the vehicle as his campaign material was strewn about.[120] He quickly jumped to his feet and began picking up the campaign literature, without his wife and others noticing what happened. Without telling many in his campaign, he went to the hospital and ended up taking a few days off because of a foot injury.[121]

When Blanton met with the new governor-elect to discuss their transition, Alexander described his predecessor as "gracious."[122] That same day, an article in the *Tennessean* briefly noted that a Nashville grand jury had heard testimony from several Chattanooga residents in "what appeared to be a spinoff of the dormant federal investigation of state pardons and paroles practices." An attorney for William Aubrey Thompson, who sometimes went by Bob Roundtree, spent more than an hour before the grand jury. Roundtree was the man who in May 1976 had offered to secure the release of a state prisoner represented by attorney Jack Lowery in exchange for money.[123]

Rather than keeping a low profile as a soon-to-be-departed governor, Blanton held a press conference and said he had once again changed his mind about whether to pardon Humphreys. "We're considering several commutations right now," Blanton said. "He's one of them."[124]

Hooker urged the Tennessee General Assembly to censure Blanton if he went through with commuting Humphreys' sentence.[125]

With his executive powers nearing an end, Blanton began issuing pardons and commutations with reckless abandon. He pardoned a probation officer working for Davidson County sheriff Fate Thomas, who later went to prison in a separate corruption case, and commuted the sentence of a top University of Tennessee basketball player.[126]

Then on Dec. 15, 1978, FBI agents arrested three members of the Blanton administration for allegedly accepting cash to release prisoners with executive clemency. Those arrested included Eddie Sisk, the governor's chief legal counsel; Charles Benson, an assistant to Sisk who handled paperwork regarding extraditions, pardons, commutations, and paroles; and Charles Frederick Taylor, a fifteen-year veteran of the Tennessee Highway Patrol, who had previously served as one of Blanton's bodyguards.[127]

When they were arrested, Sisk and Benson had $3,500 in marked bills in their pockets that had been paid to the highway patrolman in exchange for an executive clemency petition filed by an FBI informant. In addition to the arrests, federal agents could be seen throughout the Capitol complex serving search warrants to state agencies and the governor's office.

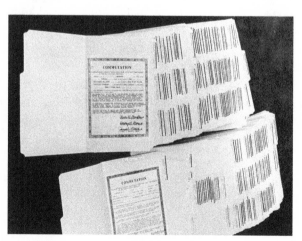

Folders containing recommendations for Gov. Ray Blanton to commute sentences are stacked on a table on January 5, 1979 (Bob Ray, *Nashville Banner*, image courtesy of Nashville Public Library, Special Collections)

Eddie Sisk, the chief legal counsel to Gov. Ray Blanton, on the day of his arrest by the FBI on December 15, 1978 (Vic Cooley, *Nashville Banner*, image courtesy of Nashville Public Library, Special Collections)

One federal agent told reporters the arrests were the result of the FBI investigation that was thought to have been wrapped up earlier in the year.

When Benson was arrested, he was carrying two signed documents directing the warden of Tennessee prisons to release two inmates, one of whom, Larry Ed Hacker, was the alleged mastermind behind the 1977 brief prison escape of James Earl Ray, the assassin of the Rev. Martin Luther King Jr.[128]

The arrests of Sisk, Benson, and Taylor were possible because of the use of a confidential source, surveillance, and audio and video recordings. According to FBI affidavits, a conversation between Taylor and the FBI's informant captured the highway patrol officer saying he was aware of twelve other sentence reductions pending, with another thirty set to be done during Blanton's final week in office.

After the arrests, Blanton's spokesman said the governor was "stunned" and had "no knowledge" of the alleged issues that led to the arrests of his aides.[129]

With less than a month before Blanton was set to leave office, the governor remained stalwart in his plans to move forward on additional commutations.[130]

When Blanton was subpoenaed to appear before a federal grand jury,

Charles Benson, left, is booked following his arrest in July 1977 (Dean Dixon, *Nashville Banner*, image courtesy of Nashville Public Library, Special Collections)

he faced questions for two hours. Afterward, the governor stood by his administration's pardons and commutations, saying he would reaffirm every executive clemency that took place. At the time, there were questions over the binding authority of his clemencies because a Blanton staffer signed the governor's name on paperwork instead of Blanton himself.[131]

Hank Hillin, the FBI agent leading the multiyear federal investigation known as Operation TENNPAR, later succinctly summarized the clemency for cash scandal: "Bill Thompson would find an inmate willing to buy his freedom. The name was passed to Sisk, who would check the inmate's record. If the record was relatively clean—murderers were OK, but no child molesters—then Sisk had the parole board review the inmates' chances for early release. The clemency document would be drawn up by the board and sent to Sisk, who would carry it to Ken Lavender's office to get Ray Blanton's signature. And then Sisk and Thompson were a little bit richer."[132]

Hooker, who had filed a lawsuit asking for a temporary injunction to prevent Blanton from granting clemency, called for the judge handling the case to "be the governor" on executive-clemency-related matters until Alexander took office. At the same time, Hooker called for Blanton to resign immediately.[133]

Tennessee attorney general William Leech, who was representing Blanton in the Hooker lawsuit, challenged the judge's ability to limit Blanton's executive authority. "These are troubled times in our state, but reason must prevail," Leech said.[134]

In less than a month, Leech would take a drastically different approach.

## BLIND LOVE

Five days into 1979, Blanton held his first press conference since the arrests of Sisk, Benson, and Taylor. While speaking to reporters, the governor disclosed, for the first time, documents he had received ahead of his grand jury appearance indicated that he was a "target" of the federal investigation. "There is not any question of me being a target of the grand jury, or they wouldn't have subpoenaed me before it," he said, while once again denying knowledge of any bribes that were exchanged for executive clemency.[135]

On Jan. 10, 1979, Blanton appeared before the Tennessee General Assembly for the final time as governor. Delivering his farewell State of the State address, an emotional Blanton said any arrogance he showed while governor was the result of his appreciation for the state. "My love for Tennessee is not so blind that I can't see the imperfections we have," he said. "But the shortcomings are far outweighed by the potentials and the actual progress that has been made."[136]

Reflecting on his accomplishments while in office, Blanton noted improvements in the state's fiscal environment and corrections system. He touted how his trade missions had boosted Tennessee's profile abroad, leading to millions of dollars in investments and the creation of thousands of new jobs. The state's unemployment rate also dropped from 9 percent to 5 percent while he was in office.

Blanton made no mention of the specific controversies he faced, including the ongoing federal investigation, other than to say he would "never willingly do one single thing to hurt this state or its people."[137]

As Blanton entered his final week in office, he began to signal plans to take action on additional clemencies. He asked for the files of Humphreys and Eddie Dallas Denton, who was convicted of murdering three people. The Denton case was controversial because FBI affidavits indicated that, when the three Blanton aides were arrested, records showed $100,000 was being offered for Denton's release.[138]

Blanton also prepared paperwork to commute the sentences of sixteen inmates, including ten convicted murderers, who had been working at the governor's mansion.[139]

With expectations that Blanton could commute the sentences of at least two dozen inmates, including Humphreys, in his final days, McWherter—the House Speaker—warned that a mass use of executive clemencies by Blanton could force the state to swear in Alexander earlier than his previously scheduled Jan. 20 inauguration.[140]

Alexander's transition team downplayed such a possibility, saying he planned to have his regularly scheduled inauguration.[141]

Then all hell broke loose.

## GUTS VERSUS BRAINS

In a late-night gathering at the Capitol on January 15, 1979, Blanton met in his office with his corrections commissioner; his legal counsel, Robert Lillard—who in 1971 had been investigated by the legislature for allegedly accepting money for securing the release of an inmate; and Secretary of State Gentry Crowell as the governor considered dozens of commutations. Blanton ended up signing paperwork to commute the sentences of forty-nine inmates, including Humphreys, and pardoned three others. Among the group granted clemency were twenty-four murderers whose sentences were reduced or ended. Only fourteen of the fifty-two inmates granted clemency had the recommendation of the state's parole board. Surprisingly, Denton's sentence was not acted upon.[142]

While signing Humphreys' paperwork, Blanton said to Crowell, "This takes guts." The secretary of state replied, "Yeah, well some people have more guts than they've got brains."[143]

When Blanton emerged from his office shortly after 11 P.M., he announced what he had done and indicated he was prepared to grant executive clemencies in six or seven more cases before he left office. The governor attempted to justify his action by explaining that the state was under a court order to reduce the prison population. "The commissioner told me that some prisoners are still sleeping on the floor at the main prison. Some of these actions will help that," he said.[144]

Humphreys was quickly released from prison and asked his attorney if he was dreaming.[145]

Reactions to the governor's actions were unabashed. Alexander said they were "sickening." Hooker called them a "disgrace" and a betrayal of the Democratic Party. McWherter said he deplored the moves, vowing to work to prevent a similar situation in the future. Republican state senator Victor Ashe said Blanton "must be a sick person." US senator Jim Sasser,

[**Above**] Gov. Ray Blanton speaks to reporters in the state Capitol in Nashville on January 15, 1979 (Don Foster, *Nashville Banner,* image courtesy of Nashville Public Library, Special Collections)

[**Left**] Senate Speaker John Wilder (D-Mason) speaks at a hearing in 1977 (*Nashville Banner,* image courtesy of Nashville Public Library, Special Collections)

a Tennessee Democrat, called Blanton's decision the "grossest breach of a chief executive's power perhaps in the history of Tennessee."[146]

The governor's late-night clemencies made national news, with Associated Press articles being published the next day in nearly every state and drawing the attention of national outlets like the *New York Times.*[147]

Lt. Gov. John Wilder said Blanton's decision may have been influenced by a state attorney general's opinion that said Alexander could be sworn in at midnight on Jan. 15. That same day, Alexander, McWherter, and Wilder discussed the potential of swearing in the new governor early. But Alexander rejected the idea.[148]

Blanton, meanwhile, disputed that his decision was motivated by the attorney general's opinion.[149]

## A SUDDEN AND SURPRISE DEPARTURE

On Wednesday, January 17, 1979, Hal Hardin, a thirty-seven-year-old US attorney for the Middle District of Tennessee, placed a phone call to Alexander's transition office shortly before noon. Hardin, who was inside Nashville's federal courthouse, began the call by telling Alexander he was not calling him in his official capacity as US attorney. At that moment, he was a concerned Tennessean.[150]

Before calling the governor-elect, Hardin had heard from an FBI agent who told him the agency had intelligence that Blanton was considering more pardons, including some of the people who were actively being investigated. One of the concerns Hardin faced was the potential for Blanton to release any number of Tennessee inmates, which at the time included James Earl Ray.

With the FBI agent's warning in mind, Hardin—a self-described yellow dog Democrat who had been named to his post by President Jimmy Carter—urged Alexander, a Republican, to take office early as governor.

After hanging up the phone with Hardin, Alexander, who at the time of the phone call was writing his inaugural address, eventually came to the conclusion that it was necessary to take control of the governor's office before Blanton did anything else that could further damage the state. Throughout the day, Alexander's closest advisors, along with McWherter and Wilder, were brought into the fold, as was Attorney General William Leech, another Democrat, to help think through various scenarios that could occur that would hinder the plan to take office early.[151]

"This was basically a coup," Alexander later recalled. "It was not the kind of thing we did in the United States of America."[152]

One of the concerns was what could happen if Blanton found out about the plan. Alexander noted Blanton was in charge of the forty thousand Tennessee National Guard members, whom the governor could have ordered to surround the Capitol. Alexander said although neither he nor McWherter or Wilder wanted to proceed with the early inauguration, the trio ultimately concluded it was necessary.[153]

During the afternoon, Hardin and Leech, along with Bill Koch and Hayes Cooney, two lawyers in the attorney general's office, met at a hotel in downtown Nashville to hash out any final legal concerns about having Alexander swear in early. After reaching a consensus, Koch was sent to inform Tennessee Supreme Court chief justice Joe Henry about the plan. Henry didn't share the news with his fellow justices.[154]

As early evening approached, reporters gathered outside McWherter's

US attorney Hal Hardin appears in federal court in July 1977 (*Nashville Banner*, image courtesy of Nashville Public Library, Special Collections)

Former state House Speaker Ned Ray McWherter of Dresden, right, celebrates his election to governor with his son, Mike, on November 4, 1986. At rear is then US senator Al Gore (Mark Lyons, *Nashville Banner*, image courtesy of Nashville Public Library, Special Collections)

office in the Legislative Plaza office building. Inside, McWherter was meeting with Wilder, Leech, Secretary of State Gentry Crowell and a member of the Speaker's staff.[155]

Around 5:30 P.M., reporters followed the group of officials as the makeshift parade headed from the legislative office building to the nearby state Supreme Court building.[156]

Shortly after, Alexander, his family, staff, and others began to gather inside the Supreme Court's robing room, a small private room where the justices gather before entering the courtroom. Inside the robing room, packed with a crowd that included Alexander, McWherter, Wilder, Leech, and Crowell, discussion turned to whether to notify Blanton of the forthcoming action. McWherter was recommended for the task. Once McWherter was connected to Blanton, he handed the phone to Leech, who informed the governor of the decision.[157]

When the group of officials made their way into the courtroom minutes before 6 P.M., they were met with the host of reporters who had followed them from the legislative building. Alexander began by reading a joint statement on behalf of himself, McWherter, and Wilder.

"The United States attorney for the Middle District of Tennessee has informed each of us that he has substantial reason to believe that Governor Blanton is about to release one or more persons, prisoners who are targets of a United States investigation into alleged payoffs for pardons and commutations of sentences. That information, taken with other information of the last several weeks, causes each of us to believe that it is in the best interests of the people of Tennessee that the governor-elect assume office immediately. We believe the taking of the oath should be done publicly, and in each of our presence. The state attorney general has given us each his opinion that the assumption of the office under these circumstances is constitutionally valid," Alexander said.

"These are not very happy days for Tennessee. It is not a happy day for me. I believe though that we have been responsible, and that we have kept the faith with the people by this decision."

The chief justice then delivered the oath of office to Alexander.

When Blanton emerged from his private home two hours later, he said the day's actions left a blemish on the state's record. "I am saddened and hurt for the state of Tennessee that this clandestine action has taken place this evening," he said. Blanton, however, didn't blame Alexander for the early swearing in, saying, "I feel for the new governor to be put into this situation." Once again, Blanton offered no sign of remorse or apology for his actions. "History will record what we did as the right and proper thing," he said.[158]

The historical record on Blanton would not prove so kind.

Although most of Tennessee's political reporters were busy chasing the historic and abrupt transfer of power from Blanton to Alexander, Nashville TV weatherman Brian Christie took a different approach: He wrote and recorded a song that lambasted the departing governor for his latest escapades. Sung to the tune of "Chattanooga Choo-Choo," Christie's song "Pardon Me Ray" was a sudden smash hit, playing on Nashville radio airwaves within hours after Blanton was forced out of office.[159]

TV weatherman Brian Christie, who wrote the "Pardon Me, Ray" parody, appears on set in 1979 (*Nashville Banner*, image courtesy of Nashville Public Library, Special Collections)

An hour after the song hit the airwaves of WKDA on a Wednesday evening, the station received a thousand requests to play it again. Copies of the song, which were sold at Ernest Tubb Record Shop in downtown Nashville, were selling so fast one worker said he hadn't seen anything like it since the death of Elvis Presley.[160]

Blanton's troubles became the subject of late-night TV jokes. "I understand Johnny Cash is really upset," Johnny Carson quipped in his *Tonight Show* monologue. "There are no more prisoners for him to entertain."[161]

## "THE MOST INVESTIGATED GOVERNOR" IN STATE HISTORY

For all the urgency to force Blanton out of office early, the investigation into his involvement in the pardon scandal dragged on for several more months. In March 1979, after a grand jury listened to an estimated sixty witnesses, indictments were handed out to six men: Sisk, Benson, and Taylor, as well as William Aubrey Thompson (aka Bob Roundtree), former Blanton advisor John Paul Murrell, and Nashville attorney Dale Quillen. The men were charged for their roles in running an executive clemency bribery and extortion scheme during the entirety of Blanton's time in office.[162]

Blanton was only mentioned once in the indictment, with him not being accused of any wrongdoing. An FBI agent warned, however, that the investigation was not over.[163]

When the case went to trial for five of the defendants, a federal appellate court judge declared a mistrial because of reports of an effort to bribe jurors.[164]

Over time, the defendants would face a host of different outcomes.

Thompson pleaded guilty in February 1981 after agreeing to testify against the others in exchange for a shorter prison sentence. While awaiting trial for the clemency case, Thompson was sentenced to one year in prison for failing to file income tax returns in 1972 and 1974 and two years for underestimating his income in 1973. Thompson's decision to cooperate in the clemency case allowed him to ensure the two and a half years he faced in prison for his role in the scandal could be served concurrently with his other prison sentences.[165]

In March 1981, Sisk and Taylor pleaded guilty to arranging executive clemency for state inmates in exchange for bribes. Like Thompson, Sisk and Taylor agreed to cooperate. Both men were sentenced to five years in prison.[166]

Benson was acquitted in May 1981, and charges against Quillen were dismissed.[167]

Murrell, a liquor store owner, was sentenced to two years in prison after he was convicted of conspiring with an agent with the state Alcoholic Beverage Commission to extort money from a nightclub owner.[168]

Beyond those initial indictments in the clemency scandal, several other officials in the Blanton administration, as well as others unearthed by federal investigators, were indicted and sentenced to prison as a result of the federal inquiry.[169]

Blanton's brother, Gene, was convicted of income tax fraud and sentenced to a year in prison. He also pleaded guilty to rigging state road contracts and was sentenced to three years. Jake Blanton, the governor's uncle, pleaded guilty to income tax evasion and bid rigging. He was sentenced to five months in prison for both charges.

A patronage chief for the governor pleaded guilty to a count of mail fraud in connection with bid rigging on state contracts. She was sentenced to eighteen months in prison. Blanton's Davidson County patronage committee chair pleaded guilty to mail fraud for his involvement in a liquor license conspiracy and was sentenced to thirty days in prison.

The former executive director of the Alcoholic Beverage Commission was sent to prison for three and a half years for extortion. The former chairman of the Alcoholic Beverage Commission pleaded guilty for failing to report a liquor license conspiracy to authorities and was sentenced to sixty days in prison. A former Alcoholic Beverage Commission agent was convicted of extortion.

A Nashville paving company owner was convicted of bid rigging and was fined.

A road contractor was charged with perjury for making false statements to a grand jury about his company's involvement with B&B Construction, the Blanton family business. The road contractor was also charged with mail fraud in connection to a bid-rigging scheme.

The head of a construction company also owned by the Blanton family business pleaded guilty to bid rigging and was sentenced to three years in prison and another year in prison for creating a shell company to bid on state contracts.

A Nashville architect pleaded guilty to income tax charges stemming from kickbacks he received on state housing contracts and was given one year's probation.

A former county school superintendent was sentenced to twenty-five months in prison for lying to a federal grand jury looking into the clemency scandal.

Blanton ultimately wasn't charged with a crime in the clemency scheme, continuing his streak. "I'm the most investigated governor in Tennessee history but . . . I've never been indicted for any crime," he once boasted.[170]

## ALLEGATIONS FINALLY STICK

Blanton's multi-year streak of avoiding federal charges ended on October 29, 1980, when a twenty-three-member grand jury returned a twelve-count indictment alleging Blanton and two associates collected profits in return for obtaining a liquor license for a Tennessee business owner. Blanton faced additional charges including conspiracy to defraud the state, extortion, obstruction of interstate commerce, mail fraud, income tax evasion, and lying on his income taxes.[171]

Also named in the indictment were Clyde Edd Hood Jr., an assistant to the governor, and James Allen, Blanton's former campaign manager and a consultant. Federal prosecutors alleged the trio of defendants used their

Clyde Edd Hood Jr., center, a former assistant to Gov. Ray Blanton, is seen in April 1981 (Vic Cooley, *Nashville Banner*, image courtesy of Nashville Public Library, Special Collections)

influence to obtain twelve liquor licenses for friends from the Alcoholic Beverage Commission when Blanton was governor.[172]

Blanton became the first governor in Tennessee history to be indicted on criminal charges. When the case went to trial, it lasted eight weeks, culminating with a jury deliberating for forty-five hours over six days before finding Blanton guilty on eleven counts. Hood and Allen were also found guilty. Hood was sentenced to eighteen months in prison, while Allen was given a two-year sentence.[173]

Blanton, who was fifty-one years old at the time, was sentenced to three years in prison and fined $1,000 per offense for a total of $11,000. He could have been sentenced to up to seventy years.[174]

## ONE FINAL FIGHT

After serving nearly all of his three-year sentence in the hoosegow, Blanton was released in May 1986. He spent thirty days in a halfway house before becoming a fully free man. In early 1988, a federal judge threw out nine of the eleven charges of which Blanton had been convicted, after the judge noted a recent US Supreme Court decision made changes to the nation's federal mail fraud statutes.[175]

In May 1988, Blanton announced yet another bid for public office, this time running for the Eighth Congressional District. Making his campaign announcement, Blanton argued he had been the victim of a Republican-run Department of Justice that was focused on taking down a Democratic governor.[176]

He finished third in the August Democratic primary, netting just 7,200 votes, compared with winner John Tanner's 45,000 votes to secure the nomination. Tanner would end up serving in Congress until 2011.[177]

After his final election loss, Blanton struggled to make ends meet, borrowing from friends and family while he tried to find work. Eventually he ended up becoming a car salesman. In 1991, a judge ordered him to spend ten days in jail for failing to make alimony payments to his first wife.[178]

Rather than fade into obscurity, Blanton spent much of the final years of his life trying to clear his name and relitigate the federal case against him. In 1992, a Memphis State University law professor raised questions about whether Blanton faced a fair trial because of issues with the attorney who represented him. After a federal judge denied a motion to order a new trial for the former governor, Blanton made his case before

Jim Allen, center, a former campaign manager for Gov. Ray Blanton, right, awaits court proceedings in June 1981 (Bob Mack, *Nashville Banner*, image courtesy of Nashville Public Library, Special Collections)

the Sixth Circuit Court of Appeals. The appellate court upheld the lower court's ruling, denying Blanton's request.[179]

Three months later, Blanton died after a struggle with liver disease. He was sixty-six years old.[180]

## A SCANDAL FROM BEYOND THE GRAVE

For most politicians, death would be the end of the story. But for Ray Blanton, tales of corruption went beyond being buried six feet under.

In June 2021, Hamilton County district attorney Neal Pinkston breathed new life into investigations of Blanton. Pinkston said local officials had finally solved the forty-two-year-old cold case murder of Samuel "Wild Bill" Pettyjohn, a Chattanooga liquor store owner.

Murdered in February 1979, Pettyjohn was found at his liquor store where he was shot multiple times, his trademark cigar still smoldering in his hand. At the time of his death, Pettyjohn was found with $100,000 in cash and jewelry on hand, with an unfired .38-caliber pistol nearby. Seven .45-caliber shell casings were found on the scene. Also discovered was a case containing a recording device and several recordings, which were eventually removed from the crime scene and never recovered.[181]

After his death, a Hamilton County grand jury charged two men with killing Pettyjohn, who was facing a trial himself for murder and arson for his role in a 1974 explosion that destroyed half a city block. The charges against the two men were later dismissed, leaving the case unsolved until Hamilton County officials launched a cold case investigation in 2015.[182]

Pinkston's cold case unearthed information that before his murder, Pettyjohn and William Aubrey Thompson, the former Blanton administration official who was later sentenced to prison and went by the name Bob Roundtree, would visit prisoners in Tennessee and tell them they could secure their freedom for money. The duo collected what was paid and provided the money to Blanton's office. Pinkston said Pettyjohn helped Thompson secure the early release of Larkin Bibbs, who was convicted of second-degree murder but released in 1975 after Blanton granted him executive clemency.[183]

Pettyjohn's role would eventually be discovered by federal investigators, who called him before a grand jury. After he agreed to cooperate, Pettyjohn was murdered.[184]

Over the course of the cold case investigation, it was revealed that William Edward Alley, a bank robber who died in 2005 while in federal prison, was behind the murder of Pettyjohn. Alley was paid between $25,000 and $50,000 to murder Pettyjohn, investigators determined after interviewing several witnesses who alleged the contract killing was ordered because the liquor store owner was cooperating with the FBI on the investigation of Blanton.

"Pettyjohn knew too much about illegal activities and his cooperation with federal authorities placed other individuals' freedom, including that of Governor Ray Blanton, at severe risk," a Hamilton County grand jury determined in its June 2021 findings, marking the end of the long-lasting trail of corruption attributed to Blanton.

The news would have been welcome to Hank Hillin, the late FBI agent who had headed the investigation into Blanton's activities as governor.

"Sam Pettyjohn, the huge, likeable black man from Chattanooga with the nine diamond rings set in gold, had been found shot to death in a convenience market he owned," Hillin recalled in 1985. "Robbery was not a motive, because none of his rings was missing.

"Though no evidence was ever developed to identify his killer, I always believed that the people who paid for Larkin Bibbs' release from prison were responsible for Sam Pettyjohn's death."[185]

In a May 1, 1982, photograph, Dinah Shore, left, Gov. Lamar Alexander, President Ronald Reagan, and Jake Butcher take part in the World's Fair opening ceremonies (*Knoxville News-Sentinel* - USA TODAY NETWORK)

# TWO
★ ★ ★
# The Butcher Collapse

THE 1982 WORLD'S FAIR was a transformative event for Jake Butcher and the city of Knoxville.

It had been eight years since an American city had hosted the world exposition, which brought participants from around the globe to its host city for months at a time. The closest thing to a World's Fair the state had ever seen was the Tennessee Centennial and International Exposition in Nashville eight decades earlier. The selection of Knoxville made it the first southeastern US city to host the World's Fair.[1]

Not everybody was enthralled by the idea. Just as Knoxville officials were in New York to complete a $20 million bond to help bankroll the event, they were met with a front-page *Wall Street Journal* story questioning whether such a "scruffy little city" could pull it off. "What if you gave a World's Fair and nobody came?" the headline read.[2]

It certainly wasn't the first time Knoxvillians felt slighted by their depiction in national accounts. Best-selling author John Gunther in 1946 described Knoxville as having an "intense, concentrated, degrading ugliness."

The World's Fair was supposed to change all that. The main theme of the 1982 fair was "Energy Turns the World," with organizers choosing it in part due to the growth of the environmental movement and the 1970s oil crisis, which had caused Western nations to face gas shortages and price increases. Promoters of the Knoxville fair were hoping to rejuvenate a city that was experiencing suburbanization, racial and class divides, and a slow economy. To prepare the city, seventy-two acres of downtown, largely near the University of Tennessee's campus, were converted from an abandoned railroad yard into the host site. Among the structures built on the site were a twenty-six-story building known as the Sunsphere, complete with 24-karat gold glass panes, and a six-story cantilevered structure known as the US Pavilion, which cost $21 million alone to build. A 150-foot-tall, 240-passenger Ferris wheel, known as the Giant Wheel, was erected as one of thirteen rides located at the fair's Family Funland amusement park on Neyland Drive, near the University of Tennessee Volunteers' huge football stadium.[3]

By the time the fair opened in May, supporters of the exposition, along with many of Knoxville's 175,000 residents, were fully convinced it would be a success.[4] Tennessee US senator Howard Baker said the Knoxville exposition would be one of the "most memorable and meaningful world fairs in history." President Ronald Reagan, who delivered an opening day speech behind a bulletproof enclosure, declared, "All Americans can be proud of this World's Fair that we open today."[5] He was joined by members of his cabinet and singer Dinah Shore, a Tennessee native, as well as state and federal politicians. The state legislature even held a one-day special session in the city to commemorate the launch. Although the city had been transformed, outsiders remained skeptical. Days after the fair opened, a *Washington Post* reporter wrote Knoxville's global gathering "seems a blend of stubborn provincialism, the realities of recession economics, and a vision of America that idolizes the shopping mall."[6]

The years-long effort to bring the fair to Knoxville was spearheaded by Butcher, a forty-six-year-old silver-haired banker who had twice run for governor of Tennessee as a Democrat. Although he lost the 1978 general election to Republican Lamar Alexander—Butcher netted 523,495 votes, or 44 percent of the total ballots cast—the East Tennessee businessman remained a popular figure in government and politics.

Butcher was put in charge of the effort to land the fair by Republican Knoxville mayor Kyle Testerman, who in 1975 asked for a study to explore the potential for hosting the fair because of the success of the 1974 exposition in Spokane, Washington. Butcher worked with Baker, who as a US senator secured a meeting with members of President Gerald Ford's cabinet to discuss the idea. In 1977, President Jimmy Carter threw his support behind the effort to bring the fair to Knoxville. A year later, the president announced the approval of $12.4 million in federal grants, which were partially secured by Democratic US senator Jim Sasser of Tennessee. Another $9.9 million federal grant awarded in 1980 helped with the construction of a three-hundred-room hotel and with building the Sunsphere, a new office building, a garage, and the US Pavilion

Democratic gubernatorial candidate Jake Butcher, center, is joined by singer Isaac Hayes, right, at a campaign stop in July 1974 (Owen Cartwright, *Nashville Banner*, image courtesy of Nashville Public Library, Special Collections)

exhibition hall. The city of Knoxville took out $46 million in bonds to cover the cost of the fair.[7]

For Butcher, the fair represented a redemption of sorts. He remained a political force both inside and outside Tennessee despite having twice failed in his quest to become governor. After Carter was elected, Butcher was considered for a cabinet post until he let it be known his focus was winning state office.[8]

Butcher was so deeply connected to Carter that when the former president and his family visited the fair in early October, the Georgia Democrat attended a reception hosted by Butcher. That day Carter reflected on his pledge of federal support for the fair as "obviously one of the best decisions I made in office."[9]

By the time the World's Fair officially closed on October 31, more than eleven million visitors had come to Knoxville, including Reagan and Carter, former vice president Walter Mondale, Bob Hope, Glen Campbell, Kenny Rogers, Crown Prince of Jordan Hassan bin Talal, and Philippine president and First Lady Ferdinand and Imelda Marcos.[10]

"We did it," Butcher boasted as the fair closed. "You ain't a'braggin' when you gone and done it."[11]

Butcher's braggadocio was hardly surprising: the fair was known as Jake's Fair.[12]

Far from being a man of modesty, Butcher was an impeccable dresser who loved Dewar's scotch and lived in a $1.2 million, thirteen-bathroom mansion known as Whirlwind that was located on twenty-six acres. He owned a $2 million jet, a $600,000 helicopter, a $500,000 yacht, two Florida condos, and a $2.2 million Georgia farm with Hereford cows and a gated entrance that read "Home of the Big, Bold Breed."[13]

And although Butcher was seemingly on top of the world as the Knoxville fair closed on that warm October day, his bubble quickly burst. The very next day, the Federal Deposit Insurance Corporation, or FDIC, dispatched 180 agents on a raid of twelve banks owned by Butcher and his brother.[14]

## ROOTED IN BANKING

Born in 1936 in the rural East Tennessee town of Maynardville, population 675, Jacob Franklin Butcher was the first of two sons to Cecil Hilgue Butcher and Kate Walters Butcher. The couple welcomed Jake Butcher's younger brother, Cecil Hilgue Butcher Jr., who went by C. H., into the world in 1938.[15]

Before the boys were born, Cecil Butcher Sr., along with two other men, formed Southern Industrial Banking, a small loan company that helped local residents buy refrigerators, cars, and farm equipment.[16]

As the Butcher boys grew up, they worked on their father's farm and later at his bank. When C. H. Butcher Jr. initially flunked out of college, his father told him to go to work or get out of his house. He enlisted in the Army, where his bunkmate was Charley Pride, who would later become a country music star. After his stint in the military, C. H. Butcher got a degree in banking and soon followed in his father's footsteps of owning a bank while Jake built a gasoline distributorship.[17]

Like his brother, C. H. Butcher enjoyed the finer things in life. In 1981, he bought his wife a $165,000 Rolls-Royce with a bar and telephone for Christmas. He owned condos and boats in Florida and farms in Kentucky and Tennessee. Among the quarter horses C. H. owned was one named Impressive, which came with a stud fee of $15,000 for "20 seconds of copulation."[18]

But in many ways the brothers had their notable differences. A gruff and rough-around-the-edges man, C. H. largely shied away from politics other than a brief stint on the Union County Commission.

Banker C. H. Butcher Jr. is led to a court hearing in Chattanooga in handcuffs in February 1986 (Bill Goodman, *Nashville Banner*, image courtesy of Nashville Public Library, Special Collections)

Unlike his brother, Jake Butcher gravitated toward politics. In 1970, Butcher expressed a desire to become the state treasurer, after he supported Stan Snodgrass, a conservative Nashville Democrat, in that year's Democratic gubernatorial primary. Snodgrass lost his bid for the nomination, but Butcher's interest in politics continued. When lawmakers reconvened in Nashville in January—the Tennessee legislature chooses who will serve as state treasurer—Butcher was defeated by a single vote by former state representative Thomas Wiseman.[19]

By 1972, his name was already being floated for other elected offices, including as a potential candidate in the 1974 gubernatorial campaign. When he officially launched his campaign for governor in May 1974, Butcher—who became the eighth Democrat to seek the party's nomination—said it was time for there to be "fewer professional politicians in government."[20] The primary eventually featured twelve candidates, including Snodgrass, Wiseman, and former US representative Ray Blanton, who ended up winning the crowded race.

Shortly after he lost in the gubernatorial primary to Blanton by two percent of the vote, Butcher briefly considered running for Congress.[21]

But he instead launched another gubernatorial campaign in 1978. Pitted in a primary election against seven other Democrats, including Bob Clement, who would go on to represent Middle Tennessee in Congress, and Nashville mayor Richard Fulton, Butcher faced criticism over his personal finances. The primary turned extremely bitter, with Clement calling for Butcher to disclose details about his family trusts and Butcher responding by calling him "Little Bob."[22]

"It is now apparent that whether or not we engage in the debate, our opponents are going to continue gutter-type mudslinging campaigns. It may be that's the only kind they know how to conduct . . . the time has come for them to put up or shut up," Butcher said days before a primary debate.[23]

With a solid base of supporters from his previous run for office, Butcher ended up winning his party's nomination. But as he campaigned in the general election, he faced a headwind of opposition, including by some in his own party, for an ongoing series of scandals and bad press facing then governor Ray Blanton.

Heading into the general election, Butcher faced Republican Lamar Alexander, who had lost his first gubernatorial campaign in 1974 in the wake of the Watergate scandal. A former Nixon White House aide, Alexander was in the market for an image overhaul. Over the ensuing four years, he worked to burnish his credentials as everything the scandal-plagued Blanton was not. Instead of a three-piece suit, Alexander wore a plaid shirt and hiked across the state, presenting himself as a man of the people and projecting himself as someone who could restore integrity to the office.

As he squared off against Alexander, Butcher sought to make hay out of Alexander's role in securing a church charter to allow a Ruby Tuesday restaurant—then a small Tennessee-based chain—to circumvent Gatlinburg's ban on selling mixed drinks. Alexander responded by launching attacks on Butcher's United American Bank, which had a new bar located on top of its Knoxville building and had financed two private bars in Gatlinburg—including a Ruby Tuesday. The back-and-forth may have been lost on casual voters. A *Tennessean* cartoon on the eve of the race coincided with a Tennessee visit by President Jimmy Carter. It depicted the Democrat expressing bewilderment during a briefing on state politics: "This is very confusing—the Republican's running against Ray Blanton and our guy is running against somebody named 'Ruby Tuesday.'"[24]

Alexander prevailed, earning 55 percent of the vote to Butcher's 44 percent. After the race was over, Butcher wrote a letter to the editor saying he was proud of his campaign, which he said was a positive effort.[25] "Winning the Democratic nomination for governor was one of the great honors of my life," he wrote. "And even though I did not win the general election, I pledge to work in the private sector to contribute whatever I can to the future of our state."[26]

With his failed bids for public office behind him, Butcher turned his attention to his business and the World's Fair.

What made the Butcher brothers stand out in Tennessee by the time the World's Fair came to Knoxville was their relatively rapid financial success. In 1982, C. H. Butcher reported having $105 million in assets and $75 million in debts. Jake Butcher's assets that year were valued at $77.9 million, with $40.2 million in debts.[27]

The Butcher brothers amassed their wealth, and their respective debts, largely because of their banking practices. They first went into business together in 1968, when a small bank in Anderson County, Tennessee, was up for sale. The brothers borrowed money from a Memphis businessman and outbid the other banks that wanted to buy it.

By 1971, the brothers entered the Knoxville market by starting a new bank just outside the city in the small town of Powell. Over the next decade, the Butcher brothers continued to add to their banking portfolio. In 1975, Jake Butcher managed to secure a $16 million loan in two weeks to buy 30 percent of the stock in a bank he later renamed the United American Bank of Knoxville.

By 1982, C. H. controlled twenty-two banks in Tennessee and Kentucky, while Jake had added branches of United American Bank in Memphis and Chattanooga, and two locations in Kentucky. In total, the banks the brothers owned had more than $1.7 billion in assets.

Not satisfied, Jake wanted to bolster his banking operations by adding the Third National Bank in Nashville, which was the second-largest bank in the state at the time with assets of $3.5 billion. In the midst of the World's Fair, Jake bought eighty-eight thousand shares of the bank, making Nashville's business community nervous.

The speed and magnitude of the Butcher brothers' financial dealings impressed many in Tennessee, including Democratic state House Speaker (and later governor) Ned Ray McWherter, who once said Jake would "own the whole state. He'll own the Capitol building."[28]

The Butcher brothers' empire was not only admired by politicians like McWherter, their financial ties to state and federal officials were also deep. After the 1976 presidential election, Carter named Butcher to his inaugural finance committee. The Butchers' banks also loaned millions of dollars to various officials, including US representative Harold Ford Sr., members of then governor Ray Blanton's administration, state House majority leader

Tommy Burnett, state House minority leader Tom Jensen, and a series of other lawmakers.[29]

The Butchers' ties to state officials were so deep, they received $100 million in state money from Tennessee treasurer Harlan Matthews' office to help alleviate cash flow problems at the United American Bank.[30]

Underneath their effort to amass wealth through acquiring new properties, the Butcher brothers' banking operations were far from financially sound. After federal investigators began examining the Butchers' banking empire, they discovered questionable and downright illegal activities. Jake Butcher would frequently make loans to purchase stock in banks whose trusts were controlled by his brother, his friends, or himself.[31]

Before the FDIC launched its coordinated raid on the Butcher banks in November 1982, the agency often had questions about the banks' loans. United American Bank had loaned money recklessly, with its reserves of capital too low to be able to secure against the loss of any bad loans. At the time, when a bank's total capital-to-assets ratio was below 7 percent, the banking industry began asking questions and making demands of the bank. In 1977, United American Bank of Knoxville's ratio was 6.58 percent. By May 1982, an FDIC audit of Jake Butcher's bank said that it needed to address outstanding problems with the capital-to-assets ratio by the end of the year or there would be consequences.[32]

On several occasions, the Butcher brothers' banks were able to avoid serious issues with regulators thanks to various deceptive practices. The Butcher banks received notice when FDIC examiners were coming in for what was supposed to be a surprise visit. The banks were aided by a convicted bank felon who worked as Jake Butcher's financial consultant and who would transfer millions of dollars in questionable loans to banks that weren't facing questions by regulators. C. H. Butcher's accountant helped create new companies that took on bad loans.

The deceptive tactics, however, were unable to throw off the FDIC, which on Nov. 1, 1982, sent 10 percent of its audit force into the Butcher banks. Despite the massive, coordinated federal effort, the news media didn't initially pick up on the flurry of activity.

First disclosed in the *Tennessean*—buried on page twelve—several days after the FDIC entered the banks, the newspaper reported Butcher's United American Bank was being scrutinized by federal examiners who were conducting an audit of the bank's loans.[33]

The FDIC's review examiner in Memphis said the probe was a "routine examination" conducted annually. He noted the FDIC had no indication that there was anything wrong with any of the loans to the bank, with the examination expected to take three weeks.[34]

But as the federal probe unfolded, the picture of the Butcher banks became clear: United American Bank had issued at least $90 million in loans it probably couldn't collect on, and only had about $40 million in capital.

In January 1983, the Butchers moved at least $25 million in bad bank loans into Southern Industrial Banking, the company their father had started decades earlier to make small loans. The transaction provided temporary relief for United American—until it was eventually unearthed.[35]

Over time, state and federal investigators were able to untangle the web of deceptive banking practices that found the Butchers had relied on a group of insiders and friends, often acting on their behalf, to secure millions of dollars in loans with little or no collateral. The probe unearthed the presence of front men and women who hid loan transactions from examiners, forged documents, made illegal wire transfers, issued false financial statements, and hatched a secret plan to funnel millions of dollars into Jake Butcher's failed gubernatorial campaign. Tens of millions of dollars disappeared into secret bank accounts, and there was a complete lack of adequate state and federal regulatory oversight.[36]

In late January 1983, United American Bank reported a $2.3 million loss for the previous year, citing more than $7.5 million in bad loans during the final quarter of 1982.[37] As a result of the losses, the bank announced Jake Butcher would have some of his authority taken away while remaining as chairman. Butcher blamed the losses on a financial crisis and the "crippled" economy.

Days later, the state's Department of Banking announced it was launching its own investigation of Butcher's bank.

Despite the onslaught of investigations, United American Bank did its best to attempt to allay concerns about its business practices. The bank continued to run ads in local newspapers, including one in the *Knoxville News-Sentinel* in early February that noted how the FDIC insures customers' deposits, adding, "United American Bank assures you of its continued commitment to you and the community." Shortly afterward, United American took out a full-page ad in the paper to note that it was "not uncommon" for a bank to report financial losses.[38]

United American Bank successfully filed a petition in federal court to keep the FDIC's findings secret.[39]

Banker Jake Butcher heads for an elevator as TV cameras give chase in September 1986 (Owen Cartwright, *Nashville Banner*, image courtesy of Nashville Public Library, Special Collections)

## FINAL THROES OF THE EMPIRE

The hammer finally came down on Jake Butcher on Valentine's Day in 1983, when state and federal banking officials closed United American Bank of Knoxville after declaring it insolvent. Butcher quickly stepped down as chairman of the board. The closing of the bank made it the fourth-largest commercial bank failure in American history. Over time, more details about the Butcher banking empire's collapse revealed it was the largest bank failure in the nation's history at that point.[40]

At the time of its closing, the bank had $750 million in assets and $590 million in deposits. The bank reopened the next day after a $70.5 million merger with First Tennessee of Memphis, the state's largest bank.[41]

Less than two weeks after the collapse of the Butcher banks, the Tennessee Sports Hall of Fame named Jake Butcher Tennessean of the year. He was selected for the award because of his role in bringing the World's Fair to the state.[42]

In the months that followed, the business world that the Butcher brothers had built continued to crumble. Southern Industrial Banking filed for bankruptcy in early March. A congressional probe into the collapse of the Butcher brothers' banks was launched.[43]

In July, C. H. Butcher, whose net worth earlier in the year had been $75 million, declared bankruptcy.[44]

By August 1983, a federal judge declared Jake Butcher and one of his associates bankrupt while ordering their assets to be liquidated to pay more than $20 million in debts. Over time, Butcher's belongings were sold off to pay for his debts. A pair of llamas—a gift from Peru for the 1982 fair—a donkey, and several pieces of farm equipment were among the items sold at a two-hour auction at Butcher's mansion. Butcher moved to Florida to avoid continued scrutiny.[45]

It wasn't until November 1984 that he was indicted by a federal grand jury on dozens of charges, including falsifying bank records and siphoning off money for personal use between early 1981 and late 1982.[46]

In June 1985, Jake Butcher was sentenced to twenty years in prison after pleading guilty to using bogus loans to defraud his banks in Knoxville and Chattanooga out of nearly $15 million. The federal judge handling the case said Butcher's actions had "badly shaken" the public's confidence in the banking system. He began serving his sentence in September 1985, less than three years after the end of the Knoxville World's Fair.

In 1989, while he was still in prison, Butcher was indicted again, along with eleven others, for defrauding a former bank in Orlando, Florida. The criminal activity outlined in the 1989 indictment allegedly occurred when Butcher was awaiting trial for his earlier crimes. Butcher eventually pleaded guilty to the latter charges but was not sentenced to additional time in prison, in part for cooperating with the investigation.[47]

Jake Butcher wasn't the only member of the family to face the justice system. In February 1986, C. H. Butcher was charged with twenty-six counts of fraud for his role in Southern Industrial Banking. Eight days later, he was indicted again and charged with seventy-one counts of conspiracy and bankruptcy fraud, for his part in a scheme involving his wife and kids to hide millions of dollars in cash and other revenue sources from bankruptcy creditors.[48]

A Davidson County grand jury indicted C. H. Butcher in April for falsifying reports to state officials. He was later sentenced to five years in prison.[49]

In June, a federal grand jury indicted him for a third time, this time on federal income tax fraud charges. In August, C. H. Butcher was acquitted of the federal charges related to Southern Industrial Banking.[50]

While awaiting sentencing for bankruptcy fraud, tax fraud, and money laundering, C. H. Butcher was indicted yet again in April 1987, along with

Democrat Harold Ford Sr. of Memphis and others who were involved in a scheme concerning $1.5 million in loans that went to the congressman from the Butcher banks. The money in question dated back to when Jake Butcher was running for governor in 1978, with Ford endorsing the Democratic candidate after he received a loan.[51]

Although C. H. Butcher pleaded guilty to two counts, when the case against Ford went to trial in 1990, it ended with a mistrial after a jury failed to reach a verdict. A subsequent trial ultimately led to Ford and two former Butcher lawyers being acquitted.[52]

In July 1987, C. H. Butcher was sentenced to twenty years after he pleaded guilty to bankruptcy fraud, bank fraud, tax fraud, and money laundering. In 1993, he was granted parole after serving nearly seven years in prison. He died in 2002 at the age of sixty-four after a fall at his home.[53]

Jake Butcher was released from prison in 1992 after serving six years and eight months of his twenty-year sentence. After his release, he summed up his tumultuous journey of riding the high of the 1982 World's Fair to the collapse of his banking empire simply. "Two years and 80 months—to hell and back again," he told the *Knoxville News-Sentinel*.[54]

Jake Butcher died in 2017 at the age of eighty-one.[55]

Pat Lester of Crossville, Tennessee, joins more than seventy other bingo players in Algood, Tennessee, on May 25, 1989, when a local businessman thought he had found a loophole that let the game be played legally (Dianne Milam - USA TODAY NETWORK)

# THREE

★ ★ ★

# Operation Rocky Top

THERE WAS A TIME IN THE 1980S when Tennesseans would flock to smoke-filled old warehouses and shuttered skating rinks for relaxation. Inside, crowds would unpack their good luck charms on tables covered in dozens of sheets of paper containing an organized collection of random numbers. The game was bingo.

As patrons opened their wallets and purses—credit cards were as good as cash—to partake in an American pastime, options were seemingly limitless: they could buy regular playing cards and "pull tabs," put a dollar in a pickle jar, get in on the action of a numbers game known as the "horse race," or head over to video poker machines labeled "For Amusement Only."

While such scenes were commonplace in Las Vegas, it was allowed in Tennessee—which, with some exceptions, has had a ban on gambling for two centuries—because it was all for a good cause: charity.

Until it wasn't.

In a sense, the downfall of Tennessee's charitable bingo began in 1985 with a simple inquiry. A constituent asked an obscure, backbench Republican member of the Tennessee House of Representatives to look into a business that was running a charitable bingo operation. The mustachioed lawmaker said he'd look into the matter, not knowing what he might find.

By the time it was all over in the early 1990s, that simple inquiry had upended a complex web of deceit, lies, bribes, and illegal gambling. Secret recordings and undercover agents followed in a wide-ranging probe that ultimately led to two suicides and dozens of indictments.

And if it wasn't for James Rand "Randy" McNally III, an East Tennessee pharmacist turned politician, what would later be known as Operation Rocky Top might have had a very different outcome.

## A QUIET BACKBENCHER

McNally was born in Massachusetts in January 1944; his parents moved the family to the East Tennessee town of Oak Ridge in 1948. His father, who was known as Rand, was a physicist who had graduated from the Massachusetts Institute of Technology.

Oak Ridge, which was famous for helping create materials for the Manhattan Project—the research and development effort that led to the world's first nuclear weapon—was tightly guarded throughout McNally's childhood. Those who entered and exited had to show a badge at a gate. McNally recalls FBI agents interviewing residents about their neighbors who, like the McNallys, had moved to Oak Ridge from other states to work at one of the three national laboratory facilities. "It just seemed kind of normal," he said of his early interactions with the FBI.[1]

The oldest of seven, McNally earned a bachelor's degree from Memphis State University before attending courses at the University of Tennessee's health science campus in Memphis, where he earned a pharmacy degree. While at the University of Tennessee, McNally—who once played John F. Kennedy for a mock debate in high school—became a Republican and worked on Winfield Dunn's successful 1970 campaign for governor. He later campaigned for other Tennessee Republicans, including US senator Bill Brock.[2]

In 1978, McNally turned down an opportunity to work for Lamar Alexander's gubernatorial campaign in favor of running for office on his own after a five-term Democratic incumbent state lawmaker from Oak Ridge gave up the seat. McNally easily won the GOP nomination and later won 60 percent of the vote in the general election.[3]

When McNally was sworn into office in January 1979, he was one of twenty-two freshmen in the House who took their oath just days before Alexander's early swearing-in amid his Democratic predecessor's cash-for-clemency scandal. McNally was in the minority, with Democrats controlling sixty seats in the House to Republicans' thirty-eight. There was also one independent.[4]

During McNally's early years as a lawmaker, he was rarely written about in newspapers' coverage of the legislature. His first mentions in the *Tennessean* came in 1981, when McNally sponsored a bill to make it a felony

Sen. Randy McNally (R-Oak Ridge), who wore a wire for the Rocky Top investigation, poses with a bingo sign in his office in January 1990 (Steve Lowry, *Nashville Banner*, image courtesy of Nashville Public Library, Special Collections)

to sell fake pills and for bucking his party in casting the lone Republican vote for a Democratic redistricting plan.[5]

In subsequent years, McNally introduced legislation to lower the legal blood alcohol limit for drunken driving and bolster punishments for tampering with food products, potable liquids, or pharmaceuticals.

In December 1982, McNally was elected floor leader of the thirty-eight House Republicans. He was re-elected to the position in 1984.[6]

When Rep. W. C. Herndon Jr., a Camden Democrat, had a heart attack while he was debating a bill on the House floor in 1984, McNally and another colleague tried to revive the freshman lawmaker and World War II veteran. Herndon was later pronounced dead at a nearby hospital.[7]

Despite McNally's rank within the House, reporters widely viewed him as a bumbling backbencher. He was known around the Capitol as "Senator Radon" and a "space cadet." Unbeknownst to his colleagues, McNally would go on to spend two years surreptitiously recording members of the Tennessee General Assembly.[8]

## CHARITY OR A LOTTERY?

McNally got to be involved in what became Operation Rocky Top— the codename for the multi-year federal probe into illegal gambling in

Tennessee—after he received a phone call in the fall of 1985 from a member of an East Tennessee chapter of the Fraternal Order of Eagles, a charitable group focused on health-related issues. The member told McNally about the local branch of the Army and Navy Union, a veteran organization the caller alleged was running a bingo operation that fell outside the confines of state law.[9]

At the time, bingo was allowed in Tennessee so long as it was considered for charitable purposes, with all other forms of gambling remaining illegal.

Tennessee has had a complicated history with gambling. In 1787, the first recorded lottery in the territory of Tennessee, which was still part of North Carolina, helped pay for building a road. In subsequent years, privately run lotteries were used to help individuals and businesses make money until they were outlawed by the legislature in 1809 for fear that they encouraged "idleness and dissipation."[10]

The state had eleven "quasi-public" lotteries between 1819 and 1829 that allowed individuals and organizations to operate a lottery to pay off debts. Lotteries were used to build wagon trails, construct a hospital and other projects in Nashville, and fund schools including Nashville College, Cumberland College, and Peabody College, which is now part of Vanderbilt University.[11]

In 1829, the Tennessee Supreme Court ruled in *State v. Smith and Lane* that private lotteries were gambling. The case arose after the defendants were charged with gaming because they were running private lotteries. State law said at the time anyone convicted of gaming was disqualified from holding any office "of trust or profit" for five years.

In his opinion, Justice John Catron, who later served on the US Supreme Court from 1837 to 1865 after being appointed by President Andrew Jackson, offered a sharp rebuke of the lotteries. "Not only ruin and beggary, but drunkenness, is almost uniformly the effect of gaming," he wrote.[12]

Praising the legislature for adopting a "wise policy" that punished gambling, Catron added, "Had Tennessee not used means to suppress such profligacy, she would be a disgrace to civilized communities."[13]

In addition to the state Supreme Court's ruling, the Tennessee legislature approved a law in 1829 that made unauthorized lotteries illegal. By 1832, state lawmakers had entirely abolished lotteries in Tennessee. And two years later, a convention led to the adoption of a new state constitution that enshrined a provision making state lotteries illegal.[14]

"The legislature shall have no power to authorize lotteries for any purpose; but shall pass laws to prohibit the sale of lottery tickets in the State," Article XI, Section 5 of the 1834 state constitution read. A similar provision was included in the 1870 state constitution. The ban existed until voters approved a constitutional amendment in 2002 to create a state-run lottery to fund education. Sports gaming was legalized in Tennessee following a landmark US Supreme Court ruling in 2018.[15]

Before and during McNally's early days in the legislature, lawmakers frequently considered making changes to allow some form of gambling in Tennessee. In 1971, at the encouragement of the Catholic dioceses in Memphis and Nashville and veterans' groups, the General Assembly approved a law that exempted bingo from the state's ban on gambling. The law allowed nonprofit groups to use bingo operations to raise money.[16]

In 1975, a court case resulted in a ruling that pinball gambling machines—which were only legal in Nevada at the time—did not fall within the state's ban on gambling. Soon there were fifteen thousand pinball gambling machines in Tennessee, grossing an estimated $100 million per year.[17]

In 1979, lawmakers had passed a measure that declared both pinball and bingo gambling illegal.[18]

After the bill was approved, two Catholic bishops tried to lobby Alexander to veto the measure, despite the governor vowing to sign it. One aspect of the new law, which Alexander signed, gave the pinball industry until 1982 to phase out operations, while bingo halls were set to be shuttered forty days after the law was enacted. A subsequent legal challenge led to a court injunction that allowed bingo halls to remain open for the rest of 1979.[19]

When lawmakers returned to Nashville for the 1980 legislative session, a top priority was to once again legalize bingo. Ultimately, lawmakers passed a bill to allow bingo in Tennessee to continue, with Alexander signing it into law the same day he approved a separate bill to restructure the Tennessee Bureau of Investigation. The new bingo law allowed operations to continue through July 1983 but added new restrictions, including a requirement for charities to file annual reports if their bingo proceeds exceeded $5,000. As a result of the new law, eight hundred permit applications were sent out to prospective operators.[20]

In October 1981, Tennessee attorney general William Leech issued an opinion after a Nashville charitable solicitations board asked the state's top attorney for an explanation about the difference between the city's and

Tennessee attorney general Bill Leech in the state supreme court chamber in June 1978 (Bill Goodman, *Nashville Banner*, image courtesy of Nashville Public Library, Special Collections)

state's charitable solicitation laws. In his opinion, Leech said expenses of bingo operations and charitable raffles, including prizes, could not exceed 25 percent of the game's gross receipts. The opinion essentially reversed previous guidance issued by the attorney general's office that the 25 percent could not include prizes. At the time, bingo operators throughout the state would often pay back upward of 90 percent of their gross receipts through monetary prizes.[21]

The *Tennessean* explained the effect of the opinion by noting that, under the previous interpretation of the law, a bingo operator that made $1,000 could have paid out $900 in prizes while giving as little as $75 to charity. Under Leech's 1981 opinion, $750 of the $1,000 made by a bingo operator had to go to charity, with only $250 remaining for prizes and expenses.[22]

"I think it ought to close down all the bingo operations in the state of Tennessee," said Secretary of State Gentry Crowell, whose office oversaw charitable gaming.[23]

In response to Leech's opinion, the Tennessee legislature once again tinkered with the state's bingo laws when another bill was passed in 1982 that placed limits on bingo prize amounts, added new restrictions on where an organization could operate, and set how many days they could be open. But the bill also entirely eliminated the 1983 end-date for bingo in Tennessee and removed the 25 percent limit outlined in Leech's opinion.[24]

Leech issued another consequential opinion in 1984, when he said bingo was illegal in Tennessee because it violated the state constitution.

The opinion was originally requested by Democratic representatives John Ford of Memphis and Don Dills of Dyersburg. But when Leech had completed his findings, the two lawmakers withdrew their request, preventing it from being released. Sen. Carl Koella, a Maryville Republican, subsequently requested an opinion on the matter, allowing Leech to release it.[25]

In the opinion, Leech said bingo games and raffles were forms of a lottery.

Even more than Leech's 1981 opinion, the 1984 study of the state's bingo law was a direct threat to those running bingo operations, including churches. The year before Leech's opinion was issued, bingo games had grossed $50 million in Tennessee. Less than a month after the opinion was released, five Catholic churches and a Jewish congregation filed a lawsuit in an attempt to block the state from revoking their bingo permits. The plaintiffs said revoking their bingo permits would eliminate a "major means of support" for their operations. A Nashville judge sided with the plaintiffs, declaring bingo constitutional.[26]

As the case was appealed to the Tennessee Supreme Court, the General Assembly once again responded to Leech's bingo opinion through legislation. Sponsored by Sen. Steve Cohen and Rep. Mike Kernell, who were both Memphis-based Democrats, a bill introduced in January 1985 defined any bingo-related funds as charitable contributions. In less than two months, the bill sailed through both chambers, despite the secretary of state urging lawmakers to repeal the law that exempted bingo from the state's gambling laws. Alexander allowed the bill to become law without his signature.[27]

The new law forced Attorney General Mike Cody, who had replaced Leech in the summer of 1985, to drop the state's appeal to the state Supreme Court.[28]

## BEGINNING WITH A BRIBE

By the time McNally was encouraged in the fall of 1985 to look into the Army and Navy Union—the veteran group McNally's constituent had alleged was running an illegal gambling operation—there was plenty of suspicion about bingo.

Earlier in the year, state officials had requested records about how two loosely defined church organizations were spending their bingo money. In March 1985, a federal grand jury was reportedly looking into the churches. In April, the *Commercial Appeal* reported state and federal investigators were examining Tennessee's bingo industry.[29]

In May, the newspaper reported a federal grand jury was looking into profit skimming, mail fraud, and tax evasion at Memphis bingo games. By June, federal investigators were reportedly examining general sessions court judge Ira H. Murphy, a former state lawmaker, who was listed on the paperwork for a bingo application.[30]

To begin looking into the Army and Navy Union, McNally stopped by the bingo operation and discovered it was offering prizes that were above what was allowed. He reached out to the secretary of state's office and asked for information about the group. McNally's inquiries ended up getting the initial caller inspected by officials. "That kinda twerked me up a little," he recalled in 2016.[31]

When McNally called one of the names associated with the Army and Navy Union's state paperwork, he was eventually able to reach someone who told him he could get state approval by filling out some basic information. "I'm thinking, it certainly doesn't smell good," McNally recalled.[32]

While he was continuing his probe, McNally said he was approached by three of his colleagues in the legislature, who encouraged him to work things out between the Army and Navy Union and the Fraternal Order of Eagles. Shortly thereafter, another member of the legislature asked Mc-Nally to have lunch with Jim Long, a bingo lobbyist. Reporters working at the Capitol said Long was known for his secretive demeanor. He was an almost invisible figure whose presence was known but he wasn't as engaging as other lobbyists.[33]

Long, who lived next door to Donnie Walker, the state's chief bingo regulator, ran what was commonly known as "The Association." Formally called the Bingo Association, professional gamblers operating charity bingo halls would pay $500 a month for what was widely viewed as protection money.[34] Some of the money paid to The Association went to Walker. In return, the paying members would be warned before state inspectors entered their bingo halls to make sure there was nothing suspicious happening.[35]

At the encouragement of his colleagues, McNally agreed he would meet with Long. And so on a Thursday afternoon in February 1986, McNally and Long lunched together at The Hermitage, Nashville's first million-dollar hotel whose guests and visitors have included US presidents, Charlie Chaplin, Babe Ruth, and John Dillinger.[36] Located steps away from the state Capitol, The Hermitage was the go-to hotel for pro- and anti-suffrage supporters before Tennessee ratified the Nineteenth Amendment, decades before it hosted Long and McNally as they discussed bingo and politics.[37]

During their conversation, Long said something that McNally remembered "stopped me cold."[38]

Long told McNally, "Some of our friends like their money a little at a time and some of them like it all at once." The East Tennessee Republican said he was bothered by the fact that a legislator could regulate how they received a contribution.

Uncertain of what to do, McNally took the weekend to think about his interaction with Long. "I didn't want to overreact," he recalled. "I didn't know who to go to. I'd gone to the secretary of state's office and it just was not working out at all."

On the following Monday—before lawmakers returned for their first day of session for the week—McNally, who was a member of the Rotary Club, went to the downtown club meeting in Nashville. As he listened to the prayer at the meeting, something triggered him to act. He considered his options of whom to reach out to. The secretary of state's office was a non-starter. Another option was the Tennessee Bureau of Investigation. There was also the Nashville police or East Tennessee officials. He settled on reaching out to the FBI.

When he cold-called the local office, he was told someone would call him back. A few minutes later, he received a phone call from FBI agent Richard Knudsen.

McNally briefly shared his story with Knudsen, who told the lawmaker he and Roger Farley, a TBI agent, were concerned about bingo. "He said there's been a lot of smoke but there hasn't been a lot of fire," McNally remembered.

Before McNally entered the scene, Knudsen said federal agents had been exploring allegations into Tennessee officials that for the most part went nowhere. Knudsen, who had worked under Hank Hillin, the lead FBI agent who zeroed in on former governor Ray Blanton with Operation TennPar years earlier, said McNally kicked their investigation to a new level.[39]

The two agents made arrangements to meet McNally at his legislative office in Nashville, inside the War Memorial Building. The agents suggested that the bingo men were testing McNally to see how he would react. If Long or Walker followed up, the agents encouraged him to tell them everything was fine.

About a week later, McNally was at a legislative reception when he was approached by Long and Walker. Like he had rehearsed with the two agents, McNally said he was fine and had no questions for the two bingo men.

McNally followed up with the FBI and TBI agents, who said he should meet with the bingo men if they asked. Days later, as McNally was heading to a committee meeting in the legislature, Long walked up to the lawmaker and handed him a white envelope while expressing appreciation for McNally. The interaction was brief, with Long walking away seconds later. As McNally started to walk to his committee meeting, he was conflicted about what to do. Missing the committee meeting might raise suspicions, he thought. But he settled on going back to his office and calling the FBI and TBI agents, who told him to leave the envelope in his pocket.

Knudsen, another FBI agent, and Farley picked up McNally in an unmarked car and headed to the parking lot of a McDonald's in downtown Nashville, right across the street from the *Tennessean* and the *Nashville Banner*, the city's main newspapers. Inside the car, the three agents, who were wearing gloves, peered into the envelope Long had handed McNally and found three hundred-dollar bills. "At that point I felt a little insulted that you could purchase a legislator for $300," McNally recalled.

The agents told McNally the bingo men were once again testing him. They asked him whether he would continue to work with them. While with the agents later that day, McNally called Long to express his appreciation for the money. When he asked Long whether he should report the money as a contribution, the bingo lobbyist said it wasn't necessary.

As McNally continued his involvement in the investigation, the agents set certain parameters. He wasn't allowed to ask for money or record just anyone on a secret recording device that was added to his home phone.

In July 1986, McNally met Long for dinner at the Regas Restaurant, a Knoxville culinary staple that opened before the Great Depression and operated until shutting its doors in 2010.[40] At the time, lobbyists' interactions with lawmakers were freer-flowing than they are today. Lobbyists could buy lawmakers' meals. Even if a lobbyist wasn't able to attend a dinner, it wasn't uncommon for them to provide the lawmaker with their credit card or give the legislator "walking around" or "suit and cigar" money.[41]

And although Tennessee still had several dry counties, post-workday, late-night options were plentiful in Nashville when lawmakers were in town.

For years, there was a Monday night tradition around the Capitol called "choir practice" in which lobbyists would host lawmakers at a local restaurant and split the cost of the bill. The cost-splitting method was in part because state law at the time required lobbyists to file a disclosure if they spent over $50 a week on a lawmaker. Then there was "The Kremlin," an after-hours gathering at a hotel across the street from the Capitol where lawmakers, lobbyists, and others would drink and socialize. Another option was the "Capitol Hill Club," which took place at another hotel but included journalists in the mix. The laissez-faire relationship between lobbyists and lawmakers was highlighted when a top liquor lobbyist testified during a 1975 legislative committee meeting that he would pick up the tab for any booze lawmakers would get from the Hermitage liquor store across the street from the legislative office complex.[42]

Jim O'Hara, a *Tennessean* reporter who covered the legislature in the 1980s, said there was always "an undercurrent of what seemed like petty corruption all the time."[43]

## AN UNDERCOVER LAWMAKER

Before heading into the Knoxville restaurant to meet with the bingo lobbyist, McNally was outfitted for the first time with two recorders, including one with a transmitter that allowed the agents to hear the conversation in real time. Long told McNally over a meal about how illegal bingo operations in Tennessee worked.

Long said McNally should get a lobbyist who is close to him and when there is a close vote in the legislature, the lobbyist could "barter" his vote and the two would then split the money. Long was open about lobbying practices in Tennessee, citing specific votes and lawmakers whom lobbyists had influenced. During the dinner, a code word—Dr. Emory—was announced on the restaurant's paging system. McNally excused himself to the bathroom, where he met an agent who told him the tape was about to run out. When the dinner ended, McNally worried the evening had been a failure because he didn't get any more money from Long.[44]

But with the recording in hand, the FBI agents were able to appeal to officials in Washington, DC, to make the case a higher priority and bring in more resources.

Before working with McNally, Knudsen had been the case agent for an investigation that arose from the arrest of Michael Burnett, an international conman who had come to Nashville in 1984. Also known as Michael Raymond, Burnett spent three decades engaging in nefarious activities, including theft, fraud, and ordering murders, before he became an informant for the FBI.

Knudsen came across Burnett in 1984, when the agent found him and an associate in a van in Belle Meade—a posh, small city located southwest of downtown Nashville—near a home they were planning on robbing. Inside the van, agents found weapons, including a handgun and a machine gun. In an effort to broker a deal, Burnett—who had an established history with law enforcement and the justice system—told agents he was paying bribes to city officials in Chicago and New York. For the next eighteen months, Burnett worked as a confidential informant in an operation that ultimately led to the fall of two powerful New York politicians.[45]

With the experience of Burnett's case under his belt, Knudsen made the decision to bring an undercover agent into Tennessee to join their investigation. One of the agents who wanted the job at one point went out to a local bar, got drunk, and apparently made an ass of himself, Knudsen recalled.[46]

Rather than hiring that agent, Knudsen brought in Ken Walsh, who he said was a serious professional FBI agent who reminded him of an accountant. Using the name Ken J. Wilson, Walsh posed as an Atlanta-based bingo supply company official and financial consultant, who hired David "Peabody" Ledford, a lobbyist and former lawmaker. Ledford introduced Walsh to the bingo officials, gaining their trust by engaging them and even contributing $200 to both the state Democrats' and Republicans' annual fundraisers in 1988.[47]

Sporting horn-rimmed glasses and a beard while maintaining a presence around the legislature from April 1987 until September 1988, Walsh rented a one-bedroom apartment overlooking the Cumberland River a few blocks from the Capitol. In December 1987, Walsh asked Ledford to monitor legislative developments for a bingo company he said he owned. The company was allegedly interested in building a bingo supply plant in Tennessee. For compensation, which was ultimately paid by the FBI, Ledford shared with Walsh information about bingo-related developments in the legislature and introduced him to lawmakers, lobbyists, and even a reporter.[48]

During the 1988 legislative session, Walsh was part of several private strategy meetings with lobbyists who were discussing that year's bingo bill. A veteran lobbyist remembered Walsh as someone who was a passive observer in the meetings, which often included Walker.

In addition to Walsh being deployed to Tennessee in 1987, McNally was outfitted with more recording equipment beyond the device at his house that allowed him to tape telephone calls. Once, when secretary of state Gentry Crowell called him, McNally picked up the call on a phone that didn't have the recording device. He started talking and quickly

Undercover FBI special agent Ken Walsh, right, sits in a Senate hearing room on February 29, 1988, next to lobbyist David "Peabody" Ledford, left, bingo figure W. D. "Donnie" Walker, and secretary of state Gentry Crowell (Rick Musacchio - USA TODAY NETWORK)

hung up—convincing Crowell they had been cut off. By the time he called back, McNally had moved to the phone that was outfitted to record conversations.

Beyond phone recordings, investigators initially wanted McNally to wear cowboy boots or carry a briefcase that held a recorder. McNally balked—he didn't wear boots or carry a briefcase and thought it would look suspicious. They finally settled on placing a recording device on his back, underneath his suit jacket, that had a microphone attached to it. One day, when McNally, who had been elected to the state Senate in November 1986, was walking out of the upper chamber, Sen. Milton Hamilton, a Union City Democrat, patted him on the back. He noticed something under McNally's jacket. Hamilton asked McNally if he was carrying a pistol. Thinking on his feet, McNally explained one of his suspenders had come loose.

The incident forced a change in how McNally carried the recording device. While shopping one day, McNally—who was a runner—bought a pair of neoprene thigh braces that he would use to hold the recorder. One wire of the device went to his shirt buttons, with another used for a toggle switch that allowed him to turn the recorder on and off.

He ended up wearing a recording device around the Capitol for more than two years. At the beginning, McNally was scared to wear the wire but over time he grew accustomed to strapping on the device four days a week during the legislative sessions of 1987, 1988, and some of 1989.

Over the years, McNally had several notable interactions with the various players involved in the bingo scheme.

In September 1986, while he was meeting Long and Walker in the parking lot of an East Tennessee hospital, the undercover surveillance vehicle that was recording their interaction was approached by local police who were looking for someone. The undercover agents told the police they were keeping an eye on the hospital after a recent prison escape. The police officers then moved to McNally, Long, and Walker, who told the officers McNally worked at the hospital. Unbeknownst to the local cops, Walker and Long were handing off a $1,000 bribe to McNally under the eye of federal agents.[49]

During the 1987 legislative session, Walker was so convinced that McNally was "on the hook" that he offered the senator a $10,000 bribe to vote for a bill to legalize betting on horse racing.[50] The vote on the bill was set to be close, with a Memphis racing promoter paying Walker $24,000 to deliver the decisive vote in favor of the bill. Days before the vote, McNally told reporters he was likely to oppose the bill, citing the "trouble" the state was having controlling bingo. McNally ultimately turned down the bribe and voted against the bill.[51]

## AN INVESTIGATION OF ANOTHER SORT

The 1987 legislative session was a high-stakes time for bingo in Tennessee and not only because McNally and Walsh were secretly recording their interactions on Capitol Hill.

A handful of the usual bingo- and gaming-related bills were introduced by lawmakers that year. One measure would have allowed the "Association for Retarded Citizens" to conduct off-site bingo games. Another would have prohibited bingo operators from participating in games or owning buildings. In March, a bill described as a "housekeeping" measure by its sponsor was unanimously approved by the Senate Judiciary Committee.[52] Despite widespread support for the bill, several committee members questioned what the bill actually did—after the vote was over.

After the measure was approved in the House, it faced pushback in the Senate, with the sponsor trying to allay concerns by saying it was simply trying to clean up the state's bingo law and make it conform to practice.[53]

Tennessee attorney general Mike Cody in October 1980 (Don Foster, *Nashville Banner*, image courtesy of Nashville Public Library, Special Collections)

The legislation sought to broaden the state's charitable bingo law by allowing churches, schools, and philanthropic, fraternal, and veterans groups to run bingo games. Under the bill, such groups could operate "bingo, raffles, and similar games of chance." The measure also would have removed a requirement that sponsoring organizations inform the Internal Revenue Service after someone won more than $500.[54]

The House and Senate passed the supposedly innocuous "housekeeping" bingo bill, and while it was awaiting Gov. Ned Ray McWherter's signature, attorney general Michael Cody issued an opinion, requested by McNally, challenging the constitutionality of bingo.[55]

In his opinion, Cody noted how the vast majority of the money earned from the state's bingo operations was not going toward charities. "Data compiled by the secretary of state demonstrates that the charitable purpose underlying the creation of the exemption for charitable bingo has, in practice, not been served," Cody said in the opinion. "In reality, many organizations are generating dollars primarily for larger prizes and to fund the operation of the game themselves."[56]

After Cody issued his opinion, McNally said it suggested the state's bingo law had "evolved" and violated the state constitution's prohibition on lotteries. Crowell conceded that Cody's opinion "borders on saying bingo may in fact be a lottery." Walker, the bingo lobbyist, said Cody's analysis was "bogus."[57]

Citing Cody's opinion, McWherter vetoed the bingo bill, which he deemed unconstitutional. It was the Democrat's only veto of his eight years in office. The week before, McWherter had suggested it might be time to do a complete review of the state's bingo laws and regulations.[58]

Less than a month later, the *Tennessean* began publishing its own comprehensive review of bingo in the Volunteer State, launching what would be a twenty-part series that picked up where the newspaper's previous coverage and Cody's opinion left off. In 1986, the paper reported the FBI was investigating allegations of kickbacks and other financial benefits for the state's bingo regulators.[59]

Like Cody, the newspaper noted how a review of the state's 280 licensed bingo games indicated that only 2 percent, or $1.03 million, of the total amount raised in 1986 went to charity. A total of $33.2 million was returned to gamblers.

The first story—published on May 10, 1987—highlighted how operators of bingo halls were conducting illegal games, including by offering pull tabs to increase their revenue. The article quoted Jim Roberson, the former director of charitable solicitations in the secretary of state's office, as saying that charitable bingo was "a farce and fraud." Roberson called for the state to treat bingo for what it really was: big-time gambling.

For more than a month, the *Tennessean* explored different aspects of the bingo industry, interviewing owners and operators, players, state officials, and even lawmakers, including McNally, who was secretly wearing a wire at that point.

"As bingo is today, a lot of people are taking advantage of what the legislature intended," said McNally in the newspaper's third story in the series. "If they are not violating the law, they are certainly circumventing the intent."[60]

The series followed daily developments and retraced the history of bingo in Tennessee in addition to breaking news. The groundwork had begun months earlier, when reporter Jim O'Hara watched the "housekeeping" bingo bill get approved in the Senate committee. Also in the audience keeping a watchful eye were Long, Walker, and Ledford. After the meeting, O'Hara went back to the *Tennessean* and met with its legendary publisher John Seigenthaler, who assigned Phil Williams, a police beat reporter two years removed from college, to work with O'Hara. As the reporters pored through documents and explored the world of charitable bingo, Seigenthaler decided to have secretive meetings where they could make decisions outside the newsroom. The paper rented out a room at the nearby Union Station Hotel, hosting reporters and some guests for discussions that were catered. Meanwhile, Seigenthaler, who was close with Cody, regularly had discussions with the attorney general as the two swapped ideas about bingo.[61]

The cloak-and-dagger approach to covering the story wasn't unfounded. In 1976, Seigenthaler fired *Tennessean* staffer Jacque Srouji for working as an undercover FBI agent, an allegation she denied. Her links to law enforcement had been revealed after she testified before a congressional hearing about FBI papers she had been given access to about an inquiry into a plutonium worker's death in an automobile accident. When a staffer sought further information from the FBI, an agent said he couldn't speak about Srouji further because she had a "special relationship" with the bureau. Seigenthaler said he had fired her after she acknowledged answering questions from agents about two other *Tennessean* staffers.[62]

As the reporters began searching through government documents in the bingo investigation, they began to notice irregularities. Financial reports from separate bingo halls across the state were notarized by the same person who lived out of state. Some former heads and founders of charity groups had no idea the groups were being used for bingo operations. The further they dug and the more people they interviewed, the more O'Hara and Williams realized there was something suspicious happening that sounded less like charity and more like gambling. O'Hara remembered hearing about a bingo game in Fayetteville that operators walked out of at the end of the night with garbage bags full of cash.[63]

Oftentimes, the games were found in massive warehouse-type buildings, where a few dozen to hundreds of people would be found sitting at tables as they played dozens of bingo cards.

Players would bring dolls and other good luck charms with them as they played. Many of the players were middle-aged to elderly working-class women.[64]

"I figure it's my money and I can spend it any way I want to," a woman named Janice told a *Tennessean* reporter in May 1987. "People are going to gamble, regardless. They're going to find a way if they have to do it with two bugs running down a sidewalk."[65]

During breaks, players would line up to buy "pull tabs" or "tear-offs"—paper games that were essentially modeled off of slot machines. To win, a player would need to pull paper tabs back that all aligned, with payoffs ranging from $1 to $100.

Pull tabs were so prevalent at bingo halls, they were estimated to account for up to half of the revenue for operators. Despite their popularity, pull tabs weren't always a winning option for players. Knudsen recalled how manufacturers of pull tabs would provide bingo hall operators with an envelope containing the winning cards. He said some of the bingo operators were "so damn greedy" they never added the winning cards into the mix of pull tabs players would purchase.[66]

Many bingo halls included video poker machines, which were officially labeled as being for amusement purposes only. The presence of the video poker machines came despite the fact that they were ruled in 1983 to be illegal gambling devices, with state officials confiscating them. Other gaming options for players included "pickle jars" or "fish bowls," in which players put a fee, typically a dollar, inside a glass container with the jackpot going to whoever drew a lucky number.[67]

As the *Tennessean's* reporting continued, other reporters took notice. The *Tennessee Journal*—a weekly newsletter with a focus on state government and politics—noted the paper's "extensive review" had found that state-sanctioned bingo had "actually become a massive gambling industry that enjoys state protection and minimal state regulation."[68]

The daily newspaper revealed how bingo halls fraudulently obtained state documents, charities illegally lent their names to bingo operators in return for some of the proceeds, and bingo operators skimmed cash and paid kickbacks, as well as described the prevalence of rampant illegal gambling and prizes that exceeded state law. The paper also exposed the interconnected relationships between those working in the industry and state officials.[69]

As the newspaper's stories continued to come out, other investigations kicked into higher gear. By November 1987, a grand jury was formed in Memphis, with federal prosecutors calling state officials overseeing bingo before the panel.[70]

The scrutiny of the state's bingo industry throughout 1987 led Attorney General Mike Cody and Secretary of State Gentry Crowell to call for abolishing bingo by January 1988. Later that month, lawmakers introduced bills to do just that. But by the end of the 1988 legislative session, the General Assembly had adopted a bill that moved bingo under the purview of the Alcoholic Beverage Commission, enacted accounting rules to require bingo cards to be marked with a specific price, and required all prizes to be paid by check. The legislation also reduced prize limits from $5,000 a day to $3,000. Per-game limits were reduced from $1,000 to $500.[71]

In late May, the Internal Revenue Service launched a probe into Walker and Ottis T. Cato, a South Carolina bingo operator and massage parlor owner, who investigators said was one of the biggest professional gamblers in the southeast. Cato owned Chattanooga bingo halls that investigators said were operating under the names of charities that were tax exempt. Days later, a second grand jury formed, this time in Chattanooga.[72]

The years' worth of undercover operations and secret recordings finally began to see the light of day in August 1988, when two bingo operators in Memphis were indicted by a federal grand jury on fraud and conspiracy charges for their roles in using churches as fronts for illegal gambling. The indictments were the first to stem from the investigation dubbed Operation Rocky Top.

Days later, the *Chattanooga Times* reported Sen. Jim Lewis, a Democrat from South Pittsburg, had received a $22,000 loan from William McBee, a Benton County developer who was a major financier of bingo halls in Tennessee. In November 1988, a third grand jury had formed, with a focus on Walker and Evelyn Hunnicutt, a pinball and video poker dealer who had been prominently featured in the *Tennessean*'s twenty-part series.[73]

By January 1989, the floodgates were open on the federal and state probes. Investigators were looking into allegations that McBee had a "hit list" containing the names of Walker and Lewis—the state senator who had borrowed the $22,000. Two bingo operators and a trio of men hired by McBee to kidnap and rob a bingo hall operator pleaded guilty.[74]

Then in late January—just days after the start of the legislative session—the next bombshell rocked state government. Walker, who had left his role as the bingo regulator to become an industry lobbyist, pleaded guilty to racketeering, tax evasion, and offering a $10,000 bribe to McNally in 1987 in exchange for a vote to legalize betting on horse races. Walker also admitted to helping set up illegal bingo operations when he was the state's chief bingo inspector.[75]

Walker's plea agreement, and his promise to help investigators, for the first time fully revealed McNally's role in Operation Rocky Top. Investigators said "a significant number" of indictments were likely to follow.[76]

Reactions to the news were mixed. As word spread around the Capitol, conversations were hushed and guarded.[77] The *Tennessean*'s Jim O'Hara, who was covering the legislature at the time, said everyone at the Capitol was surprised at McNally's involvement. Some around the statehouse were angry that McNally had broken an unspoken rule of remaining loyal to the institution. "At the same time . . . we were really proud to see that somebody in that morass actually had an ethical compass," O'Hara recalled.[78]

Tom Humphrey, another longtime Capitol reporter, for the *Knoxville News Sentinel*, remembered a Democrat referring to McNally as a "grandstanding son-of-a-bitch."[79]

Crowell said he would have fired Walker if he had known about his misdeeds. Gov. Ned Ray McWherter reportedly told an aide anyone under his jurisdiction who was guilty of violating the public trust would be forced to resign. But Tom Hensley, the prominent liquor lobbyist known as the "Golden Goose," said the news "shouldn't affect anything."[80]

In the weeks and months that followed, the indictments and guilty pleas continued to mount. Among those charged were McBee, S. J. King, who admitted to participating with Walker to extort money from bingo operators, state election commissioner Tommy Powell, and Long, the bingo lobbyist who first met with McNally in 1986.[81]

House majority leader Tommy Burnett, who had once been a rising star in the Democratic Party and widely viewed as a potential future gubernatorial candidate, was called before a federal grand jury. Burnett, who was re-elected to the legislature in 1984 while serving ten months in prison for failing to file his income taxes, was indicted in November.[82]

While prosecutors charged dozens of officials with various state and

State representative Tommy Burnett (D-Jamestown) attends a House floor session in May 1977 (Dean Dixon, *Nashville Banner*, image courtesy of Nashville Public Library, Special Collections)

Secretary of State Gentry Crowell, nicknamed "The Godfather," attends a roast on the occasion of his birthday in December 1982 (Bill Thorup, *Nashville Banner*, image courtesy of Nashville Public Library, Special Collections)

federal crimes throughout 1989 for their roles in the state's illegal bingo operations, two other elected officials took matters into their own hands.

On December 12, Secretary of State Gentry Crowell, who had served in the role since 1977 after two terms in the General Assembly, shot himself in the mouth with a .38-caliber pistol on the porch of his home in Lebanon. Crowell had faced months of scrutiny, appearing before two grand juries. Known as "The Godfather," a nickname he had earned during his legislative days, Crowell shot himself two weeks after he appeared before the second grand jury in Memphis. For eight days, Crowell lay unconscious in a Nashville hospital with the bullet lodged in his brain until he was removed from life support.

Crowell was the second elected official in a matter of months to take his own life while facing scrutiny from investigators. In July, Rep. Ted Ray Miller, a Knoxville Democrat, killed himself with a 12-gauge shotgun inside the bedroom of his home.[83] Miller, whose nickname was "Little Caesar," had been under investigation for months as officials looked into allegations that he extorted $30,000 from an attorney in exchange for blocking a bill seeking to stop a Knoxville incinerator project.[84] Miller, who signed a formal agreement with the US attorney for the Middle District of Tennessee to return the thousands of dollars in bribe money he received, took his life the day he was expected to be indicted.[85]

In the decades after Miller's and Crowell's suicides, the Tennessee statehouse would be rocked by other sudden and violent deaths, including in 1998 when, days before the November general election, state senator Tommy Burks, a two-plus-decade Democratic incumbent, was shot and killed by his Republican opponent, Byron Looper, who had officially changed his middle name to "Low Tax" but still failed to gain popular support. A few years later—in 2002—the statehouse was once again faced with the sudden loss of a colleague after Rep. Keith Westmoreland, who had been charged with seven counts of indecent exposure, killed himself.

## FROM SCANDAL TO REFORM

In the days before Crowell turned a gun on himself, reporters covering the secretary of state said he defended himself as someone who wasn't a crook.[86] Reporter Tom Humphrey said he once wrote a piece that said if stupidity were a capital crime, then Gentry Crowell would be staring at the gallows. When Humphrey ran into Crowell shortly after, the secretary of state fixed his gaze into the air as the reporter greeted him. He told Humphrey he was staring at the gallows. The next day, Crowell shot himself.

At the time of Crowell's death, twenty-five people had been indicted as part of Operation Rocky Top.

Despite the suicides of Miller and Crowell, the federal and state investigations pressed on, with more indictments coming down throughout 1989 and 1990.

Recapping his work for the Department of Justice, US attorney John Gill noted how the joint investigation involved all three of the state's US attorneys, the FBI, the IRS, the Tennessee Bureau of Investigation, and several state prosecutors.

"The Democratic administration in Tennessee has been seriously shaken and pressure has mounted for ethical reform in the state government," he wrote in a memo to superiors.[87]

By the time the investigation ended in the early 1990s, about one hundred people across Tennessee had been convicted for their roles in illegal gambling.[88]

Bingo officially became illegal in Tennessee in February 1989 after the state Supreme Court found the state's charity bingo laws were unconstitutional.[89]

Although the death knell of the state's bingo industry came through a judicial decision from the state's highest court, the scrutiny of reporters,

State representative Ted Ray Miller (D-Knoxville) speaks on the House floor in January 1984 (Dave Findley, *Nashville Banner*, image courtesy of Nashville Public Library, Special Collections)

State senator Tommy Burks (D-Monterey) attends a committee meeting in Nashville on November 23, 1983 (*Nashville Banner*, image courtesy of Nashville Public Library, Special Collections)

investigators, and McNally all played undeniably important roles in bringing down one of the largest corruption scandals in Tennessee history.

In the wake of the scandal, lawmakers introduced various reform efforts, including creating an independent campaign finance system, an issue that had previously failed to gain much traction. Lobbyists' interactions with legislators also began to be reeled in, much to the chagrin of many lawmakers who enjoyed their largesse.

In 1989, the legislature passed a law to create the Registry of Election Finance, a seven-member board tasked with enforcing the state's campaign finance laws with the ability to impose civil fines on violators. The law also made it illegal for a lobbyist to loan a credit card to a lawmaker or pay for their hotel room and required reports to be filed by lobbyists who spent more than $50 a week or $500 a year on a lawmaker.[90]

As the scandal continued, there was another attempt during the 1991 legislative session to approve a measure to make various reforms for the state, including strengthening conflict-of-interest disclosures for public officials, banning the use of campaign money for private purposes, and putting contribution limits in place. But as time wore on, enthusiasm cooled for such reforms.[91]

It wasn't until 1995 before lawmakers approved a serious overhaul of the state's ethics laws in the aftermath of the Rocky Top investigation. The new law completely banned lobbyists from being able to buy individual legislators meals or gifts; prohibited lawmakers from raising money during the legislative session; and implemented contribution limits on individuals and political action committees.[92]

### A FINAL PARDON

As Republican governor Bill Haslam was preparing to leave office in 2019, he went through the customary practice of reviewing clemency applications. One of the individuals under consideration was David "Peabody" Ledford, the former lawmaker and lobbyist who had introduced an undercover FBI agent to political players when the federal probe was getting underway in 1986.

Ledford had been convicted of two counts of bribery in 1991 for offering McNally cash payments of $2,000 and $3,000 to help block legislation related to solid waste companies and the bingo industry (the money for the latter had come from an undercover FBI agent).[93]

Ledford, who went on to work for then representative Jim Henry (who

Senate Speaker Randy McNally (R-Oak Ridge), center, speaks to reporters at the legislative office complex in Nashville on January 31, 2019. At left is Senate Republican leader Jack Johnson of Franklin and at right is caucus chair Ken Yager of Kingston

would later serve as Haslam's deputy), had another powerful voice speaking in favor of a pardon. McNally, who had since risen to become Speaker of the Senate, wrote to Haslam on Ledford's behalf, noting he had achieved sobriety and "made many positive changes in his life."

Haslam agreed to issue the pardon, citing the "positive contributions" Ledford had made in his Roane County community after his legal troubles ended.

State senator John Ford (D-Memphis) speaks on the Senate floor in Nashville in April 1990 (Larry McCormack, *Nashville Banner*, image courtesy of Nashville Public Library, Special Collections)

# FOUR

★ ★ ★

# John Ford and the Tennessee Waltz

FOR MORE THAN THIRTY YEARS, the Ford family machine held a firm grasp on all things political in Memphis. Harold Ford Sr. became the state's first Black congressman in 1974, the same year his brother John was elected to the state Senate. Several of their siblings held local and state office, and the widely circulated Ford family ballot of endorsed candidates often helped decide the winners and losers in the state's most populous county come election time.

Controversy often surrounded the Fords, but they seemed to revel in the attention—and in swatting back at their critics.

"Nobody in this body is more ethical than I am," John Ford declared in denouncing a 1995 bill limiting gifts to lawmakers from lobbyists. The statement was far-fetched even then. But it became all the more poignant when the Memphis Democrat became the top lawmaker snagged in an elaborate FBI bribery scheme ten years later.

The *Commercial Appeal*'s longtime Capitol bureau chief Rick Locker in 1990 said no one in the General Assembly was more colorful or controversial than Ford, whom he described as "the mouth of the Senate, liberal defender of the downtrodden yet sponsor of legislation for the rich, opinionated, powerful and outrageous, snazzy dresser, fast driver, junketeer, connoisseur of fine dining at lobbyists' expense."[1]

"I can't be humble," Ford had told the Memphis newspaper years earlier. "Because I couldn't get anywhere if I was. There is a need to get things done and sometimes I have to take an unorthodox approach. My head is screwed on right—I have not forgotten who I represent."[2]

Decades later, Ford became embroiled in the FBI's Tennessee Waltz corruption sting after boasting to undercover agents about his ability to control votes in Nashville and back home in Shelby County. "You're talking to the guy who makes the deals," Ford said as hidden microphones recorded every word.

Not that Ford was shy about speaking even when he knew his comments were on the record. When the *Commercial Appeal* called for comment about claims Ford had tried to limit the scope of a state audit into a childcare broker in Shelby County, the senator unleashed a tirade at the reporter. The paper promptly reprinted a redacted transcript of the conversation that included sixty-nine curse words by the senator, most of the f-bomb variety (and one of which was "especially inappropriate for Mother's Day," a *Commercial Appeal* columnist observed).[3]

The screed barely caused a ripple among Ford's constituents in Senate District 29, which he had represented since 1974, the first election since a federal court ruling on school busing had accelerated white flight to the suburbs. His brother Harold Ford Sr., then a twenty-nine-year-old member of the state House, took advantage of the African American share of the old Eighth Congressional District growing from 29 percent to 45 percent to defeat incumbent Republican US representative Dan Kuykendall by 744 votes.[4]

While Harold Ford was running for Congress, John Ford was making his first bid for the Senate. Two weeks before the vote, he got into hot water following a disagreement with a fellow member of the city council. Gwen Awsumb complained Ford had parked his car across two spaces in the council lot. "You can go to hell as far as I'm concerned," Ford responded. His colleagues didn't take kindly to Ford's outburst, voting 8–0 to censure him. But with several members not present or abstaining, the tally was one vote short of the two-thirds threshold needed to pass.[5]

The public attention didn't hurt Ford at the ballot box, where voters were already accustomed to his brash and confrontational style. And when Ford was sworn into the Senate, he let it be known he wouldn't change his approach.

"I'm not going to be intimidated," Ford said, gesturing to the media gallery. "I don't have anything to hide from these guys. These guys can put their cameras all around—anywhere they want to. I wasn't elected by the press. They've never written anything about me that was worthwhile."[6]

US representative Harold Ford Sr. (D-Memphis), right, is congratulated in his office by a crowd of supporters on April 9, 1993, after being found not guilty on all counts of federal bank fraud charges (Mark Humphrey, Associated Press)

Ford's remarks set the tone for the tumult that would surround him over his next three decades in office, including high-speed traffic stops, spending taxpayer and donor money on personal items, and public disputes about supporting several children by numerous wives and girlfriends. His political career finally came crashing to an end amid allegations of corruption in office.

In retrospect, it's hard to imagine any other outcome. But during his time in office, Ford developed a reputation for thriving despite repeated allegations and scandals that might have destroyed another lawmaker. It helped that Ford enjoyed the backing of enigmatic Senate Speaker John Wilder at nearly every turn.

### TRUCKER SHOOTING TRIAL

Several truckers complained to law enforcement in October 1990 that Ford had fired gunshots at them on I-40. A warrant was sworn out charging the senator with felony aggravated assault.

Ford was dismissive of the charges, initially saying he'd had a quiet drive from Nashville to Memphis on the afternoon in question. "I don't have a gun," Ford declared. "It sounds like a bunch of rednecks playing

State senator John Ford (D-Memphis) appears in court in June 1980 (Owen Cartwright, *Nashville Banner*, image courtesy of Nashville Public Library, Special Collections)

games and trying to embarrass people with an election coming up."[7]

Ford had just fallen short two months earlier in his effort to become the first of his family to win a countywide office, finishing third in a six-way contest for trustee. He faced only nominal competition in his re-election bid for the Senate, collecting 83 percent of the vote despite the pending shooting charges.[8]

The alleged incident occurred close to mile marker 104, near the exit to Lexington, where heavy construction slowed traffic to a crawl. Truck driver Nelson Kieffer of Dallas said he saw a brown Mercedes weaving onto the median and shoulder to pass stopped traffic. When trucks tried to box the car in, the driver stuck a gun through the sunroof and fired it at him, Kieffer said.[9]

Ford's car was identified from his Senate license plate that bore the number 4, and Kieffer twice identified Ford from photographs of lawmakers in the *Tennessee Blue Book*, the official state guide.

"First, he pulled up beside me and gave me the No. 1 sign. I just waved at him. Then he pulled a gun and I waved at him again," Kieffer told a reporter. "Then I seen him go for the trigger. I just ducked because I thought he was crazy."[10]

It wasn't the first—or last—time Ford had run into problems on his commute between Nashville and Memphis. In 1980, he got into an argument with a trooper who pulled him over for going 100 mph. Ford said the officer was "belligerent, arrogant, and egotistical" and that the stop was delaying his effort to get to a public ceremony at the governor's mansion. Ford called the trooper a "racist redneck."[11]

Ford also had repeatedly tried to pass legislation banning trucks from the left lanes of interstates.[12]

"Every highway patrolman in Tennessee knows me and no one said a word to me yesterday," Ford told reporters asking about the incident with the truckers. "There were five of them between Jackson and Memphis."[13]

Ford hired William Peeler, a senator-turned-lobbyist and Waverly attorney, to represent him in the case. His story also changed after the charges were filed.

"All I know is there were about four trucks out there trying to run me off the road," Ford told the Associated Press. "Why would someone like me go down the street shooting at somebody? It's the most absurd thing I've ever heard in my life."[14]

Ford posted a $2,500 bond and was released. Meanwhile, the Shelby County Sheriff's Office retrieved a 9mm Sig Sauer handgun that had been issued to Ford as a "special deputy" in 1989. He was the only person holding the honorary position to be supplied a firearm. Memphis police said Ford had two other registered handguns.[15]

Ford called it a "gross miscarriage of justice in the highest form" when he was indicted in February 1990, vowing to remain in the Senate and hold on to his chairmanship of the General Welfare Committee. In the aftermath of the Operation Rocky Top public corruption scandal, both chambers of the General Assembly had adopted rules requiring indicted lawmakers to step down from leadership positions while the charges were pending.

The Senate hadn't yet renewed its rule when Ford was indicted. The five members of the Ethics Committee initially voted to re-up the rules, with supporters arguing it didn't make sense to change them only because one of their members had gotten in trouble.

Democratic senator Tommy Burks of Monterey, the sponsor of the original standard, said, "If it was a good rule last year, when no one was indicted, it's just as good this year."

"If I had been indicted, I couldn't hold my head up," Burks said. "I wouldn't have the brass . . . like some people do and go around the state acting like there's no shame in it. There is shame in it."[16]

State senator Douglas Henry (D-Nashville) speaks to reporters outside the governor's office at the state Capitol on August 16, 1973 (*Nashville Banner*, image courtesy of Nashville Public Library, Special Collections)

The upper chamber later passed a revised version of the rule that added an "escape clause" to allow an indicted chairman to request a public hearing before the Ethics Committee.[17]

Not everyone was enamored by the rule.

"We are saying that you are guilty until you come back to us and prove you're not," said Democratic senator Andy Womack of Murfreesboro.[18]

By now, Ford's recollection of the incident had evolved to his being boxed in for more than twenty miles by several trucks in an act of "pure terrorism." He reiterated he was unarmed at the time but conceded he may have waved a black mobile phone at the truckers.

"They should have been charged with reckless endangerment for trying to run me off the road," he said.[19]

Democratic senator Douglas Henry of Nashville made the motion in the Senate Ethics Committee to remove Ford from his chairmanship until after the trial.

"I would never undertake to determine whether Sen. Ford . . . is telling the truth," Henry told the panel.

The motion failed on a 2–2 vote when only fellow Democrat Riley

Darnell of Clarksville backed Henry. Senators Curtis Person, a Memphis Republican, and Womack voted against, and Chattanooga Republican Ray Albright abstained.[20]

Ford's supporters held a champagne reception in Nashville with a "suggested donation" of $200 to help raise funds for the senator's legal defense costs. Ford was not required to disclose how much was raised on his behalf under the laws of the time.[21]

Senate Speaker John Wilder of Mason and Sen. Ward Crutchfield of Chattanooga, both Democrats, testified as character witnesses for Ford at the trial. With the jury absent, prosecutors noted Ford had his record expunged for previous arrests, including for theft in Chicago in 1966 and three more incidents in Memphis: disorderly conduct and resisting arrest in 1969, using offensive and arresting language toward a police officer in 1973, and assault with a deadly weapon in 1975. He was also convicted on a civil charge of libelous slander in 1974. Crutchfield said he had been unaware of the previous charges but maintained his opinion that Ford was a peaceful and truthful man. The judge ruled Ford's previous arrests couldn't be introduced to the jury.[22]

Wilder and Crutchfield testified Ford should be believed under oath owing to his reputation for "quietude."[23] Newspaper accounts don't indicate whether they made the claim with a straight face.

### THE CASE UNRAVELS

Ford's attorneys sought to have the trial moved from rural Lexington to Jackson, arguing the Black defendant wouldn't be able to get a fair trial in predominantly white Henderson County. The judge denied the motion.[24]

"The charges should be filed against the trucker and others for reckless endangerment from 25 minutes of terror at speeds of 60 to 65 mph," Ford said. "They tried to run me off the road."[25]

Kieffer, a part-time professional wrestler known as "The Texas Hammer," and two other truckers testified they had boxed in Ford because they feared he was drunk and likely to cause an accident. They agreed over CB radios to "cut him loose for bear bait" because they knew a Highway Patrol car was ahead with blue lights flashing.

The defense attacked Kieffer's credibility during cross-examination, persuading the judge to allow questions about a reckless endangerment charge that had been brought after Ford filed a complaint. Kieffer also was asked about being charged for writing a bad check in 1978 and theft of about $4,000 four years earlier. A Texas judge had granted deferred adjudication in the latter case.[26]

FBI agents testified at trial that a hole in Kieffer's windshield was characteristic of a ball bearing, marble, or air rifle—but not a 9mm bullet. The sheriff's office said Ford's handgun had all fifteen bullets in its magazine when the firearm was confiscated. But the FBI found only fourteen bullets when it took possession of the gun. Tennessee Highway Patrol investigators walked a mile on the shoulder and median near the site with a metal detector but didn't find a spent casing.[27]

Ford took the stand in his own defense, denouncing eyewitness accounts of him firing at truckers as "absolute lies."

"As God is my witness, I did not fire a gun at Nelson Kieffer or anyone else," he declared. "I have never in my life fired a weapon at another individual."[28]

Prosecutor Jerry Woodall acknowledged his primary witness had been weak. But the claim made by the defense team that Kieffer had engineered a conspiracy against Ford was even less believable, he said. Woodall urged jurors not to give deference to Ford because of his elected position.

"The maker of the law is not above the law," he said. "The maker of the law needs to be treated like the other breakers of the law. Don't allow this defendant to misuse the system."[29]

Ford was dismissive of the case to reporters as the jury deliberated.

"This is the flimsiest case I have ever seen in my life," he said. "They haven't proved that I've done anything except drive 65 mph on the interstate."[30]

After deliberating for about two hours, the jury returned a verdict of not guilty. Kieffer muttered to reporters that Ford had "lied to get what he got." His wife shouted at Ford from across the courthouse lawn that "you're nothing but a sleazy piece of trash."[31]

Ford shook hands with the jurors as they left the courthouse and declared he had "never lost faith in God or the people of Henderson County." He told reporters he never would have been prosecuted had he not been a well-known public figure.[32]

"I would hope that the people I represent and the people of Tennessee will see that the integrity and veracity of John Ford has not been touched," Ford said.[33]

Ford later sued Kieffer and three other truckers for intentionally blocking him on the interstate, seeking $10 million in damages. Kieffer pleaded guilty to reckless driving in connection with the incident that led to the alleged shooting. He paid a $25 fine and $278 in court costs.[34]

Ford's congressman brother, Harold, said he never had any concerns the senator would not be acquitted, alleging the *Commercial Appeal*, former US attorney Hickman Ewing, and the local FBI office had conspired to bring a bogus case.

"It's nonsense and I would expect nothing less from Harold Ford," said William Fallin, the special agent in charge of the Memphis FBI office.[35]

Senate Speaker Wilder praised the verdict, saying Ford was "a friend and he stood by me for a long, long time." The jury's decision had vindicated the Senate Ethics Committee's decision not to remove Ford from his chairmanship, Wilder said.[36]

## BACK TO FORM

It didn't take long for Ford to get back in the news. In July 1991, state records showed the senator had spent $2,306 of taxpayer money designated for printing and postage expenses on thirteen Montblanc pens.[37]

In 1992, a Shelby County sheriff's deputy pulled Ford over for speeding on I-40, but let him go without writing a ticket after a dispatcher said the senator had legislative immunity. Ford at first denied he had been involved, telling reporters it was a "case of mistaken identity." But he later confirmed he had been stopped.[38]

Also in 1992, Ford reported spending $14,843 from campaign funds on personal expenses, plus $6,000 in legal fees for Peeler, the attorney for his shooting case. Another $2,700 went toward paying rent in Nashville, and nearly $12,000 covered credit card expenses listed as "travel and entertainment." There was technically nothing wrong with spending campaign funds on personal expenses at the time, though most lawmakers recognized the negative optics of doing so.[39]

A new law passed in that year's session banned the use of campaign funds for personal purposes. It also required public officials to disclose income sources of more than $1,000. Ford abstained when it came up for a final vote in the Senate after the chamber rejected his efforts to neuter the bill. The personal income provision would come back to haunt Ford as his political career began crumbling in the early 2000s.[40]

Ford embarked on another run for countywide office in 1992, this time winning his bid for general sessions court clerk. He initially said he'd step down from the Senate to take over the $74,000-per-year job supervising

170 employees. But when it was determined the position did not fall under a ban on lawmakers holding a position with a state court of record, Ford decided he would keep both taxpayer-funded jobs. Ford hired then representative Roscoe Dixon, a fellow Memphis Democrat, as his chief public relations officer.[41]

While he was court clerk, Ford introduced legislation in the statehouse to mandate counties provide monthly car allowances for locally elected officials who request such payments in their annual budgets. He said he asked others to sponsor the bill on his behalf so he could "avoid even the appearance of a conflict of interest." The *Commercial Appeal* reported the bill was filed after Ford obtained a lease from United American Bank for a new $36,190 Cadillac. The deal was struck after Ford had moved the court's bank accounts to United American from another bank, a transfer estimated to cost more than $55,000 in lost interest and higher fees per year.[42]

When a television reporter tried to ask Ford about the deal at the legislative office complex in Nashville, the senator responded by shoving him. "He's just an impolite guy asking a lot of stupid questions about my car, about whether it was right for the county to pay for it, which it isn't," Ford said.[43]

WKRN-TV reporter Tom Atwood said Ford had become upset a week earlier when he had asked questions about campaign finance matters: "He said, 'Get out of my face. If you don't get out of my face, I'm going to slap you out of my face.'"[44]

Ford had upset his Shelby County colleagues in 1991 over Memphis State University basketball tickets. The school traditionally gave local members twenty season tickets to skybox seats, leaving it up to the delegation to decide how to distribute them. But before the tickets were sent to the chair, Ford claimed them on the delegation's behalf and handed them out to his friends and supporters. Hard feelings about the tickets didn't prevent colleagues from electing Ford chair of the Shelby County delegation in 1993.[45]

In 1994, Ford was ticketed by a state trooper for driving 94 mph in a 65-mph zone near Jackson. While at the side of the road, Ford called the state's safety commissioner, who oversees the Tennessee Highway Patrol. In a terse exchange with the trooper's supervisor, Ford was recorded as saying: "I declare legislative immunity!"

"You don't have legislative immunity," the lieutenant responded.

"The hell I don't!" Ford exclaimed.

Advisory opinions from two attorneys general had previously

determined that while lawmakers are immune from arrest in most cases while traveling to and from legislative session, they do not have immunity from traffic laws.[46]

Ford denied he had been going 94 mph but later paid a $112 fine rather than contest the case in court. He also filed a written complaint against the trooper who stopped him, claiming he exerted a "threatening demeanor." Meanwhile, Ford was recorded as telling the trooper during the stop that he "better not lay a fucking finger on me." An investigation cleared the trooper of any wrongdoing but recommended he undergo courtesy counseling.

Despite a testy relationship dating back decades, the *Commercial Appeal* endorsed Ford for another Senate term in 1994. The editorial page found that while he was one of the most controversial and outspoken legislators in state history, "he has one characteristic his constituents and other Shelby Countians appreciate: He gets things done."[47]

Ford threw his hat in the ring for Shelby County mayor in 1994, but ran an oddly subdued campaign. His brother Harold surprised many by endorsing someone else in the race. Harold Ford's chosen candidate, Jack Sammons, finished a distant second to Jim Rout, while John Ford landed just 5 percent of the vote to come in fourth.

Smelling blood in the water, county Republicans, led by Chairman David Kustoff (who would himself be elected to Congress in 2016), declared Ford as the GOP's number one target in the 1996 election. Ford's mixture of public and personal issues would give his opponents ample ammunition for attacks that would eventually lead to his being drummed out of the general sessions clerk's office and later cause his legislative career to collapse.[48]

The *Commercial Appeal*'s Marc Perrusquia reported in November 1995 that Ford had hired a woman with whom he had fathered a child out of wedlock to a $48,000-per-year job in the clerk's office. Connie Mathews was the seventh-highest-paid person on the payroll despite a professional history—she had previously marketed barbecue sauce—that didn't appear to match the qualifications of the program administrative specialist position to which she had been hired.

When Perrusquia inquired about the hiring, Ford's office said Mathews had been brought on to a temporary six-week job that was to end the next day. But Mathews' personnel file turned up no documentation of the assignment's temporary nature.[49]

The revelations emerged weeks after Dana Smith, another former employee in the clerk's office, filed a sexual harassment lawsuit against Ford, whom she also accused of fathering her one-year-old child.

Ford's then wife, Tamara Mitchell-Ford, had filed charges against Mathews two years earlier, claiming she had received harassing phone calls. She told the *Commercial Appeal* she only found out about Mathews' hiring and other allegations of infidelity in the clerk's office from the newspaper. "It's devastated me," said Mitchell-Ford, who had three children with Ford at the time (they had another child together later, after they were divorced). The interview came after Mitchell-Ford told officers her husband had punched and kicked her in the chest, stomach, and side. But she didn't file a formal complaint.[50]

Ford kept quiet about the controversy at first. But in early December, he blasted the coverage by the *Commercial Appeal* in an interview on WDIA-AM, the country's first radio station to be programmed entirely for a Black audience. The "white newspaper," the county GOP, and WREG-TV were unfairly trying to target him, he said.

"They have a way of assassinating characters of Black elected officials every time there is a major election," said Ford.[51] Days later, he issued a longer statement that appeared to be slightly more conciliatory.

"Like many others, I had children which I have legitimated and support. Like many others, I am not perfect. I apologize to anyone who feels I may have let them down," Ford said in the statement. "While I may have made mistakes in judgment, I am human like everyone else."

While he acknowledged "personal problems," Ford stressed that "in the political arena, I have done nothing illegal nor improper." He also maintained he was the subject of "a malicious attempt to assassinate my character."[52]

A week later, Ford agreed to a juvenile court consent order requiring him to pay $1,050 a month to Mathews for what turned out to be two children fathered out of wedlock. The order formalized child support payments he had already been making, Ford's attorney said.[53] A subsequent ruling determined Ford was the father of Dana Smith's child after a DNA test found a 99.99 percent probability and ordered Ford to pay child support and fees.[54]

After the dust settled, Ford quietly hired Mathews to work on his bid for re-election as clerk, though that effort never quite took flight among all the sordid revelations about his relationships. In the end, Republican Chris Turner, a former state representative, beat Ford by 2.5 percentage points. Ford blamed his defeat on "perception," not performance. He acknowledged details about his personal life may have played a role in his

State senator John Ford (D-Memphis) holds up documents during a Senate floor speech in February 1987 (Rick Mansfield, *Nashville Banner*, image courtesy of Nashville Public Library, Special Collections)

defeat but said "that's part of the politics people play."

"That's part of the game," said Ford, who remained in the Senate despite the loss of his local office.[55]

Meanwhile, Smith's $10 million sexual harassment lawsuit against Ford went to trial in federal court in late 1996. A jury awarded her $10,000 in damages, but decided against her on three of four counts. Both sides nevertheless declared victory after the verdict, with Ford exclaiming to the assembled cameras outside the courthouse: "I'm vindicated!" While it's true the jury cleared him of the quid-pro-quo allegation of demanding sex as a condition of employment, they did find him guilty of fostering a "hostile environment" at the workplace.[56]

It wasn't the last of Ford's courtroom disputes with Smith. In fact, the next big round would help sow the seeds of the end to his political career.

## ARRESTED AGAIN

Ford was arrested the following year on charges of aggravated assault after allegedly brandishing a shotgun during a confrontation with utility workers parked near his driveway. "If you don't leave, I'll blow your [expletive] brains out," Ford told the workers, according to the arrest report. He was later sentenced to probation and community service.[57]

While the charges were pending, Ford was stopped again in 1997 for driving 94 mph in his Cadillac near Dickson. Ford called Gov. Don Sundquist's office to complain it was taking too long for the trooper to process the ticket, which would cause him to miss a Senate vote. When WSMV-TV tried to interview Ford in the legislative office complex about the matter, the senator kicked the cameraman in the crotch.[58]

In 2003, Ford was put on the defensive after approving more than $1,300 in FedEx shipping costs billed to his legislative correspondence account at taxpayer expense. Many of the shipments were listed in the name of his recently divorced wife, Tamara Mitchell-Ford. Far from being contrite about the revelations, Ford refused to apologize in a Memphis press conference. "As a matter of fact, I'm proud of it," he insisted.[59]

In an out-of-character development, Ford reversed course ten days later, agreeing to reimburse the entire amount.

"I have had my integrity questioned to a degree that it has never been questioned before. Let me hasten to point out that I understand fully that I have been the subject of much controversy in the past," Ford said in a statement. "There is one major difference about the instant controversy; it could be seen as questioning my personal honesty and integrity. It is because of that fact that over the past weeks I have made statements and protested vigorously against any insinuation that I would do anything to take something from the citizens of the State of Tennessee to which I was not entitled. This effort is becoming all too consuming. I regret this entire matter, and apologize to the citizens of the State of Tennessee."[60]

The apology turned out to be the first of many cracks in Ford's armor. In a 2004 legal fight over child support payments, Dana Smith argued the senator's obligations should be heightened because of a dramatic increase in his income. Ford invoked a new state law he had sponsored the previous year that allowed courts to take into account how much parents pay to support other non-custodial children when those amounts aren't covered by court orders.

As part of the proceedings, Ford divulged that he spent part of each week with his ex-wife, Tamara Mitchell-Ford, and the rest with Connie Mathews so he could enjoy time with his young children. "I live back and forth," Ford told the judge. The problem with his statement was that it left little—or no—time for Ford to actually live within his Senate district. He stressed his official domicile remained his family's funeral home.[61]

At the end of the hearings, the judge raised Ford's child support to

Smith from $500 to $1,900 per month. At a subsequent speech to the state chapter of the NAACP, Ford lashed out at "white media" and urged the group to issue a statement in his defense.

"You watch this: They are totally unfair when it comes down to Black people, our folks. They figure, they say, 'Well, you know most Black people, they ain't got nothing; they ain't going to stand up for nobody amongst them that they feel are successful,'" Ford said. "But let me tell you this: I am one guy that has not forgotten about you."[62]

Also in early 2005, WTVF-TV reported Ford had spent $9,000 in campaign funds at the Peabody Hotel in Memphis to cover expenses related to a "reception" and "entertainment." It turned out the event in question was his daughter's wedding.

Meanwhile, Ford's outside consulting work was raising red flags in Nashville. Despite his efforts to keep his private financial information out of the public eye (disclosure could "put me in imminent danger of a lot of different things," he said), the records were first obtained by the *Commercial Appeal* and later officially released by the judge.[63]

The newspaper reported Ford had listed $237,000 in partnership income in the previous two years from a Pennsylvania company called Managed Care Services Group. TennCare contractor Doral Dental confirmed it had a governmental affairs consulting contract with the company, saying it didn't know of Ford's involvement. Ford had not included the income in his state ethics disclosures, which listed only "funeral services, real estate, and insurance."[64]

With a new Republican majority flexing its muscles in the Senate, Ford's travails were suddenly getting more scrutiny than they had when Democrats controlled the chamber. All the while, more information kept trickling out. Climate control and facilities management company Johnson Controls said Ford had helped the company land a contract with Erlanger Hospital in Chattanooga, with former manager Scott Bascue saying the senator had used his "leverage" with contacts in state government to secure the deal.[65]

Bascue said his bosses wanted him to stay on Ford's good side. The experience made him uneasy. "It didn't seem right," he said. "I was told, basically, if you want to keep your job, shut up."

Bascue said it was his job to pick up the tab at fancy dinners. "He was an expensive guy," Bascue said. "If you just had dinner with him, you were lucky if you got out of there for less than 600 bucks."[66]

The company later confirmed its deal with Ford, but said it was for a onetime fee of $15,000 (not a reported $50,000), and officials stressed they did not ask him to use "his political leverage" to land deals.[67]

One of the effects of the public scrutiny into Ford's consulting deals was that his clients began canceling their contracts. The senator was soon back in court trying to get his child support payments to Smith reduced. Ford had lost $192,000 from his gross annual income since Doral Dental canceled its contract with Managed Care Services Group, his lawyer told the court.[68]

Hauled before the Senate Ethics Committee, Ford gave an emotional defense. With his voice rising and breaking, the senator and his attorneys called his failure to disclose his consulting income an "inadvertent, innocent omission." The panel nevertheless found probable cause that Ford had failed to disclose $48,693 in consulting income in 2003.[69]

Ford in a letter urged his colleagues on the ethics panel not to widen the scope of its look into his consulting activity and his relationship with Johnson Controls.

"P.S.," Ford wrote at the bottom of the letter. "Those of us who live in glass houses should not be the first to throw stones."

Several members said they saw Ford's statement as a threat, though his attorney, Ed Yarbrough, disputed that characterization. "It was definitely not intended to be a threat," Yarbrough said. "It was a cliché. If you read it carefully, he included himself."[70]

Further revelations surfaced that Ford had also been paid $420,500 under a consulting agreement with the parent of OmniCare Health Plan, another TennCare contractor.

While the investigation was going on, lawmakers were taking up a bill to ban public officials from receiving consulting or lobbying income from any entity doing business with the state. Ford defended his record in comments made on the Senate floor.

"Some of you are suffering from a seared conscience of shame. And the worst part of it is, you don't even understand why," said Ford, who still grudgingly voted for the bill. The final version passed the House 92–3. Then representative John DeBerry, a Memphis Democrat, said the measure fueled an unfair public negative perception of lawmakers. "We are a citizen body," he said. "We're not some group of mongrel crazies that appeared out of the primordial ooze." DeBerry nevertheless ended up voting for the bill.[71]

Ford was dismissive of the new law in an interview with the *Memphis Flyer*'s Jackson Baker.

"There's conflict of interest, and there's illegal," Ford said. "Those crazy-assed rules and everything? Shit! I won't be able to make a living."[72]

In mid-May 2005, the Registry of Election Finance voted 4–3 to fine Ford for spending $15,320 in campaign funds on his daughter's wedding reception. Ford said he believed it was a legitimate expense because about one hundred of the more than three hundred guests were his constituents. But commissioners didn't take kindly to Ford listing one vendor as "Awesome Videos," when the company's full name was Awesome *Wedding* Videos.[73]

All the while, the FBI was involved in an elaborate sting operation that by the end of the month would lead to the arrests of Ford and three other sitting lawmakers. Senate Republican leader Ron Ramsey of Blountville said Ford's questionable consulting activities would have led to his being expelled had he not stepped down following his arrest.

"We would have had the votes to oust Senator Ford from office," Ramsey said. "He saw the writing on the wall."[74]

### DANCE WITH WHO BRUNG YA

Agents with the Federal Bureau of Investigation's Memphis office in January 2002 opened a probe into contract fraud within the city's school board. In May of that year, the probe was expanded to look into alleged kickbacks in the Shelby County Juvenile Court Clerk's Office.

According to a memo obtained under Freedom of Information laws, a walk-in complainant provided documents to the FBI alleging corruption on the part of state lawmakers, including Sen. Ford and Rep. Lois DeBerry, both Memphis Democrats.

"Complainant stated the facts as outlined represent a clear violation of Tennessee state law, and wished to have the FBI investigate and pursue prosecution of these representatives," the memo said. "Complainant stated he 'will not stop' until the above representatives are prosecuted."[75]

The whistleblower's identity is redacted in the memo, and the submitted documents weren't included in the records release. Subsequent records show the FBI pursued the lead on DeBerry but didn't seem particularly interested in Ford—an ironic development given the former would never be charged while the latter became the highest-profile lawmaker brought down by the sting operation. DeBerry was the second African American woman ever elected to the General Assembly and was known for delivering a rousing nomination speech for Al Gore at the 2000 Democratic presidential convention.[76]

A memo the following week added then senator Roscoe Dixon and others to the list of targets. An agent also documented developing a source who was providing information in the case. While details are redacted, the document likely refers to Tim Willis, a Democratic political operative and lobbyist who became a key player in the ensuing probe.

By early July 2003, Memphis FBI agents were seeking authorization from their superiors to offer bribes to three Tennessee state lawmakers: DeBerry, Dixon, and Rep. Kathryn Bowers. Details are redacted, but handwritten notes indicate the operation was approved a week later.[77]

Six months later, the FBI investigation had a new name: Operation Tennessee Waltz. Its purpose, according to the agents running the case, was to expose "systemic corruption within the Tennessee State Legislature . . . [by] making bribe payments for legislative influence."[78]

The cooperating witness in January 2004 recorded interactions between Dixon and several other elected officials at a Democratic fundraiser at the governor's mansion in Nashville. The next day, he recorded conversations at the legislative office complex involving Dixon, DeBerry, and three other Democratic representatives from Memphis.[79]

As part of the operation, the FBI devised a scheme under which a sham business called E-Cycle would induce lawmakers to pass legislation directing electronics recycling work to the company. The FBI agents posed as L. C. McNeil, purportedly a music business executive who was investing in the company, and Joe Carson, an affluent Miami businessman and yacht owner who headed E-Cycle. The latter was actually Joseph Carroll, a retired FBI agent who worked as a security consultant in Florida. During his thirty-year law enforcement career, Carroll had investigated corruption in more than a half dozen state legislatures.[80] McNeil's real name was never divulged because he was involved in other active cases.

The undercover agents hosted a dinner at Morton's Steakhouse in Nashville on March 22, 2004, explaining that the proposed bill, while ostensibly generally about electronics recycling, "would benefit only E-Cycle." The memo noted DeBerry briefly dropped by to introduce herself but did not stay for dinner.[81]

The E-Cycle representatives got Bowers to host another reception at Morton's on April 19. This time, agents hit the jackpot when Ford showed up unannounced and soon began regaling attendees with stories about his influence in the legislature and back home in Shelby County.

"You're talking to the guy who makes the deals," Ford said as hidden recording devices documented the discussion.[82]

"I got a brother on the County Commission, and I got a brother on the City Council," Ford was recorded as saying. "And I control the vote both places."[83]

Ford was among the public officials invited by the company to Miami, where the senator was treated to a voyage on a fifty-foot FBI yacht. The E-Cycle deal didn't come up until the undercover agent drove Ford to the airport to fly back to Memphis. But Ford appeared enthusiastic.[84]

"Book me. I'm on board," Ford said, according to a tape of the conversation. "Whatever we need to do."[85]

The next month, McNeil paid Ford $10,000 for drafting legislation for the company, adding $5,000 per month going forward. The agent complained in a September 2004 conversation that a Tennessee law already required state surplus computer equipment to go to public schools.

"I'm going to eliminate that," Ford promised.[86]

## A LOCAL OPERATOR

The FBI agents needed an established figure in Shelby County and state politics to help make introductions and persuade lawmakers to listen to the E-Cycle proposal. They ended up with Tim Willis, a young African American political consultant who had made the rounds in Memphis and Nashville.

In the summer of 1999, Willis attended a Young Democrats meeting at the Peabody Hotel in Memphis. Willis, who had been teaching at a city high school, was introduced by a mutual friend to US representative Harold Ford Jr., the nephew of John Ford. Harold Ford suggested Willis consider working for his uncle Joe Ford's mayoral campaign, and with plans of moving to Chicago a couple months later to pursue an MBA, Willis said he thought it would be an interesting experience—and pay better than his teaching job.[87]

"I had only been in Memphis nine or 10 months," Willis later recalled. "I didn't know how to get around. I didn't know anybody. Nothing."[88]

Willis began by doing what many new campaign workers do: putting up yard signs. But he was soon noticed by Harold Ford Sr., the former congressman, and quickly rose to become deputy campaign manager. After Joe Ford lost the election, Willis worked on Harold Ford Jr.'s annual "Operation Happy Christmas" charity event before the congressman's father put in a word to get him a job on the coordinated campaign supporting Al Gore's presidential bid in Tennessee.

Willis later joined the NBA Now effort to bring professional basketball to Memphis and worked on Democrat Phil Bredesen's gubernatorial campaign. But just as he was coming into prominence in Memphis, Willis was indicted on identity theft charges dating back to his college days in the mid-1990s in Mississippi, when he and a group of friends fraudulently obtained credit cards.

"I was just a kid then," Willis told a reporter after the scheme became public knowledge.[89]

Willis pleaded guilty and was sentenced to four months in a federal prison camp and three years' supervised release. He was also ordered to pay $43,519 in restitution.[90]

Before he was sentenced, Willis had consulted for Shelby County Juvenile Court Clerk Shep Wilbun, where his $105-per-hour rate included a lunch with Sen. John Ford. Federal agents descended on Wilbun's office in a wide-ranging corruption probe in June 2002. Willis' $33,000 in invoices to the Juvenile Court were subpoenaed and he was called to testify before the grand jury.[91]

According to federal prosecutors, Willis got "jammed up" for submitting phony bills while working as a lobbyist for the clerk's office. The FBI sought information about other potential corruption activity in the county, but Willis wasn't interested in cooperating at first. He was persuaded otherwise when he was caught lying to the grand jury, the FBI said. He then began telling agents about "certain corrupt individuals he knew that would accept money in return for their official action."[92]

When Willis moved to Nashville to work on the Gore campaign, he found a place to stay with another young Democratic operative named Ken Whitehouse.

"I had an open room, and I needed a roommate," Whitehouse recalled. "We got along well—he was the most pleasant of the roommates I had over time. Then he left and went back to Memphis to work on another campaign."

The two operatives lost contact, not least because Willis ended up serving time for the credit card fraud. After the Tennessee Waltz sting came to light, Whitehouse was working as a reporter for the *Nashville Post* and got back in touch. Willis spoke to Whitehouse at length about his background and experiences with the undercover operation, and some of his comments came back to haunt prosecutors at trial.[93]

For example, Willis in the interview called the E-Cycle scam his "brainchild"—something the feds vehemently denied at trial. Willis told the

*Nashville Post* he had looked at similar programs promoted in other states and wrote a detailed business plan that he said he could have used to solicit investors had the company been real. Willis also played up his access to funds and a willingness to be generous. Several trips to strip clubs, bars, and restaurants followed on the lobbyist's tab.

"I didn't like the places, but those are types of things they like to do," Willis said about lawmakers. "I'm tagging along picking up the tab everywhere we go now, I'm their personal bank account basically."[94]

Willis was calling himself "Kashflow" and touting his connection to the movie and music industries at a time when Memphis artists were gaining national attention. But while he was working undercover for the FBI, Willis' restitution payments were apparently falling behind in Mississippi to the point where authorities there considered revoking his supervised release.[95]

Probation officers wrote to the federal judge in Mississippi to explain that the FBI was paying Willis $6,000 per month to help service his "extremely large debt load," adding the public corruption probe would be severely hindered if he were forced into bankruptcy "or otherwise appear to be financially insolvent."[96]

Willis caught a break from having his probation revoked and continued working on the case. The investigation wasn't without its hiccups.

Willis returned a rental car at the Nashville airport in April 2004, but forgot his digital recording device—which was concealed within a pager—in the vehicle. The Budget Rental Car office located the pager and turned it over to an undercover agent. The device contained a recording of a conversation with DeBerry.[97]

But Willis' quick thinking also kept the sting alive when Ford began to raise doubts about the E-Cycle operation. Or, as the *Memphis Flyer* put it, Willis "bullshitted the champion bullshitter in his own office."[98]

Ford pressed Willis about how much he really knew about the E-Cycle representatives and the soundness of their proposal.

"I'm just trying to figure out why they need a bill," Ford said. "Are they legit, man?"

Willis suggested E-Cycle was a shell company for a get-rich-quick scheme. Any funny feelings Ford might be getting from the two company men, he suggested, might stem from the fact that McNeil and Joe Carson "hated each other." Willis said McNeil, whom he described as having grown up in a tough neighborhood in Chicago, might be trying to sabotage the deal.

Former senator John Ford answers questions from reporters outside the Clifford Davis Federal Building in Memphis after pleading not guilty to federal charges stemming from an FBI bribery sting on June 8, 2005 (Greg Campbell, Associated Press)

Ford was skeptical, suggesting the FBI had shell companies, too.

"Let me ask you," Ford put it to Willis. "You ain't working for none of them motherfuckers?"

Willis broke into nervous laughter and tried to deflect the questions.

"The feds ain't cut no deal with you?" Ford pressed, adding: "I got a gun. I'll just shoot you dead." When the tape was later played for the jury, they could hear static from Willis nervously shifting the recorder around in his pockets.[99]

Ford sounded worried that as a public official he might be seen as engaging in a "quid pro quo."

"Somebody could say that is corruption," he said. "It may be, it may not be. If you're gonna be charged with that, cost you $200,000 for some damn lawyer to get out of it."[100]

Prosecutors argued after Ford's arrest that the conversation was evidence he was a threat to the public, noting agents had seized two loaded handguns from the senator's office. But Ford attorney Martin Grusin told the judge his client was just engaging in "street talk."

"That's just the way John talks," Grusin said, likening his client to an "effective blowhard."[101]

Roscoe Dixon, right, and his attorney Walter Bailey on their way to federal court at the Clifford Davis Federal Building in Memphis on December 28, 2005. Dixon was charged in the Tennessee Waltz operation (Dave Darnell - USA TODAY NETWORK)

## THE HAMMER FALLS

The legislative session was drawing to a close in May 2005, when federal agents fanned out to arrest Ford, Bowers, Crutchfield, and Rep. Chris Newton of Cleveland, the lone Republican lawmaker charged. Dixon, who had resigned his seat earlier in the year to take a job as an administrative officer in the Shelby County mayor's office, also was taken into custody, along with two bagmen, Barry Myers of Memphis and Charles Love of Chattanooga.

Ford was charged with accepting $55,000 in bribes, while $12,000 went to Crutchfield, $11,500 to Bowers, $9,500 to Dixon, and $4,500 to Newton. The feds also had three thousand hours of sound and video recordings to back up their allegations.

Testifying at the first Tennessee Waltz trial of Dixon, Agent Carroll had a less than charitable view of the E-Cycle proposal.

"We had no competition because it made no sense to do business like that," he said. "The scenario made no sense. I'm surprised no one questioned it."

Recycling companies were usually paid to dispose of unwanted electronics, he said. But agents told a different story to lawmakers when they were promoting E-Cycle. At a March 2004 dinner at Prime Minister's in Memphis, Carroll told Dixon that the company wanted to "stay under the radar" because it had a corner on a lucrative market that would be strengthened by favorable legislation in Tennessee.

Dixon had introduced an E-Cycle bill but then withdrew it at the agent's request, ostensibly to pursue more beneficial language.

"We appreciate everything you've done for us," Carroll told Dixon. "We would like to kind of do a standalone [bill], a sneaky through-the-back-door standalone."[102]

In one of Ford's early court hearings, the senator was seen clutching a worn copy of a book about John DeLorean, the carmaker who famously used an entrapment defense to beat criminal charges that he had sold $24 million of cocaine to salvage his company in 1982.[103]

"The government has tried to show me and others as being corrupt and villains when, in essence, they are the ones that are corrupt. They're the villains," Ford said after pleading not guilty. "They're the ones that have been disingenuous all along. They're the ones that set up a fictitious, phony, illegal apparatus."[104]

In his lawyer's opening statement at trial, however, the entrapment defense took a back seat to arguments that Ford was doing legal work as a business consultant. McNeil had lured Ford to attend the American Black Film Festival in Miami, defense attorney Mike Scholl claimed.

"John Ford went down there as a consultant—a legitimate business-man," Scholl told the jury, noting Craig Brewer's *Hustle & Flow* was being shot in Memphis at the time and that Ford had given Willis a tip about the film being made there.[105]

Also attending the festival and the E-Cycle events was Mina Knox, a former professional cheerleader and model who had been invited by Willis. The twenty-six-year-old quickly took a liking to Ford, moving her bags to the senator's hotel room within a day of arriving.

She testified for the defense at the trial, saying McNeil spoke about producing movies during the yacht party and never mentioned E-Cycle.[106]

The jury was deadlocked on an extortion charge and found Ford not guilty of three counts of witness intimidation. But it convicted him on a single count of bribery, which led to a five-and-a-half-year prison sentence. All the other Tennessee Waltz defendants either pleaded guilty or were convicted at trial.

Ford was later found guilty of federal wire fraud and four counts of making false statements on official documents related to his taking money

Senate Speaker John Wilder (D-Mason) walks back to his desk with a resignation letter from Sen. John Ford in his hand after reading it to members on May 28, 2005 (Mark Humphrey, Associated Press)

from TennCare contractors and lobbying for them while serving in the Senate. The conviction was later thrown out on the basis that the case should have been brought in state court.

## RUSHING TO THE DEFENSE

In the first Senate floor session following the Tennessee Waltz arrests, Wilder sprang to the defense of the targeted lawmakers, offering a prayer from the well of the chamber.

"Money was being offered as bait to put somebody in jail," said Wilder, who along with Crutchfield had served as a character witness for Ford during his I-40 shooting trial. "That's wrong, and that's not your way."[107] Following an uproar, Wilder said he only meant to express his belief that "entrapment is wrong."

"I don't think the government ought to induce crime," he said. "I think when law enforcement induces a crime for political expediency, that's wrong."[108]

Wilder likened the sting to other undercover operations on Capitol Hill in the late 1970s.

"I've been there. I was the No. 1 target. The Amax Coal Co. sent $500,000 to my office in Somerville to ask my son David to be their lobbyist. He said, 'I can't do it.' They said, 'We'll give you $500,000.' They had it in a sack."

When informed about the discussion, Wilder said he called the company to say he supported their legislation already, so they need not "throw their money away." After his son refused the case, Wilder said, the company offered $100,000 to one of their business partners who was later arrested.[109]

## ETHICS IN THE EYE OF THE BEHOLDER

Tennessee House Speaker James Bomar in 1955 recommended lobbyists be required to register with the state.[110] Lawmakers discussed the matter off and on for the next decade, finally passing a bill in 1965 establishing that lobbyists had to register with the secretary of state and file financial statements at the end of each session. Ten years on, the legislature required the reports to include disclosures of gifts worth more than $25 and campaign contributions of at least $100. A related effort to require lawmakers to disclose their sources of income and ban them from doing business with the state failed.

The General Assembly in 1985 passed what became known as the "Lobbyist Relief Act," upping the threshold on reportable gifts to lawmakers from $25 to $50. A *Tennessean* editorial questioned the need for the change when only one of four hundred registered lobbyists had disclosed buying a lawmaker a meal worth more than $25 the previous year.[111]

In 1995, a new law set more limits on contributions and banned most gifts to lawmakers. Exceptions included tickets to sporting events at in-state schools and meals costing less than $50 if lawmakers from two or more legislative districts attended.

Ford was long a critic of bills seeking to tighten ethics rules, even in the wake of the federal Rocky Top investigation into illegal bingo gambling. "You've got idiots who will accuse members of this body any time," Ford said in 1989. "Some are not plain citizens; some are in the FBI. They ask you ridiculous questions."

"We're sitting up here kicking ourselves in the rear over this," Ford said. "Who are we trying to tell we're ethical? I'm telling you right now, I'm ethical. My constituents know it."[112]

Despite Ford's objections, the General Assembly passed a new law requiring lobbyists to report spending on wining and dining lawmakers—though with the significant loophole that only meals costing more than $50 required disclosure, a threshold often avoided by having lobbyists split the tab. Nevertheless, Ford was the top recipient of lobbyists' largesse when the first reports were filed.[113]

A four-year effort to require lawmakers to disclose the amount they received for consulting services finally appeared close to approval in 2004. But Ford blew a gasket about the measure when it reached the Senate floor. "This bill doesn't make any kind of sense," he thundered. "It is egregious to all of us as senators. It is silly; we ought to reject it and send a message. . . . It's going to create a situation where a lot of us are not going to want to serve here."[114]

Shortly after Ford's comments, Crutchfield, the Democratic majority leader, was caught on the chamber's audio recording system telling Speaker Wilder to tap the brakes on the bill.

"Somehow we need to put this thing over until Thursday," Crutchfield told Wilder. "John's mad and now he's ready to resign."[115]

The bill's sponsor agreed to put off a vote until later in the week. At that point, it passed unanimously—including with Ford's vote. But with the session nearing an end, the two chambers never sought to reconcile differences between their competing versions, and the bill died when lawmakers adjourned.

As longtime *Tennessean* reporter and columnist Larry Daughtrey observed after the Tennessee Waltz arrests, the FBI didn't have to try too hard to snag lawmakers.

"The agents simply rolled into Legislative Plaza and acted like everyone else," Daughtrey wrote. "They schmoozed and solicited. They offered winter trips to sunny Miami. They threw a party across the street at the Sheraton and invited the whole legislature. Whiskey and finger food flowed; a woman sang. Small talk was made. They knew how to work with the sleazy bagmen who are legendary on Capitol Hill, people with no obvious occupation, but who are always hanging around lawmakers."[116]

To Daughtrey, who had covered political scandals in Tennessee dating back to his early days with the paper in the 1960s, the response to the sting operation among lawmakers was exaggerated.

"The Capitol Hill protestations about shock and surprise were laughable," wrote Daughtrey, who died in 2016. "This Tennessee Waltz has been going on for a very long time, interrupted only by the FBI visits about once a decade."[117]

## COLLATERAL DAMAGE

The John Ford saga didn't occur in a vacuum. While the state lawmaker's legal troubles were making headlines in newspapers and television newscasts, his nephew Harold Ford Jr.—who had succeeded his father in Congress—was generating widespread enthusiasm for a US Senate bid in 2006. The seat had been opened by the retirement of former Senate Republican leader Bill Frist of Nashville, and Democrats thought their chances of gaining a majority in the chamber might hinge on winning the Tennessee contest.

Harold Ford Jr. brought a rock-star quality to the race, attracting large crowds wherever he campaigned and thrilling rally audiences with his soaring oratory. The national media closely followed Ford's exploits. The Republican nominee was Bob Corker, a former Chattanooga mayor who struggled at first to keep up with the Ford whirlwind. But his campaign eventually found a sensitive target: Ford's family.

Corker charged in a debate in Memphis that Ford had come from a family engaged in "machine-type politics." Ford tried to deflect the criticism, saying he loved his family and urging Corker to stick to the issues.[118] Ford later took to the airwaves to defend his family.

"Bob Corker's been going personal—after me, my family, and if I had a dog, he'd probably kick him, too," Ford said in a TV ad.[119]

While the focus on Ford's family might not have made a difference in other parts of the state, it was a different story closer to home in West Tennessee. The region had once been a stronghold for conservative Democrats, but much of the rural vote ended up going for Corker. Ford ultimately lost the race by 2.7 percentage points.

### DON'T CALL IT A COMEBACK

John Ford was released after serving four years behind bars in 2012. After his probation expired, he spoke at length to the *Memphis Flyer* about what he considered the injustice of his bribery conviction.

"The crime was being committed on their part," he said. "If you tried to bribe me, you would be guilty of trying to bribe me."

As for an infamous video of the undercover agent counting out hundred-dollar bills and handing them to Ford, the former senator suggested the evidence was doctored.

"All they had was what they recorded on tape. You can make a video show what you want it to show," he said. "Where's the evidence? They're the ones making a recording. There's nothing illegal about that, about somebody counting out money and giving it to you. They give you some money and talk about something else."[120]

Ford made noises about a political comeback after serving four years in prison. The former lawmaker's announcement in late 2019 that he wanted to run for clerk of Shelby County General Sessions Court—the job he once held while serving in the Senate—was the cause of much handwringing among the political set.

Ford said he would challenge the secretary of state's office about rulings that he was ineligible to hold public office as a convicted felon.

"I've got more lawyers than they've all got," Ford said with some of his bluster of old.[121]

But it wasn't to be. A 2017 court order restoring Ford's civil rights included a caveat that he was "forever disqualified from qualifying for, seeking, or holding any public office in Tennessee." Ford was kept off the ballot and has since largely faded from the political scene.

## DEBERRY POSTSCRIPT

While evidently one of the earliest targets of the FBI probe, Lois DeBerry was never charged. Undercover agents took her and Bowers to a casino in Tunica, Mississippi, and gave DeBerry $200 to gamble with. But in an official memo documenting the event, the agent said the money was "not in exchange for any specific official act."[122]

DeBerry in July 2005 confirmed she had accepted the $200 from FBI agent L. C. McNeil. DeBerry said she was standing in front of a nickel slot machine when the man who turned out to be a federal agent handed her the cash. DeBerry said she dropped the money into the machine but won nothing. (The *Tennessean* later observed the $200 would have paid for four thousand plays of the nickel slots.[123])

At a press conference in Nashville, Democratic House Speaker Jimmy Naifeh came to DeBerry's defense against GOP calls for her resignation, describing her as a "model for honesty and dignity." An analysis by legislative attorneys found a ban on accepting gifts from a lobbyist or an employer of a lobbyist didn't apply because E-Cycle had not registered. DeBerry later stepped down from the House Ethics Committee but remained as the Speaker pro tempore, the chamber's ceremonial No. 2 leadership position.[124]

By 2008, the Memphis office recommended closing the case against DeBerry, though agents couldn't refrain from including speculation about alleged misdeeds.

According to an FBI memo, "during the course of the [undercover

Rep. Lois DeBerry (D-Memphis), left, talks with House Speaker Jimmy Naifeh (D-Covington) during a House Finance Committee meeting in Nashville on May 23, 2005 (John Russell, Associated Press)

operation], it became apparent that DeBerry was extremely influential and likely had other illicit forms of income, but she felt uncomfortable receiving them from a new company on the scene."[125]

DeBerry had been contemplating a congressional bid for the seat opened by Harold Ford Jr.'s decision to run for the US Senate in 2006, but she decided not to enter the race after the revelations, the FBI report said. Following media accounts about DeBerry spending Black Caucus funds on herself, the FBI said it found what it called "questionable expenditures." But it wasn't clear whether they violated any state or federal laws.[126]

DeBerry died in 2013 at age sixty-eight.

Rep. Jeremy Durham (R-Franklin) addresses the House on the day of his ouster on September 13, 2016

# FIVE

★ ★ ★

# Representative Pants Candy

WITH HELP FROM
## DAVE BOUCHER

THE VOTES WERE IN, and the results were not good for Cameron Sexton.

It was December 2014, and the two-term Republican lawmaker sat twenty floors above downtown Nashville in the SunTrust building. He looked around a conference room as his colleagues chatted and ate hors d'oeuvres. A majority of them had just decided they did not want him to be a leader in their caucus.

Sexton had served as the House majority whip for the past two years, canvassing his Republican compatriots to determine how they'd vote on certain legislation and weighing broader legislative interests against those of party leadership. Sexton did not want to overstep his position, but he'd worked to align himself closely with Speaker Beth Harwell, a Nashville Republican who could help him ascend to greater power in the House.

But now he was officially a backbencher. No leadership role, no rank, no stature. It was the worst kind of rebuke, one that can end a political career. He wasn't defeated by the enemy—his friends had told him they'd rather move on.

House Republicans instead voted 38–34 in favor of a young lawyer to take over as majority whip.[1] First elected as a twenty-eight-year-old two years earlier, the title attorney was steeped in the influential and well-heeled conservative circles of Williamson County, a highly affluent area twenty miles south of Nashville. Outgoing, exceptionally confident, and ambitious, the up-and-comer relished both being in the spotlight and politicking behind the scenes.

His name was Jeremy Durham.

"While I'm humbled to have the support of my colleagues, I just hope the position will prove valuable in representing the desires of the people of Williamson County," Durham said in a statement at the time.

The red flags were already waving at this point. If lawmakers had cared to look, they'd have found an aggravated burglary charge and allegations of inappropriate campaign finance actions while Durham was in college. A phone call or two would have revealed a more recent grand jury inquiry and a character reference letter for a youth pastor who admitted to committing statutory rape and possessing child porn. There were also persistent rumors of inappropriate sexual conduct.

But Durham could raise money.

The caucus election marked a turning point in the lives of both Sexton and Durham. It could have been the start of a rapid rise to power for Durham—lawmakers frequently use such gigs to position themselves for a more powerful post in the statehouse or even an eventual run at Congress. And it could have been the end of Sexton.

Instead, in five years Sexton would become Speaker of the House and Durham would be little more than a black eye for Tennessee Republicans.

The path to this future exemplifies an era of Tennessee state Republican politics: it's paved with deceit, misinformation, mistakes, and malfeasance. Without question, there were those in the party who wanted Durham to fail. But he also made his own bed, using his power to harass, bully, intimidate, and ultimately prey on others. At the same time, he embodied the blatant disregard for election laws so often seen in state politics, using money given by donors on everything from airplane tickets and sunglasses to custom suits and spa products.

The media and law enforcement caught up with him eventually, issuing multiple, detailed reports that outlined a web of alleged sexual and financial misdeeds. A mountain of evidence and pressure forced his colleagues to throw him out of his seat—an action seen only once since the end of the Civil War.

On his way out, Durham cast blame on everyone else, pointing to lawmakers he considered hypocrites and a media he deemed unfairly bloodthirsty.

But it was Durham's choices that cost him nearly everything. And he may still have more to pay.

## RISING THROUGH THE RANKS

Durham was born in the small West Tennessee town of Adamsville, which had also been the hometown of the ethically challenged late governor Ray Blanton. Durham grew up the son of two small-business owners, but he knew from a young age that he wanted a future in politics.

He started developing his talents at the University of Tennessee at Knoxville, where he studied political science, joined the Pi Kappa Phi fraternity, and participated in student government. He helped raise money for George W. Bush's 2004 presidential campaign and served as a political consultant for one-term US representative David Davis, a Republican from upper northeast Tennessee.

But there was the 2003 arrest, on charges of aggravated burglary, vandalism, and theft. Durham would later wave off the incident as "college shenanigans," but a police report from the time indicates he broke into the home of his ex-girlfriend's new boyfriend after forcing the young woman to take him to the dwelling.

The charges were ultimately dropped.

The student paper also uncovered information that the student government political party that Durham led exceeded campaign finance limits. He shrugged this off as well, saying the problem was nothing more than an accounting error.

Both instances foreshadow the allegations that would ultimately force Durham from the statehouse and prompt a criminal investigation.

Durham headed back west after graduating, earning his law degree from the University of Memphis. He would make a pivotal friendship during his time in Memphis with another young and ambitious Tennessee Republican: Brian Kelsey.

Kelsey was already serving as a state representative at the time and relied on Durham to boost his own career. Durham served as campaign manager for Kelsey's successful 2009 state Senate campaign, when he ran to fill a seat vacated by Paul Stanley, a fellow Germantown Republican embroiled in his own tumultuous scandal. Stanley was the subject of a blackmail plot after having an affair with his intern. The young woman's boyfriend threatened to publicize "provocative" photographs of the senator and the intern in the lawmaker's apartment if he didn't pay up.[2]

Stanley alerted the Tennessee Bureau of Investigation, which ultimately set up a sting operation and charged the boyfriend with extortion. Stanley resigned.

In 2009, Durham moved to Franklin, a wealthy Williamson County enclave. The GOP stronghold was already something of an epicenter of Tennessee conservatism, home to the likes of then US representative Marsha Blackburn, state senator Jack Johnson, state representative Glen Casada, and more.

Shortly after settling in Franklin, Durham became the head of the Tennessee Young Republicans. One source likened his arrival to a tornado as he churned through the organization, reportedly driving away many who had previously been actively interested.

That was partially due to his at times juvenile political tactics. He didn't just yell profanities at those who he felt crossed him; he would reportedly take their email addresses and sign them up for an array of spam emails, ensuring their inboxes were flooded with garbage.

At the same time, Durham was dogged. He started to methodically establish himself, both as a local Republican and as a member of the community. He opened up a law practice and ultimately started working with a partner in 2009. He got married to Jessica, an optometrist, in a 2011 ceremony where Kelsey served as best man. Jeremy and Jessica moved to an upscale subdivision with brick homes and expensive cars.

The entire time, Jeremy weighed his own political run. For him, that came in 2012, after once-every-decade redistricting created a new Williamson County seat in the state House. Initially, the local GOP establishment was skeptical; his college antics had drawn a fair amount of attention. But they also saw someone who wouldn't be outworked. He constantly knocked on doors, went to community events, and used his capacity to be charming to win over possible voters.

"I think he worked extremely hard over a year just knocking on doors in neighborhoods and even going back to neighborhoods and talking again," Franklin mayor Ken Moore told the *Tennessean* in 2016. "He really wanted the job really bad, and he did what you have to do."[3]

He won the race in 2012, defeating a pair of primary opponents in a seat that's essentially impossible for a Democrat to grab. No one challenged him in 2014, virtually paving the way for him to hold the seat as long as he wanted it.

But Durham wanted more. More responsibility, more power, more money. And with that comes more scrutiny.

## A HISTORY OF TROUBLE

Unbeknownst to many constituents, colleagues, and political observers, Durham was again in the crosshairs of law enforcement in late 2013.

Local police thought they could make the case that Durham attempted to illegally fill a prescription for 5 mg pills of Adderall. A pharmacist at a Franklin Kroger noted Durham had tried to submit a prescription that was substantially out of date; someone had written over the date with a pen in an effort to hide the deadline to get the medication.[4]

Durham claimed it was a misunderstanding and he had other, valid prescriptions for the medication. But investigators determined he'd stopped seeing the doctor who'd written the prescription in December 2012.

A law enforcement officer approached Durham about the potentially changed prescription on June 27, 2013. Audio recordings of the interaction portray an at times frantic Durham who repeatedly denied misconduct.

At one point, the officer told Durham he'd have to read him his Miranda rights, the warning police need to give before they can arrest someone. "Shut up," Durham responded in a joking voice. Before the law enforcement officer ended the interaction, Durham suggested people in his office might have had access to the prescription before again denying misconduct.

"I don't think I did," Durham said. "I know the consequences of doing that. I've handled cases like that."

Law enforcement took their evidence to a grand jury, generally an indication police believe a crime occurred. But in January 2014, the local grand jury declined to indict Durham.

"This situation is from two and a half years ago and was fully vetted by 12 Williamson County citizens who quickly agreed that nothing illegal occurred," Durham told the *Tennessean* in December 2015.

Just two months after the grand jury declined to charge Durham, the young lawmaker used his official letterhead to make what would later amount to be a colossal political mistake. He wrote to a federal judge and asked for leniency on behalf of a youth pastor who had pleaded guilty to statutory rape and child pornography charges.

Joseph Todd Neill admitted to statutory rape of a sixteen-year-old girl who attended his church. Law enforcement also found child pornography on his cellphone described as "violent and sadistic."[5]

"Mr. Neill served as a minister for several years and comes from a very reputable family deeply committed to Christian service," Durham wrote in the letter. "As you may expect, the Neill family values reputation a great deal and the mere publicity of this situation has taken an enormous toll somewhat similar to any punishment the Court is prepared to render."

He also referenced his own run-in with law enforcement during his time in college, saying, "after much deliberation among prosecutors, law enforcement and University of Tennessee officials, I was granted a second chance in life due to many factors—not the least of which being my proven track record as a law-abiding and community-minded citizen up until that point."[6]

Durham wasn't the only person to ask the judge to show Neill leniency. But of the thirty-eight people who wrote letters on Neill's behalf, Durham was the only person not to indicate any personal connection to the man. He told the *Tennessean* a very close friend knew the Neill family, adding, "If people actually read the letter, it's pretty clear that the liberal media is just on another witch hunt."

He didn't name his friend, but Durham did have a connection to another man who wrote a letter on Neill's behalf: John Simmonds, the former CEO of Southeast Financial Credit Union, who had substantial ties to Tennessee Republicans.

Simmonds donated tens of thousands of dollars to Republicans all over Tennessee, including Durham. That included $3,000 from Simmonds and his family in 2013, and another $500 in 2014. In 2015, Simmonds and a family member donated a combined $1,500 to Durham.

The stories about the grand jury and the letter came out in rapid succession. By this point, Republican legislative leaders were notably frustrated. Some had known about the letter and the grand jury before reading about it in the newspaper, but many had not. Yet most were aware of other stories floating around the statehouse that did not paint a flattering picture of Durham.

Generally speaking, political leaders prefer to not speak out publicly against members of their own party. Most would prefer to decline comment or offer a bland statement that acknowledges the serious nature of some allegations while noting everyone should be afforded due process. But Ron Ramsey was not a typical politician.

Lieutenant governor at the time, the loud and brash East Tennessean's folksy demeanor belied the iron grip he held on the state Senate. Ramsey had spearheaded the GOP's march toward a robust majority in the legislature's upper chamber and would occasionally cast aspersions on anyone in any party who he thought had stepped out of line. It was Ramsey, for example, who had organized a united front among Republicans to

Senate Speaker Ron Ramsey speaks to a Republican gathering in Nashville on April 5, 2016

pressure Stanley not to try to hold on to his seat following revelations of an affair with his intern.

After stories about Durham's grand jury run-in and the letter to the judge, Ramsey had seen enough. He called the statehouse press corps to his spacious office one December day for his weekly media briefing.

"It's just poor judgment, I think, on anybody's part as a state legislator to write a letter to encourage a lesser sentence on child porn," Ramsey said.

"I hesitate to do it because in the end, it could always come back to bite you," Ramsey continued. "Of all the things you could think of—this wasn't shoplifting, this wasn't anything like that. . . . You'd have to think twice about ever doing anything like that, but obviously he didn't."[7]

Ramsey weighed in on the grand jury probe as well, acknowledging no charges were filed but calling the situation very serious.

"And if we have a state representative that's misusing—and I know they chose not to indict—but if you listen to the transcript [from the investigation] . . . it looks very serious to me," Ramsey said.

Ramsey had no control over Durham. In theory, voters hold ultimate sway over a politician's future. In practice, there were two lawmakers in the lower chamber who, if they chose to do so, could hasten the end of Durham's political existence.

One, Nashville Republican and House Speaker Beth Harwell, had already taken actions behind the scenes to try to scare Durham straight. A classic establishment Republican, Harwell served decades in the

Beth Harwell presides on her last day as House Speaker on January 8, 2019

Tennessee legislature before becoming the first woman in state history to earn the Speaker's gavel. She was politically savvy, practiced, and polite. It was a style that clearly served her well in her legislative career, but one that would be repeatedly tested as she tried to deal with the ballooning Durham situation.[8]

The challenge that Durham presented Harwell was both political and ideological. After being elected Speaker, Harwell frequently faced push-back from the right wing of the House Republican Caucus, which included Durham. Members would test boundaries and her patience as she tried to keep the chamber on track even while moving the body in a more con-servative direction after she was elected Speaker in 2011. While Harwell needed to keep the caucus united to pass legislation, punishing Durham too much could imperil her grasp on the top leadership position. Later signifying how challenging the Durham situation was for Harwell, she won her final re-nomination for Speaker by just ten votes in November 2016. Before the stories about the grand jury and leniency letter raised eyebrows, other anecdotes about Durham were making their way back to Harwell. The statehouse is a place brimming with gossip and rumors spread by politically motivated people. It's also an environment where constitutional authority doesn't always mesh well with traditional human resources. It's a culture where people bestowed with substantial power are routinely in a position to impact the futures of very eager, earnest, and young legislative staffers.

Harwell never publicly disclosed the nature of the stories she had heard, but they were clearly troubling. They didn't prompt her to go to the police or to the press, but she knew she had to do something. She decided to ask legislative human resources leader Connie Ridley to speak with Durham about his behavior. Ridley wore many hats at the legislature. But in general, if someone had a problem with a lawmaker or someone else at the legislature, her office would have some role in alleviating it.

No one had filed a formal complaint against Durham at this point. But Harwell determined Ridley needed to tell Durham about "appropriate professional behavior and all that entails," the Speaker later told the media.

Ridley provided her own, equally vague description about the meeting.

"I let him know I was getting a fair amount of feedback from various sources about his behavior. . . . I stressed to him that obviously if it was not appropriate, then that was something he needed to be aware of," Ridley said.[9]

Harwell chose to disclose the news of the Ridley meeting after the stories about the grand jury and leniency letter were published. The nature and timing of the trifecta of damaging stories prompted some of Durham's House colleagues to take action: they set the wheels in motion to discuss removing him from his legislative leadership position.

Demoting a state lawmaker is one of those punishments that resonates keenly in the statehouse but typically does not make it onto the radar of the average voter. But it should have been a clear message to Durham: the two highest-ranking Republicans in the statehouse publicly lamented his actions, a clear sign of trouble.

Yet he had an ally, a powerful protector who also happened to be that second lawmaker who played a key role in determining Durham's fate.

House Republican Caucus chair Glen Casada was a fellow Franklin lawmaker who at the time viewed Durham as a protégé. Casada's ongoing support for Durham would prove crucial in the young lawmaker's attempts to hold on to power. Casada led every House Republican meeting, so it fell to him to chair the session where many anticipated deciding whether to oust Durham from legislative leadership. It was early January 2016, weeks after the damaging stories and only days before the start of another legislative session.[10]

Great politicians know how to inspire, to find the right words in the right moment to effect change. Politicians who've ascended to power know how to use procedure to their advantage. Republicans only needed a majority of their caucus—about thirty-four lawmakers at the time—to support pulling Durham from leadership in order to seal his fate. But Casada told his colleagues that in order to discuss Durham's behavior or ouster, they first had to vote to suspend the typical rules for a GOP caucus meeting.

Rep. Jeremy Durham attends a House Republican Caucus meeting in Nashville on January 27, 2016

This vote required the support of two-thirds of all elected House Republicans, not just those present at the caucus meeting. That day, it meant forty-nine votes to even talk about Durham's future. The issue received forty-eight. Durham had survived at least for the time being. The grand jury probe and leniency letter were speed bumps, new blemishes on the record of the ambitious lawmaker. Durham blasted the proceedings as a "kangaroo court," saying they were driven by the "liberal media." He also brushed aside Harwell's statement that she had HR speak to Durham about unspecified behavior. "I didn't know what she was talking about," he said.[11]

The win was short-lived. Within days, Durham would step down from the leadership role. That's because at last, the stories that had circulated the statehouse for months started to come to light. House leaders knew about those tales even before the caucus meeting. They chose to keep them a secret. But the women started to speak out.

## LATE-NIGHT TEXTS AND THE START OF ANOTHER PROBE

In one text message, sent after 10 P.M., Durham said he missed her. In another, sent at about 1:30 A.M., Durham asked her for pictures.

The woman, then in her mid-twenties and someone who had worked in various capacities at the statehouse, said during the 2013 legislative session Durham repeatedly sent her texts and Facebook messages. Some were sent very late. His intentions were obvious. Another woman said she received dozens of messages from Durham; at least one, sent after 1 A.M., also asked for pictures.

"For me, I was just trying to engage professionally, from one professional to another. And he crossed the line: You don't text and constantly message on Facebook and ask to meet up at bars in the evening," the woman told the *Tennessean*.[12]

"He would come up with these ideas and I would just be like, 'Are you crazy?'"

In total, three women revealed receiving inappropriate late-night messages. The newspaper granted anonymity to all three, as each described legitimate fears of public backlash, and published a two-part investigation in late January 2016.

The women also scoffed at the idea that filing a formal complaint with the legislature would do more good than harm. The *Tennessean* noted the legislature's sexual harassment policy was overly secretive, not conducive to providing the open accountability and punishment needed to ensure people were safe.[13]

"I go tell someone in HR, oh, this representative did this to me, you know," the woman said. "I mean, I know those things are supposed to be anonymous, and no one's supposed to know who it was. But someone would have known by the time I walked back across the street to the plaza."

Durham denied sending the messages after they were described to him by the *Tennessean*. Instead, he zeroed in on the fact none of the women were named in the story.

"Not having seen the texts, not knowing who the other party to the conversation is, when they were sent, what exactly they say, whether I was responding or initiating the text stream, it is simply impossible to respond," Durham said in an email to the newspaper. "Furthermore, the fact that there has never been a complaint filed makes me question your continued use of anonymous and unverified sources."[14]

But few questioned the veracity of the information. Instead, scrutiny of Durham and Republican legislative leaders only intensified in light of the Sunday front-page investigation.

The story also indicated legislative leaders knew of at least one woman alleging sexual harassment against Durham before the caucus meeting weeks earlier that was focused on his future. Rep. David Alexander, a

Winchester Republican, said he was contacted by a woman who wanted to discuss her allegation at this caucus meeting.

Alexander said he took the information to Ridley and House majority leader Gerald McCormick. Later, Alexander discussed the allegation on a conference call with Ridley, a legislative attorney, and a member of Harwell's legislative staff. Harwell chief of staff Scott Gilmer and Casada knew about the allegation before the caucus meeting as well.

The group decided against allowing the woman to speak at the caucus.

"I think the general response was that it would be a bad precedent, just to get somebody who shows up at a caucus meeting and goes after a member, without going through a formal process," McCormick said.

Harwell denied anyone ever filing formal or informal sexual harassment allegations against Durham, despite knowing of the woman who called Alexander with an allegation. She said she did not know the nature of that complaint, but her chief of staff told Alexander to direct the woman to Ridley's office.

Days later, McCormick acknowledged he was approached by two different people with broad allegations of inappropriate behavior by Durham. One told him the unprofessional action took place during the summer of 2015, the other during the 2015 legislative session.[15]

"I did not ask for or receive specific details, and I immediately told both individuals that they should report this to Connie Ridley and the Speaker's office to file a formal complaint. Both women refused to go through the formal process, and they only shared the complaint with me on the strict condition that I not share their identity with anyone else," McCormick later told reporters.

Hours after the *Tennessean* published its investigation into text messages and the sexual harassment policy, the House Republican Caucus issued a statement saying Durham had stepped down as majority whip. But three minutes after his GOP colleagues sent out the release, Durham denied the move.[16]

"I'm talking it over with my family but have not made a decision. Nothing should've gone out," Durham said in an email to the *Tennessean*. "Watching Broncos game at the moment."[17]

Durham would eventually confirm his resignation from the leadership post, but the bizarre back-and-forth showed a growing rift between Durham and several members of House Republican leadership. He blamed his colleagues for being distracted by a "targeted media campaign" but suggested stepping away from leadership should allow everyone to focus on the work of the legislature.

That same afternoon, Harwell called for a review of the statehouse's sexual harassment policy.

The Speaker went further the following day. Joined by then Tennessee Republican Party Chairman Ryan Haynes, the pair called on Durham to resign from the legislature altogether. Harwell and other leaders suggested Durham needed to spend time with his family, seek help, and step away from Nashville.

If he had left then, it's likely very little else about his behavior would have become public. But quitting was not in Durham's nature. He chose to fight.

"I've never sexually harassed anyone, and I'm sorely disappointed that members of my own party would rush to such judgment given the that [*sic*] no complaints were ever filed and the general lack of evidence suggesting I did anything wrong," Durham said in a statement.

Late January is typically a time when lawmakers are energized and ready to take on a new legislative session. The zeal doesn't always necessarily translate to legislative work, as legislators tend to leave the bulk of their lawmaking until the last possible moment. That January, as lawmakers returned to Nashville, members of both parties pounced on the Durham scandal.

Several House Republicans not part of leadership and many Democratic lawmakers called for the creation of a bipartisan committee to review sexual harassment in the statehouse. Gov. Bill Haslam, a former Knoxville mayor known more as a policy wonk than a cutthroat politician, said Durham needed to ask himself whether he could effectively serve his constituents.[18]

Democrats, the minority party in Tennessee since 2008, wanted heads to roll. Mary Mancini, leader of the Tennessee Democratic Party, called for Harwell, McCormick, and Casada to resign. They did not step down, but the leaders did appear to acknowledge that everyone wanted more than a polite request for Durham to go home.

Just days after the *Tennessean* published the text message investigation, House Republicans held another caucus meeting to discuss Durham's future. But it was Lt. Gov. Ramsey, in a position to offer blunt advice without having to consider the ramifications for a member in his own chamber, who first publicly brought up the idea of an ouster.[19]

Harwell agreed. If he would not leave on his own, the Speaker decided it was incumbent on legislative leaders to show him the door. It was time to talk about expulsion.

She confirmed she had attorneys reviewing the process, carried out only one other time in Tennessee in more than 150 years.[20]

The last expulsion process in the Tennessee House took place after Rep. Robert Fisher, an Elizabethton Republican, was indicted in 1979 for allegedly accepting $1,000 in exchange for killing legislation. In 1980, the House began the process of expelling him. Lawmakers asked then attorney general William Leech for his thoughts—Leech suggested giving Fisher a chance to defend himself before any expulsion vote, and for the legislature to create a committee to investigate the allegations.

That legislative committee ultimately recommended removing Fisher. His attorney was allowed to speak on his behalf, but the House voted 92–1 in favor of removal.

Harwell and the legislature tried to follow the same playbook. On January 28, Harwell also announced she had asked Tennessee attorney general Herbert Slatery to investigate Durham's "ongoing situation."[21]

In Tennessee, the attorney general is appointed by the state Supreme Court. It's a unique process that's supposed to remove politics from the position. While Slatery was a Republican, he wasn't known as a firebreather. A close friend and former legal counsel for Haslam, Slatery was seen as everything Durham was not: reserved and apolitical.

Harwell's hand was forced a bit on the Slatery investigation by perhaps the only politician less reserved than Durham: the freewheeling Ramsey. Apparently reveling in a scandal plaguing the lower chamber, Ramsey told reporters in late January that Durham had engaged in an affair with a fellow representative who resigned as a result.

"Obviously we don't want the press lynching anybody, but nobody forced, the press didn't force somebody to send text messages after midnight asking for pictures," Ramsey told reporters.

The press "didn't force somebody to have an affair with another state rep and force them to resign," he said.

By that point, it was one of many rumors swirling around the statehouse. But Ramsey had breathed life into another serious allegation.

Ramsey did not name the fellow lawmaker, but there were two who'd recently resigned: GOP Reps. Mike Harrison and Leigh Wilburn. Durham's office used that lack of specificity from Ramsey to both deny the misconduct allegation and make the situation even more bizarre.

"He categorically denies having any physical relationship with former representatives Harrison or Wilburn," a Durham assistant said in a statement.

Harrison, who left the legislature to take over the county mayors association, laughed when asked if he'd had an affair with Durham.

"Are you serious?" he asked a reporter. "Oh Lord, have mercy. No, I didn't have an affair with Jeremy Durham."[22]

That left Wilburn. A West Tennessee lawyer serving her first term in the statehouse, Wilburn announced in December 2015 she would resign, "due to unforeseen circumstances involving my immediate and extended family and my business."[23] She declined to comment about Durham through a family member reached by the Associated Press.

If the situation was not unraveling for Durham before, it certainly was now. Despite his nature to fire back, the Franklin Republican decided to live to fight another day. He offered up a political olive branch, one he thought would keep the expulsion dogs at bay.

The same day news broke of the AG investigation and the alleged affair, Durham announced he would be taking a leave of absence from the legislature. His leave, for up to two weeks, would allow him to seek unspecified treatment.[24] House Republican leaders supported the move, painted as an effort to spend time with his family and evaluate the ramifications of his decisions.

Nothing slowed down during Durham's days away from Nashville.

Despite asking the AG to investigate Durham, Harwell abruptly announced the creation of a legislative committee that would lead the inquiry. Slatery would report his findings to the lawmakers, who in turn would make recommendations about actions involving Durham's future.[25]

The committee formally gave Slatery subpoena power for his investigation, a relatively rare move. It meant the attorney general could demand documents and interviews in a fashion akin to a typical police investigation.

"I'm concerned about that a little bit because it could open Pandora's box here," Rep. Andrew Farmer, R-Sevierville, and a member of the committee, told the *Tennessean* about the scope of the investigation.

He wasn't wrong. Back at the statehouse after his self-imposed hiatus, Durham told a local newspaper Slatery's office requested he turn over all electronic devices and access to his personal email for the investigation.[26] Durham agreed to hand over his state-issued iPad, and he learned Slatery had obtained a copy of the hard drive for his legislative desktop computer.

But he declined to turn over the rest of the requested information.

This happened many times over for Slatery. His office repeatedly asked for documents and data that could shed light on Durham's behavior. Requests also went to news outlets and legislative staffers. It was months before Slatery offered the results of his inquiry. But the sweeping investigation prompted drastic action in April, a move that put the increasingly infuriated Durham in another corner.

Despite the negative attention, Durham announced his intention to seek re-election in early April. In a statement, he vowed to uphold constitutional conservative values, "regardless of outside pressure from establishment politicians or special interest groups." But days later, the attorney general offered initial findings from his investigation. The results were vague but scathing.

"Based upon the information gathered thus far, Representative Durham's alleged behavior may pose a continuing risk to unsuspecting women who are employed by or interact with the legislature," Slatery said in a letter to House officials obtained by the *Tennessean*.[27]

Slatery indicated his office had interviewed thirty-four people at that point. The memo detailed broad misconduct, ranging from abuse of power to inappropriate sexual acts. According to media reports, the memo indicated Durham:

- *"Occupied a superior position of power to the women."*
- *"Obtained personal contact information from the women under the guise of legislative business or another legitimate reason."*
- *"Initiated contact about non-legislative matters and attempted to meet the women alone."*
- *"Usually involved alcohol in his interaction with women."*
- *"Made inappropriate comments of a sexual nature or engaged in inappropriate physical contact with some women."*

Slatery also found numerous women who said they feared nothing would be done if they reported Durham's behavior, another indictment of a flawed sexual harassment policy at the legislature.

Harwell, at that point already impatient with Durham's refusal to step down, took immediate action. She banished him from his legislative office and banned his access to nearly every legislative staff member and intern. A Durham assistant and Ridley packed up the embattled lawmaker's belongings and pushed them across the street to a separate state building.

The report and subsequent exile raised all kinds of constitutional

Attorney general Herbert Slatery, right, speaks to Rep. Jerry Sexton on the House floor on
February 3, 2020

questions. If this were any other workplace, Durham would likely have
been fired. But the legislature is unique: voters pick their representative,
and it takes extraordinary action to boot that person from the gig.

There are ethics committees in the House and Senate, purportedly created to examine allegations of misconduct. But they were little more than
figureheads: at the time of the AG's Durham investigation, the House
Ethics Committee hadn't met in six years. The Senate Ethics Committee
hadn't publicly met in more than a decade. Both chambers had high-
profile misconduct allegations during that time, but the committees remained dormant.

Durham's new attorney raised questions publicly. Bill Harbison was
a Nashville legal legend: a highly respected lawyer then serving as the
president of the Tennessee Bar Association, Harbison had defended the
marriage of a gay couple before the US Supreme Court just months earlier.

Now, he would represent Durham.

"We find it surprising and unfair, frankly, that a report would be released without our having had any opportunity to know what was being
investigated or what was being discussed," Harbison said in a statement.[28]

Despite Slatery's initial findings and Durham's office move, he still had
key supporters in the legislature and in his district. As the Slatery investigation lingered, Durham's defenders became slightly more outspoken. A

Rep. Rick Womick (R-Rockvale) speaks to Republican colleagues on behalf of his unsuccessful bid for House Speaker on December 10, 2014

group of Williamson County women, including a school board member and the local GOP county chairwoman, met with Harwell to discuss the Durham investigation. Some indicated they either thought Durham was being treated unfairly or went to simply show support for their lawmaker.

Rep. Rick Womick, R-Rockvale, went much further. A frequent Harwell critic and consummate legislative backbencher, Womick called the Durham investigation a "witch hunt" and questioned Slatery's authority to investigate Durham. State senator Mae Beavers, R-Mount Juliet, also questioned why Slatery was participating in the investigation if there had been no formal complaints against Durham.[29]

The delayed release of Slatery's report also called into question the legislature's ability to expel Durham. Lawmakers generally wrap up their session every year in the spring. By late May, Slatery was still working to complete his review as lawmakers gaveled to end their regular work.

Within days of Slatery releasing his initial report, several Republicans announced they planned to run against Durham in the primary. They included Sam Whitson, a retired US Army colonel. But Durham proceeded with campaigning as though nothing was wrong. And he had high-profile support. Casada and state senator Jack Johnson, R-Franklin, one of the more influential members of the upper chamber, attended Durham's reelection campaign kick-off in late May 2016.[30]

But yet another shoe was about to drop, one that would put Durham in the crosshairs of a whole new set of regulators and ultimately cost him some of his closest supporters. It wasn't the numerous stories about the women that did in Durham for Casada. At least publicly, Casada said it was the money.

## MONEY PROBLEMS

There's probably someone like Tom Lawless in every state capital city in America. But there's only one Lawless.

The bespectacled attorney was one of those guys who knew everybody in Tennessee Republican politics and was a member of the Nashville elite. His face was painted on the walls of The Palm, the downtown power lunch spot just down the road from the Ryman Auditorium.

As is so often the case with political elites, Lawless found himself appointed to what has at times been an obscure governmental agency: the Tennessee Registry of Election Finance. In theory, it's an organization established to ensure political candidates follow very specific laws crafted to bolster public confidence in their elected leaders. In practice, it had more of a perfunctory role: an apology or a good lawyer could help wayward actors avoid any serious ramifications.

Lawless, and most everyone else in Nashville, learned of the alleged new transgressions when Slatery tipped off the registry about some possible money issues. The AG's team found that Durham may have moved campaign funds into an account he used through his private work as a title attorney. It had been illegal to use campaign funds for personal purposes since a 1992 law passed in the aftermath of the Rocky Top public corruption scandal—this was the registry's bread and butter.

Drew Rawlins, then the registry's executive director, told the *Tennessean* about the referral from Slatery and why it warranted an investigation. He noted the attorney general had a sworn statement from a man named Benton Smith, who previously had worked for Durham's campaign and title company. He said he moved campaign funds to one of Durham's personal accounts.

"On or about May 25, 2015, Rep. Durham wrote me a check out of his campaign account in the amount of $2,000.00 which I endorsed and deposited into the title company's operating account at his direction," Smith wrote in the statement. "The proceeds for this check were used to pay expenses of the title company."[31]

Tennessee Registry of Election Finance board members Tom Lawless, right, and Tom Morton attend a meeting in Nashville on September 7, 2022

In classic fashion, Durham flat out denied any financial impropriety. He called Smith a disgruntled employee and told the *Tennessean* he could produce bank records proving he never moved the money that Smith claimed. He never provided those records to the paper.

Lawless and his colleagues on the registry board ultimately determined there was enough smoke, voting to audit the lawmaker's records going back to 2014. That meant subpoenas for bank records, interviews, and analysis. Initially, Lawless was reticent to condemn Durham.

"I'm just concerned that it appears that everybody's out to get Mr. Durham," he said. "So far I've got some concerns over what we've received from the attorney general's office, but we need more information before we can go forward."

Things quickly began to change. To that point a fervent supporter, Casada suddenly determined the accusations of financial shenanigans were a step too far. Slatery's staff revealed text messages between Durham and Smith that appeared to show the lawmaker directing his employee to inappropriately use campaign funds.

"If everything is true and those are his words, yes, I do think he should resign. That's just behavior that cannot be tolerated by the public from an elected person," Casada said.[32]

In some ways, Casada's about-face on Durham was similar to what he said in 2007 when Rep. Rob Briley, a Nashville Democrat who fled the scene of a car accident and led police on a high-speed chase, was facing charges of evading arrest and vandalism.[33] "At this point in his life, he is out of control and should not be making laws that the rest of us live under and he does not," Casada said of Briley.[34]

Despite repeatedly defending Durham in the face of multiple credible allegations of sexual misconduct, Casada also suggested the use of campaign funds for personal purposes "violates the trust of the people and can't be tolerated from an elected person."

"This is empirical, this is measurable, it's his own words indicting him, where the harassment charges were, she said this and he said this," Casada explained. "There was nothing to show who was right or who was wrong. It was rumors, hearsay, that kind of thing. This is Jeremy's own words saying, 'Do this, take money out of my campaign account and put it in my business account.'"[35]

It was another public knock from a former ally. But it wasn't the final straw, by any means.

Despite the financial revelations, there was something of a calm before the storm. Rep. Billy Spivey, a Lewisburg Republican who served on the committee purportedly leading the legislative inquiry into Durham, suggested in mid-June that it had lasted too long and "reeks of a political witch hunt."[36]

But his views were in the minority. Most watched and waited, with rumors continuing to circulate about what now two different sets of investigators could find.

Unbeknownst to many, the attorney general also sought information from the *Tennessean* about its original investigation into Durham. Slatery and his team formally requested the paper either provide a message to the women who spoke anonymously with reporters or to reveal their identities to investigators. While the intent was clearly to further the state's investigation, it was still an extraordinary ask from a law enforcement agency to a press outlet. The *Tennessean* declined to provide this information to the attorney general.

By early July, there were signs Slatery's probe was nearly complete. Although it had lingered for some time, it was anticipated he'd finish before the upcoming primary election. While Durham had coasted to previous victories, the lingering investigations and public distancing by former allies did not bode well for his re-election hopes.

Finally, the legislative committee created to lead the investigation announced a meeting. It's relatively rare for any committee to meet when lawmakers are not in session, and word quickly spread: the final report would likely be released at this gathering. Durham and his team immediately reacted. They filed a lawsuit seeking in part to prevent the public release of the attorney general's findings. They also argued the AG had no authority to investigate Durham in the first place.[37]

"If the report is released at this time, Rep. Durham will suffer immediate and irreparable harm if the report is released mere days before early voting starts. The releasing of the report days before the election will render a final judgment ineffectual as the damage to Rep. Durham's re-election efforts will already have taken place," the lawsuit stated.[38]

Harwell called it unfortunate for Durham to drag out the process. The AG and his team prepared to battle the request in a judicial proceeding called for the day before the legislative committee was to meet.

In a filing, Slatery painted a very different picture for the judge. Releasing the report would serve the public interest, he argued, noting Durham had repeatedly declined to participate in the investigation. That included never agreeing to allow Slatery to review his personal phone—while providing the phone could help his argument that he was innocent, turning over evidence against himself could obviously hurt Durham.

Durham had previously vowed to be open with investigators, Slatery argued. He pointed to a previous radio interview, in which the embattled lawmaker told the host, "If I did it, I will own it and I will take responsibility. . . . The more evidence out there, the better for me."[39]

"It is a case in which [Durham] wants only to prevent the House from investigating allegations about his use and abuse of his position of power as a member of the House," Slatery wrote, referencing one of Durham's arguments in the initial filing.[40]

The court ultimately sided with Slatery. Sure the report could harm Durham, Nashville chancellor Russell Perkins determined. But he said the public's ability to review the investigation's findings outweighed any argument offered by Durham.[41]

The stage was set for the public release. And Slatery delivered.

## THE JANE DOES

It was the morning of July 13, already shaping up to be another Tennessee summer scorcher. Generally, the state Capitol complex would be something of a ghost town, with the bulk of lawmakers back home concentrating on their re-election campaigns.

But on that day, the complex was buzzing.

The legislative committee leading the Durham probe was meeting. But they were almost a secondary attraction. At that point, everyone knew Slatery's long-anticipated report would be released.

The report blew away expectations, surprising even some of Durham's harshest critics. The thirty-two-year-old former rising star was accused of inappropriate sexual conduct with twenty-two women, Slatery's team determined, outlining sweeping allegations of harassment in dispassionate but striking detail about predatory sexual behavior.[42]

"Representative Durham's behavior created an environment that made a number of the women uncomfortable interacting with him in the workplace," the report said. "Many of those who continue to work for or with the legislature avoid or refuse to be alone with Rep. Durham, a situation which adversely effects their ability to perform their jobs in the same manner as their male counterparts.

"With few exceptions, the women who related incidents felt they could not report Rep. Durham's behavior because nothing would be done, and they did not want to lose their jobs or be considered 'untrustworthy' by employers, clients, or other legislators. Most were fearful and extremely anxious about having their identities revealed publicly."

Durham declined to be interviewed by investigators, who also outlined issues they'd had in their efforts to obtain information from him. He was under no legal obligation to participate, but Slatery's team painted a picture that he went out of his way to avoid providing text messages, electronic devices, and other information.

The scope of the alleged misconduct was sweeping: Slatery's team did seventy-eight interviews with seventy-two witnesses, speaking with lawmakers, legislative staffers, lobbyists, and many others. They also reviewed Durham's state-issued laptop and iPad along with a slew of texts or messages sent via social media. The investigation painted a clear picture: Durham knew he had power over these individuals, and he used it to his personal advantage.

Durham allegedly brought numerous women into his legislative office for sex, at least one who was as young as twenty. He pressured them, using his position of power and alcohol to force them into situations that made them well beyond uncomfortable, the report stated.

The twenty-year-old said she met Durham in May or June of 2014, right after she had finished her junior year in college and while she was working on a political campaign. The pair started talking, at first about politics. She described an initial meeting as "very professional" but eventually, text messages became "flirty."

Rep. Jeremy Durham leaves a caucus meeting at Legislative Plaza on January 27, 2016 (Samuel M. Simpkins - USA TODAY NETWORK

In June, he asked her to hang out with him at Legislative Plaza, and she agreed. She thought spending time with a lawmaker was cool, she told investigators. It was clear this was not a professional meeting: Durham brought a cooler of beer, despite the woman not yet being of legal drinking age. He suggested they move to some couches in an office near his own. They began to kiss and eventually had sex, according to the report.

"Afterward, they talked and watched a baseball game in his office, during which time Rep. Durham told her, 'I better be careful, or I could end up falling for you.' About 45 minutes later, he drove her back to her car," the report stated.

The woman later texted Durham that she felt sick about what they'd done, but he told her it wasn't a big deal, she told investigators. Conversations continued. In August 2014, Durham and the student had sex at the lawmaker's home, she told investigators. Soon thereafter she returned to college, but Durham eventually asked again to hang out.

It was the day he was elected to serve as House majority whip, she told investigators. After seeing her at the Legislative Plaza he allegedly texted, "I would like to see you naked around midnight." The woman told investigators she went to his legislative office around midnight. Durham was intoxicated, and they had "sexual contact," according to the report.

By May 2015, Durham was still texting the woman, but she'd started to doubt his previous statements about getting a divorce from his wife, she told investigators. She said she eventually told him to leave her alone and blocked his number, the report stated.

"Jane Doe #38 was visibly emotional during the interview and cried when talking about her sexual encounters with Rep. Durham. She stated she had considered working for the legislature at one time but after her experience with Rep. Durham, she no longer has any interest. She stated that she was very stupid and naïve and 'politics was very new to me,'" according to investigators.

Another person, who at the time of meeting Durham was an intern, described an interaction with him at a legislative party. Typically, interns aren't supposed to go to such parties, but she'd received "special permission" from the lawmaker for whom she worked, the report stated. So did several other interns or young staffers; all listed by the report were women.

Durham repeatedly approached her, the intern said. At first, he offered to help her get into law school, obtaining her cell phone number in the process. As he drank more, though, the intern told investigators he became more aggressive.

Eventually, he convinced her to go out on a patio with him. As soon as they were alone, he moved "toward her in an 'aggressive, very flirtatious manner.'" The intern knew he wanted to kiss her. She moved away, pointing out that he was married and that she had a boyfriend. Durham reportedly shrugged it off, telling her they had a "connection." But once another woman walked onto the patio, he left, the intern said.

The episode caused substantial emotional distress for the woman. She told investigators she left the party, crying as she told her boyfriend that a lawmaker tried to "make a move on me." The next day, the lawmaker for whom the intern worked said there was a rumor circulating that she'd gone home with Durham. This infuriated the intern; she texted Durham in an effort to get him to squelch the story, but she told investigators he didn't take her seriously.

She reported the interaction with Durham to the legislative intern supervisor almost immediately. The supervisor said to inform her if Durham texted again; she told investigators that she also told her boss about the allegation. That person made a note of the incident but indicated the intern did not want to make a formal complaint, according to the report.

The intern told investigators the entire episode was foundational in her decision to take a different direction in life. After that evening, she was ridiculed by other interns and generally found she'd lost faith in a life in politics.

"She was very emotional in the interview and stated that the incident with Rep. Durham and the aftermath 'completely turned me away from wanting to be a part of the political process, one that I have been very passionate about my whole life,'" the report stated.

When she spoke with investigators, she was already working in a different field.

By the time investigators spoke with a woman identified as Jane Doe #24, she had also left her job at the statehouse. She had been a legislative staffer, leaving in part due to her interactions with Durham, she told Slatery's team. The staffer worked for a lawmaker with whom Durham was close, so he was around the office frequently. At one point, he made a comment about the staffer's breasts, she told investigators. Like others interviewed, she said she felt uncomfortable but didn't want to "rock the boat" for fear it would hurt her employment prospects.

From there, the inappropriate conduct escalated, she said.

Durham got her phone number and invited her to a bar in downtown Nashville. The staffer said she was flattered and figured it was a gathering of lots of people from the legislature. But when she arrived, it was just Durham. He eventually sat next to her in a booth, put his arm around her and continued to get close. She said she thought his intentions were clear.

After Durham walked her home, the staffer rebuffed the lawmaker's request to go up to her apartment. Durham then allegedly put his hand on her back and kissed her. The staffer told investigators she reminded Durham he was married and said something to the effect of "this is not going to happen." He laughed and left, according to the report.

From there he constantly texted her, sometimes late at night, sometimes asking for pictures. The staffer assumed he wanted her to send him naked photographs, the report stated. On another occasion, he kissed her on the neck, she told investigators. The staffer said the lawmaker for whom she worked found out, and after the 2013 legislative session she was not rehired at the statehouse. She left politics, giving up her longtime dream of becoming a lobbyist, she told investigators.

The report did not accuse Durham of sexual assault or any similar offense. But it did repeatedly mention power dynamics and note the women interviewed at times felt their livelihoods depended on maintaining his good favor.

"As Jane Doe #46 explained, the inappropriate text messages Rep. Durham sent a fellow lobbyist 'put her between a rock and a hard place' because lobbyists have to be careful how they answer a legislator," the report stated. "She said, 'If you piss them off, they are the ones with the vote; they have the trump card. They can make or break you.'"

In fact, investigators noted this was generally considered a well-known dynamic at the Capitol, involving more than just Durham.

"As legislative clerk Jane Doe #12 explained, when she told Rep. Durham that his requests for drinks with her in 2013 were inappropriate because he was married and she was engaged, she said his response was, 'Welcome to Capitol Hill,'" the report stated. Another woman told investigators he gave her a similar line after she rebuffed his advances, telling him she was engaged and he was married.

A male lobbyist told the AG's team—in front of a female lobbyist also being interviewed by investigators—that women have to take unwanted sexual advances from legislators.

"No direct evidence was presented to the office that Rep. Durham's vote was actually affected by a lobbyist's response. However, a lobbyist's livelihood depends on her/his ability to maintain a professional working relationship with legislators in order to advocate on behalf of clients' interest in bills pending before the Legislature," the report said.

Other female lobbyists corroborated many of these accounts, telling investigators about their colleagues reporting "creepy experiences" with Durham, according to the report. Another lobbyist also reported Durham tried to trade a vote on a bill for some sort of personal interaction.

This lobbyist told investigators that during the 2015 legislative session, she was assigned by her bosses to lobby Durham on a piece of legislation. She met him at his office and began to discuss the bill, but he reportedly only wanted to talk about drinks. Durham repeatedly mentioned that he had mixers in a mini-fridge and booze in his drawer, inviting her over for drinks if she was around the legislature at night before showing her the contents of the fridge.

She said she thought her conversation about the legislation was "white noise" for Durham. Frustrated, she left. Durham poked his head out of his doorway and said, "I'm for your bill but I'm going to expect something in return," the lobbyist told investigators. Angry at this point, she said she responded, "We have the votes. We don't need yours, thanks."

The lobbyist told her bosses about the interaction. The bosses then told a male lawmaker, according to investigators. After the *Tennessean* published its investigation in January 2016, the lawmaker reached back out to the lobbyist to see if she wanted to file a formal complaint against Durham. She decided against it, she told investigators, because she was afraid she would not be able to confidentially tell her story. She said she was afraid her family would read her name in the newspaper or that her reputation at the statehouse would be harmed.

Slatery's report was full of similar stories. One lobbyist told investigators she went to Durham's office at least seven times and "he's never looked at my face," instead staring at her chest. That person's firm wouldn't send her alone to lobby Durham. Another lobbyist said Durham at one point texted her very late at night about getting drinks, and she found her interactions with him "terribly inappropriate" and he "creeped me out."

Another female lobbyist said Durham approached her at a reception in January 2016—days before the *Tennessean* published its investigation about inappropriate text messages but after he had been warned about his behavior—and commented on her looks.

"Are you working out? Keep doing what you're doing. It's working for you," he reportedly said, looking the lobbyist up and down and looking at her "below the neck," according to the report.

A woman described in the report as being associated with the legislature in 2014 said Durham told her he had a crush on her. She reminded him they were both married, but he continued to hit on her. He later texted something to the effect of "your smile gave me chills," the report stated.

Nothing seemed to deter Durham. One lobbyist told investigators she and a friend socialized with Durham and his wife at a 2013 conference in Chicago. After the event, the four agreed to have drinks together and all got in a cab. A heavily drunk Durham allegedly sat between the lobbyist and his wife, at one point taking his hand and rubbing the lobbyist's thighs. She told investigators it gave her the "heebie jeebies" and prompted her to not go for drinks with the Durhams after all.

The incident from the report that received perhaps the most subsequent attention was an allegation involving Durham, mints, and his pants. At least three people independently told investigators about an incident that earned him a nickname that would be plastered on television and print stories for weeks: "Pants Candy."

During a meeting with Durham at some point in either the 2013 or 2014 legislative session, a lobbyist saw a bowl of mints on the lawmaker's desk. The lobbyist asked for one, but Durham declined.

"He then stood up behind his desk, put his hand in his pocket, and moved it around in a manner that made 'quite a display' of accentuating his genitalia. He then pulled an unwrapped, dirty mint from his pocket and said something to the effect of, 'I think this is the piece you want,'" the lobbyist told investigators.

From then on, lobbyists began referring to Durham as "pants candy," she said. In addition to corroborating the general tenor of the conversation, two other people interviewed by investigators stood up during their interviews and demonstrated how Durham had fiddled with his pocket, as described to them by the lobbyist, the report stated.

Investigators interviewed several lawmakers as well. Some said they'd heard of or seen inappropriate conduct. Others acknowledged being approached by lobbyists or others who had stories of alleged misconduct. But one defended Durham. Referred to in the report as Rep. Jane Doe #33, the legislator told investigators she and Durham were "best friends" who socialized regularly. She denied ever seeing or hearing about anything inappropriate by Durham before reading the *Tennessean's* investigation. She told investigators she had talked about the articles with Durham. He denied the allegations and they'd "laughed about it," she said.

## THE EVER-DEFIANT DURHAM

Durham and his team were not laughing the day the report was released.

In a statement issued to the media the same day of the report's release, Durham's attorney Bill Harbison criticized the investigation and its findings without denying any specific allegations.

"Even though nobody ever filed a complaint of sexual harassment, the investigation goes into alleged details with allegations from witnesses whose identity is completely anonymous," Harbison said.[43]

"Unlike any normal legal proceeding where there is an opportunity to confront witnesses, get notice of subpoenas, or, at the very least, understand the exact allegations against a person, this investigation has been secretive and deceptive from the very beginning. We believe that no fair-minded person should judge Jeremy Durham based on a one-sided, anonymous report."

Durham was offered the chance to speak with investigators and offer witnesses who would participate in the investigation. He did not. This was also not a normal legal proceeding—it's not every day a legislative committee tasks the attorney general with investigating the conduct of a lawmaker—but Judge Perkins had recently ruled in favor of releasing the report.

Protesters hold up signs demanding Rep. Jeremy Durham's ouster in the House chamber on September 12, 2016

In classic legislative fashion, the lawmakers leading the committee investigating Durham did nothing with the findings.[44] While they thought there was enough evidence to expel him from the legislature, the members ultimately decided they should leave it to voters to determine Durham's fate. The August 4 primary was only a few weeks away, and the lawmakers thought it might be a challenge to bring back their colleagues in time for a special legislative session.

But the investigation was not an "act of futility," Speaker Harwell argued, almost yelling in response to a question at a press conference after the report was released. "This may be one of the few times in his life he has been held accountable."[45]

Casada went into overdrive working to distance himself from his one-time protégé. He told reporters Durham lied to him, called the report's evidence "indisputable" despite previously raising questions about the sexual impropriety questions, and predicted his colleague would not win re-election.

The ever-quotable Lt. Gov. Ron Ramsey went off on Durham with both barrels. The day after the report's release he called him despicable and said he'd push Harwell for a special session to expel Durham if he were re-elected.

"When someone like Jeremy Durham says 'Welcome to Capitol Hill,' it makes you want to smack him in the mouth," Ramsey said.[46]

Gov. Bill Haslam and Ryan Haynes, head of the Tennessee Republican Party, reiterated that Durham should step down. Durham's Williamson County colleagues from the state House and Senate joined in on the bandwagon, calling on him to vacate his seat. So did Franklin mayor Ken Moore.[47] With criticism coming from all sides and little vocal support, Durham called a press conference for the next afternoon at his attorney's office in a high rise in downtown Nashville.

Up to that point, at essentially every turn of the investigation, Durham chose to fight. He'd left his leadership post and temporarily left the caucus, but he'd refused to leave his seat or step away from re-election. He'd repeatedly questioned the veracity of the allegations reported in the media while accurately noting many if not most were tied to people anonymously quoted.

Given his track record, it was anyone's guess what Durham would say during his press conference. Wearing a dark suit, white shirt and light tie, Durham stepped up to a microphone and podium to read a statement. The two-minute prepared remarks embodied so much of the Durham known to lawmakers, constituents, and many others around the statehouse: defiant but calculating.[48]

He opened by immediately denying the bulk of the allegations in the report. While not pointing to a specific comment or interaction, he said "the great majority of the anonymous allegations in the AG report are either completely false or taken completely out of context." But, he acknowledged, a handful of the report's interactions were true. He never mentioned which allegations, instead stating that some of his communications were "less than professional." Arguing his intentions were harmless, he said he still took full responsibility for the never-specified communications and apologized.[49]

"This type of behavior is something that will never be a problem again going forward but I do accept full responsibility for those past actions. This is something my wife and I have fought hard to work through so that we can improve our marriage," Durham said.

He did expressly deny having or attempting to have sexual interactions "with any of the individuals in the report."

Eschewing his conciliatory tone, he again blasted the investigation and its process. He argued he was never allowed to "understand the allegations against me" or exactly who made them, cross-examine those witnesses or present his own evidence. He did not note that investigators tried to interview him, allowed him to provide witnesses for them to question, and asked for documents from his phone or other devices that in theory could have corroborated his denials.

Again, he attempted to liken a legislative inquiry to a criminal proceeding, arguing he was not afforded due process at least in some part because of a vendetta from Harwell.

But, in what was characterized as an about-face in the *Tennessean*, Durham closed with what has become an oft-used political tactic: a professed desire to focus on his family.

"Right now, I'm focused on spending time with my family during what has been a very difficult time for us. But most importantly I love my wife and I must focus on spending time with my family," Durham said.

"Therefore, I am suspending my campaign for re-election to the House of Representatives. I ask for your respect and your privacy for my family during this difficult time."

His comments and decision not to leave office were immediately met with criticism. Both Harwell and Ramsey unloaded again.

"Representative Durham's denials are insulting to the brave women whose testimony was detailed in the report. Representative Durham needs to make absolutely clear he is not seeking re-election," Harwell said in a statement.[50]

The lieutenant governor said refusing to resign "is an affront to the women of this state and the taxpayers who pay his salary."

While Ramsey and Harwell had repeatedly criticized Durham, the report left neither unscathed. The investigation broadly demonstrated a culture and a workplace that were far from the shining city on a hill so often alluded to by its inhabitants.

Interns did not feel comfortable telling their bosses when they felt a lawmaker crossed the line. Lobbyists feared losing their jobs, credibility, or respect if they told anyone a legislator tried to kiss them or sent late-night texts. And in some instances, the lack of a so-called formal complaint appeared to entirely derail accountability, despite administrators' and legislative leaders' knowledge that women would have to come back to work the next day knowing the person allegedly harassing them would go unpunished.

"It's very rare that people lie about being victimized in some way. One of the best things we can do is believe and support the victims when they experience something like this," said Rachel Freeman, vice president of programs at the Nashville Sexual Assault Center. "We need to think through our response as a community and a society about what we're communicating by not holding an alleged offender accountable."

The same day Durham announced his decision to suspend his campaign, Harwell and Ramsey formally approved a new workplace harassment policy for the legislature. In the works since Harwell's announcement following the initial *Tennessean* investigation, the new policy was at least in part crafted to restore confidence that workers at the legislature would be protected.

Many changes were predicated on transparency. In Tennessee, lawmakers and legislative staff have personnel files that are open to the public. But until the new policy, any harassment or other workplace transgressions would not appear in those files. Now, Harwell noted the public would see the final results of investigations that determined misconduct had occurred.

Lawmakers in both chambers would also be forced to go through sexual harassment training, already a common requirement in many other workplaces in the private sector. The policy also included a mandatory reporting requirement, meaning anyone at the legislature in a "supervisory position" who learned of or received a complaint would need to report it to legislative leaders or the head of legislative administration.

At the same time, Harwell argued there was nothing that could have prevented Durham's actions, noting the allegations appeared to violate the legislature's previous human resources policy. The sentiment was not supported by Slatery's investigation, or by the numerous media reports that came out after its release. Investigators zeroed in on the dynamics of culture and power, twin driving forces that often left the vulnerable or unsuspecting in precarious positions. Throw in booze, masculinity, and the party atmosphere so many seek in Nashville, and it created an environment where misconduct was rife.

"I think that this went on for so long speaks to a culture," one lobbyist told the *Tennessean*. "It went on for way too long. I knew about Jeremy Durham three years ago. So did everybody else. Everybody knew the Pants Candy story. Everybody!"[51]

A female Republican lawmaker who had been harassed by one Republican and one Democrat during her time in the legislature told the paper she understood why some of the women whom Durham harassed did not file a formal complaint.

"When someone does something like that to you, you don't know what to do or how to act," the lawmaker said. "It's a personal decision, it is something that is going to impact and change your life."[52]

As Durham denied the allegations but nixed his re-election and legislative leaders blasted him, the Capitol Hill rumor mill was at full speed. Despite calls for people not to try and figure out the names of the people anonymously quoted in the attorney general's report, it became something of a parlor game for Nashville insiders.

The politicians were the easiest to spot: Harwell was clearly interviewed, as was legislative administrator Connie Ridley. Others steeped in the legislative culture likely sussed out many more, even those who provided some of the most intimate allegations. It was at once both an attempt to find accountability and the enactment of some of the women's worst fears. The greater public may not know they participated, but many a politico could determine or guess at the identities of the Jane Does.

Within weeks of the report's release, some of the women whom investigators interviewed were being harassed. In one case, a woman received packages with derogatory messages at the home of a relative. Casada confirmed learning of the messages. He denied they came from Durham, but would not provide additional details about their source to the *Tennessean*.[53]

The harasser sent emails to colleagues of the woman who received the packages, haranguing her and advocating that she be fired due to behavior detailed in the attorney general's report. Casada said the messages were frustrating, but there was nothing he or the attorney general could do.[54] It was more evidence that despite the report, as well as the public allegations against Durham and assurances from leaders that he was a bad apple, the legislature had a culture problem.

Now, more than ever, it was clear Harwell wanted accountability. She announced her desire for a special session to remove Durham, pushing her Republican colleagues to sign off and agree to return to Nashville for an ouster.

Remembered by few, the state campaign finance officials quietly plodded along, reviewing evidence of possible Durham misdeeds. Known by even fewer, at the same time federal law enforcement decided they too were interested in Durham.

## THE FEDS TAKE AN INTEREST

Shortly after Durham's decision to not resign, legislators zeroed in on what became a key issue in whether to remove the lawmaker from his seat: state health benefits and his pension. In Tennessee, state lawmakers are part-time employees. But if they serve a certain amount of time, they're eligible to retain state health coverage and receive a pension once they turn fifty-five. Durham was eligible to receive lifetime health and pension benefits if he served out the remainder of his term.

To Durham's critics, a special session to oust the lawmaker to deny him his state benefits was the obvious next step. Not everyone was quite so enthralled with the idea. Casada announced he would only back a return to Nashville if lawmakers could also weigh removing Rep. Joe Armstrong, a Knoxville Democrat under federal indictment related to an alleged scheme to buy cigarette tax stamps, advocate for a bill to increase their value, then seek to sell them at a profit. Casada's move was seen as trying to depress support for the special session among Democrats.[55]

In Tennessee, lawmakers have the ability to call themselves into a special session but two-thirds of the members of both the House and Senate must sign on to a petition.

In early August, on the final day to sign the petition, only twenty-seven lawmakers had done so. The attempt had failed miserably and suggested an overall lack of support for ousting Durham if the matter ever reached a vote.[56]

That same week, Durham officially lost to Sam Whitson in the Republican primary election. By the time Durham had suspended his campaign, election officials said it was too late to get his name off of the ballot. In the aftermath of the vote it seemed as if Durham would be allowed to quietly leave the General Assembly at the end of his term, with lawmakers focused on their own elections.

Then news broke that the state campaign finance probe's preliminary findings uncovered $191,000 in discrepancies between bank records and disclosures from Durham's campaign. A few days later, the *Tennessean* reported federal investigators, too, were scrutinizing Durham's campaign finances.

In late August 2016, criminal defense attorney Peter Strianse confirmed he had been hired by Durham.[57]

"The US Attorney's Office in Nashville has opened up a matter based on the allegations that were carried in your newspaper," he told the paper. "I think the government has an open mind about what they're investigating."

The feds sent Durham two subpoenas related to allegations of possible campaign finance and tax crimes, Strianse told the paper. He said his client was innocent and would cooperate with the investigation. The confirmation of a criminal probe forced Durham back into the spotlight. He may not have faced formal punishment for the sweeping sexual misconduct allegations, but here was proof that law enforcement thought his financial dealings were worthy of further scrutiny.

Rawlins, the executive director of the state campaign finance watchdog, confirmed he'd spoken with federal prosecutors. Lawless—the top Republican leading the Registry of Election Finance's probe of Durham—told the paper the state investigation was ongoing, but so far what he'd seen appeared to indicate the possibility of serious wrongdoing.

Days before the confirmation of a federal investigation, state campaign finance experts had published a broad overview of some of their findings. It noted Durham used his campaign funds to invest in several different ventures and loaned out campaign funds to individuals. It's illegal to use campaign funds for personal purposes.[58]

The same week the *Tennessean* reported on the federal investigation, it also confirmed Durham had invested funds from his campaign, a political action committee, and his own bank account into the business of a wealthy Republican donor. The donor, Andy Miller, confirmed he'd spoken with state officials in accordance with their investigation but said he thought they'd been satisfied by his answers to their questions.[59]

In the middle of the news about state and federal investigations, Durham also closed his title company. It was the same one where former employee Benton Smith told the attorney general he'd transferred campaign funds, a key catalyst in prompting the state campaign finance probe.[60]

Amid the Durham scrutiny, Haslam called a special legislative session. It wasn't related to Durham; instead, the governor wanted lawmakers back in Nashville to tweak a law related to drunk driving that could've cost the state $60 million in federal money. Haslam specifically did not add a Durham expulsion vote to his special session call—the governor has the power to essentially tell lawmakers what's on their agenda during a special session. However, he said if the House decided to take up a resolution to boot Durham, he wouldn't get in the way. Harwell pounced on the opportunity.

"There will be a motion and a vote on expulsion, and I welcome the opportunity to vote for it," Harwell said in early September, days after Haslam called the special session.[61]

Strianse, Durham's attorney, argued trying to vote on Durham's fate during the special session would not be allowed. If the governor did not include a Durham motion in his request for a special session, then such a vote would be "unconstitutional," he said.[62]

That didn't dissuade Harwell in the slightest. She and legislative leadership pushed forward with their plans to include a Durham expulsion motion during the special session. It would soon be time for lawmakers—at that point reticent to formally expel a colleague—to cast a vote on Durham's future.

Durham appeared livid: he told a local television station that the expulsion effort was similar to a "medieval beheading."

"If they provide me a legitimate opportunity to present my own evidence and face my accusers, I wouldn't miss it. But it must be fair," Durham told WKRN-TV in Nashville.[63]

Harwell confirmed Durham would be allowed to speak during the session. It raised an important question, and fear, among some: would Durham name people in the attorney general's report?

At that point he had not publicly identified anyone he suspected of participating in the investigation. However, the day before the start of the special session, Durham sent an eight-page letter to his legislative colleagues. The motivations seemed clear, if not explicit: Durham threatened to reveal names unless the expulsion effort was called off.[64]

"Due to the way this situation has been handled, my family finds itself in the position of wanting to largely clear my name by releasing names and text messages of many Jane Does while also wanting to not make the situation a bigger circus than it has already become," Durham wrote in the letter.

"I've prepared a document responding to each and every Jane Doe—with names—and with text messages stored on a cloud. But that process should be handled according to House rules—not in a public expulsion proceeding."

In the letter, he argued he was routinely mistreated, convicted in the court of public opinion without the benefit of having an opportunity to clear his name. He argued he should be allowed to face his accusers. Durham said he was ready to "accept a mild degree of fault" but wanted to blast leaders and the process before doing so.

He labeled all of the allegations in the attorney general's report as anonymous hearsay. That's inaccurate: many of the people interviewed by investigators provided their own experiences, not information relayed by others.

Durham correctly noted that the only other recent legislative expulsion, from 1980, came in response to a case of bribery. He pointed out that although Slatery's team talked to people who suggested Durham may have bartered with his vote, they found no direct evidence that his vote was swayed by any untoward action.

Perhaps his most brazen play was trying to use the older legislative sexual harassment policy against leadership. The former policy had language promising any information related to a complaint would not be made public, and no one involved with the complaint—including the person making the accusation—would "be allowed" to discuss the allegation.

In theory, this was crafted to both allow for anonymous complaints and prevent rumors from leaking about unsubstantiated claims. In practice, it was one of the worst parts of the policy; experts told the *Tennessean* it essentially muzzled possible victims, and the prospect of trying to prevent someone who was sexually harassed from telling family or a therapist is unreasonable. One expert likened it to a "gag order" for victims.[65]

Durham tried to argue that the legislature didn't follow the policy, seeming to imply that information about complaints became public. However, as he himself and others noted in the Slatery report, no formal complaints were made against Durham before the start of the attorney general's investigation.

The letter went on, saying Slatery's team never offered him a fair chance to tell his side, instead trying to ambush him. He said the notion that he had "inappropriate sexual contact" with twenty-two women was not supported by the report findings either, arguing that texting "what's up" and "offering a simple verbal compliment" did not constitute inappropriate sexual contact.[66]

This was not the Durham who said he would accept some culpability and apologized the day after the release of the report. This was the fighter, the man who worked hard to get the seat he had and wasn't prepared to go out with a whimper.

He went on to launch something of an attack against one of the women from the report. He didn't identify her by number, but suggested he knew that she was "rewarded" with a new state job after giving "false anonymous accusations." Durham also said he knew thirteen of the sixteen lobbyists interviewed, suggesting their clients or issues made them biased.

The lawyer trotted out his legal acumen as well, trying to argue that any of the alleged conduct from the investigation wouldn't meet the definition of sexual harassment under Tennessee law. Never mind that lawyers from the attorney general's office determined his actions constituted sexual harassment—there were caveats in the law that made it "literally impossible" for him to meet some of the components of the term's definition, he said.

Durham ended the letter by suggesting he suspected he would be a "political instrument for election year grandstanding" if he attended his own ouster session. Some of his colleagues even nearly came to blows arguing over who got to sponsor the expulsion resolution, Durham suggested (without providing any evidence).

So, in protest, he said, he planned to skip the session unless House leadership "institutes some level of fundamental fairness." It was a wide-ranging, last-ditch effort to convince his colleagues that he was the wronged party and the entire process hardly amounted to what was required to oust a duly elected official from the legislature.

To call it a longshot was an understatement.

Typically, before the General Assembly votes on a particularly important or contentious issue, legislative leaders get an idea of where everyone stands. The day before the House met to discuss the Durham expulsion resolution, both Harwell and Casada said they had the sixty-six votes needed to successfully remove Durham.

"I would be shocked if it was less than eighty [votes in favor of expulsion]," Casada told the *Tennessean*.[67]

The outcome felt both expected but uncertain: it was hard to predict what would happen with Durham. Not only the final tally, but what he would do if he did decide to speak for himself before his colleagues cast their votes.

There was no indication legislative leaders responded to Durham's letter. But the Franklin Republican did change his mind, showing up at the statehouse with a large leather folder tucked under one arm. His attendance—and that folder—appeared to catch some lawmakers off guard. GOP leaders called a break in the proceedings for what the *Tennessean* described as an emotional plea from House Speaker Beth Harwell for support to prevent anyone from publicly identifying women who'd accused Durham of sexual misconduct.

"I'm asking the Speaker if I can go into recess to remind the caucus that it is paramount to protect the Jane Does—the innocent women who are brave enough to come forward," Casada said moments before the start of session.

Harwell's voice broke as she asked her caucus to support the motion. "Don't do this to these women. Don't you dare," she said.

Eventually state representative William Lamberth, a Republican former prosecutor from Sumner County, made a motion that no one who spoke could identify any of the women who'd provided information under the condition of anonymity with the attorney general. He also implored

Rep. Jeremy Durham attends a floor session on the day of his ouster from the House on September 13, 2016

the media not to print the names of women if Durham did say them during the hearing.

Fears that Durham would go on the attack proved to be justified minutes later.

The Franklin Republican eventually walked up to the lectern that stands in the middle of the House floor, facing out toward the rank-and-file and standing in front of the House Speaker's pulpit. He launched into a speech that lasted nearly thirteen minutes, where he again focused largely on what he considered the fatally flawed process of the investigation as opposed to individual allegations.

"No matter how guilty you think I am, there are aspects of this situation that should bother you," Durham said.

After finishing, he appeared ready to head back to his desk. But Lamberth got to his feet, asking Durham to answer questions. Perhaps to the surprise of some, Durham complied.

Lamberth thundered away at Durham, asking about the allegation he had sex in his legislative office with a twenty-year-old, among others included in the Slatery report. The lawmaker said he felt betrayed by Durham.

House Democratic Caucus chair Mike Stewart of Nashville questioned Durham next. Also a lawyer, Stewart walked Durham through a series of clearly prepared questions. Again, Durham stayed at the lectern, ready to answer them. His posture was relatively casual, his tone not aggressive.

But he was clearly in attack mode.

Stewart asked him to point out which allegations in the report were true. He declined, instead suggesting it "would be much more fun to talk about the ones that are false." And then he pointed at that large binder, hinting that what it held inside would be damaging to some of the lawmakers seated before him.

"I assure you, you don't want me releasing some of the things that are in this binder," Durham said. The statement came less than an hour after he'd criticized the media for reporting that the lawmaker had threatened to name accusers.[68]

At least one lawmaker did come to Durham's defense, be it only on procedural grounds. Rick Womick resumed his role as a thorn in Harwell's side, standing to speak out against a process he agreed had not afforded Durham due process. The argument didn't go far in the House. Lawmakers noted expulsion is not the same as a court proceeding, and to compare the two would be misleading.

Abruptly, Durham appeared to have had enough. He'd already seemed prepared to storm off, but remained to answer additional questions. As more lawmakers asked him about the report, though, Durham grabbed his binder and strutted out of the chamber. Journalists chased after him as he walked down the Capitol's marble steps. He specifically declined to give comments to some but spoke briefly with a handful of television journalists before climbing into his Toyota RAV4 and driving away.

In the statehouse above him, his colleagues were preparing to vote. Leaders expected the measure to easily exceed the requisite of two-thirds of members, but they also noted that several lawmakers were unable to attend the special session. Others, like Womick and fellow Republican representative Andy Holt of Dresden, suggested they would not vote on a resolution they considered to be taken up unconstitutionally during the session.

In the end, the measure squeaked by, receiving seventy votes in the ninety-nine-member chamber. Ten lawmakers were excused from attending the floor session and another eleven were registered as failing to cast any vote at all—including Durham himself and several of the far-right faction of the Republican caucus. Four lawmakers officially abstained, including Holt and David Byrd (who would later face calls for his own ouster over allegations of sexual misconduct with high school basketball players when he was their coach in the 1980s). Just two members voted against the ouster, Republican representatives Courtney Rogers of Goodlettsville and Terri Lynn Weaver of Lancaster.[69]

Despite the relatively close margin, legislative leaders were relieved. Harwell said she was pleased with the vote, although she suggested some Democrats could have done more during the hearing.

Durham's legislative career was done. He went on to sue the legislature and state government in an effort to regain his benefits, arguing the proceedings were unconstitutional. He lost, repeatedly, most recently in November 2021 before the US Court of Appeals for the Sixth Circuit.

In the days after his ouster though, Durham did not fade quietly out of the spotlight. Just weeks after his expulsion, Durham was also booted from a University of Tennessee football game. The avid Vols fan reportedly smacked a supporter of the rival Florida Gators in the face, causing his sunglasses to spiral away down a row at Neyland Stadium in Knoxville. Local law enforcement escorted the suddenly former legislator out of the game.[70]

Durham himself gave several television interviews, apparently revealing some of what was in his leather binder. He told WSMV-TV that one legislator who voted in favor of his ouster had smoked marijuana at the Capitol and others had consumed alcohol in legislative offices. He said he'd seen Williamson County GOP colleague Rep. Charles Sargent kiss women at Legislative Plaza. He also said he'd seen Casada give hugs, "but I can't even, like, send a remotely flirtatious text message."

Sargent acknowledged an occasional hug or "peck on the cheek" with women he knew. Casada said he sometimes hugged women, and men, and thought "hugging is proper if done correctly."[71]

Political fighting would continue. But the real fuel for the ongoing fire involving Durham came from the long-simmering state campaign finance investigation.

## A RARE REBUKE

Expulsion in no way dissuaded state campaign finance officials from continuing their probe.

Initially, registry board chair Tom Lawless had cautioned the public against assuming Durham was guilty of financial malfeasance. But as officials dug deeper, his tone began to change. There were the preliminary findings, indicating odd loans and other payments. Then reports came out in October 2016 that, leading up to his expulsion, Durham spent $1,000 in campaign funds on University of Tennessee tickets. He was not the only lawmaker to spend campaign money on a sporting event, but it remained illegal to use political contributions for personal purposes.

The *Tennessean* also reported that Durham and a crew of other Republican lawmakers—including Spivey and Holt—went on a seaside trip together and stayed at the home of a wealthy school voucher advocate. The advocate paid for their stay and for an ocean fishing trip for some; all of the lawmakers who went on the trip at some point co-sponsored legislation in support of vouchers.[72]

To the public, it was a steady trickle of information showing seemingly questionable actions or judgment. But behind the scenes, the information investigators found was even more shocking. The registry's initial investigation included broad allegations that Durham provided campaign finance loans or gifts, but included few details. Yet in February 2017, the *Tennessean* revealed that one of those payments—$20,000—went to a friend and professional gambler.[73]

The news came out days before the registry was set to reveal its final, formal findings. It turned out to be just the tip of a very large and lavish iceberg. Officials determined Durham had violated state campaign finance law at least five hundred times.[74]

The allegations were sweeping, specific, and at times comical: he reportedly used campaign funds to buy fancy sunglasses, spa treatments, and suits. Durham spent nearly $1,500 for someone to mow the lawn at his home, trying to justify the expense by saying he hosted campaign events at the house. He spent another $541.70 on a plane ticket for his wife to accompany him on a trip.

He loaned his wife $25,000, in addition to the loan to the professional gambler, and made a $100,000 investment into the business of a prominent donor.

The registry determined he broke at least six laws and did so repeatedly for years.

In a move that mirrored his approach to the Slatery report, Durham had his attorney, Peter Strianse, petition the registry to not release its findings. Speaking at the registry's meeting on Durham's behalf, Strianse argued his client was again denied due process and wasn't allowed to offer a real response to the allegations. Not swayed, officials took actions that telegraphed they would fine Durham. A *Tennessean* analysis determined he could face a staggering $7 million in fees, far more than the typical punishments issued by the registry.

Generally, the campaign finance oversight agency fined lawmakers a few hundred or a few thousand dollars. But with Durham, they decided to make an example. The registry issued more than $465,000 in fines against Durham, by far the largest punishment ever levied by the agency.

"It puts people on notice that the board takes the campaign finance law very seriously and if it's violated, they have no problem assessing civil penalties," Rawlins, executive director of the registry, said after the June 2017 decision.

Durham tried to appeal the punishment. But the agency stood its ground.

Lawless, who was an electoral college delegate for President Donald Trump in 2016, seemed to be outraged by the level of contempt Durham appeared to show toward even the most basic financial practices.

"It's just the proverbial onion, and just every layer you get to just gets worse," Lawless said about the registry's findings.[75]

While an administrative law judge temporarily ruled in Durham's favor and drastically reduced his fine, the ruling was eventually overturned. Strianse would later argue during a 2021 court proceeding that Durham could not both adequately provide information to the registry and effectively protect himself against a federal criminal probe. Strianse contended registry members had adopted a "scorched earth" approach to the proceedings and singled out Lawless and Democratic registry member Hank Fincher for intemperate comments about his client that he said were made "so they could read about themselves in the *Tennessean*."[76]

Nashville chancellor Anne Martin appeared to agree with some of Strianse's arguments during the September 2021 hearing, at times describing what she viewed as "vitriol that seemed to infuse the process" leading up to the fines being levied. But she ultimately upheld the registry's original penalty. Durham promptly mounted an appeal, which was turned back by the state court of appeals.

The federal criminal probe ultimately never materialized into charges against Durham. Instead, in the fall of 2021, it was revealed that Durham was an "unindicted co-conspirator" in the criminal investigation of state senator Brian Kelsey, who said Durham provided information against the best man at his wedding in exchange for not being charged. Kelsey pleaded guilty to federal campaign finance charges before having a last-minute change of heart. It's unclear if that federal investigation was the same probe as the one involving Durham in 2016 and beyond.

If there's any enduring legacy of the Durham legislative scandal, it's the changes to the legislature's sexual harassment policy. It was tested almost immediately. In early 2017, a newly elected West Tennessee Republican was accused of sexual misconduct.

A fair and carnival operator voted into office in 2016, Rep. Mark Lovell was accused of sexual harassment after he spent an evening during the legislative session in Nashville attending a series of lobbyist-funded receptions. Accounts vary about what exactly Lovell did, with some sources telling the *Tennessean* that Lovell grabbed a woman's breasts and buttocks. Others said he inappropriately touched another woman. After the incidents, a woman filed a formal complaint with the legislature, which led to an investigation. Lovell denied the allegations.[77]

After the investigation began, Harwell's chief of staff handed Lovell a resignation letter and suggested he step away from the legislature. Unlike Durham, Lovell complied with the request, signed the letter, and ended his tenure in the General Assembly after less than one hundred days in office.

The letter ultimately made it into Lovell's legislative personnel file, along with a memo indicating he was found guilty of misconduct.[78] All of that information would have been private if not for the sexual harassment policy changes prompted by the Durham saga.

Harwell left the legislature, as did Casada and others, but the sexual harassment policy remains in place. Whether it works effectively to prevent future legislators whose behavior "may pose a continuing risk to unsuspecting women who are employed by or interact with the legislature"—as Slatery once described Durham's actions—remained to be seen.[79]

Rep. Glen Casada celebrates after being elected House Speaker on January 8, 2019

# SIX

★ ★ ★

# Casada's Crash Landing

AFTER YEARS OF PLOTTING, Republican representative Glen Casada finally reached the pinnacle in the state House with his election to the all-powerful position of Speaker in January 2019. But there were plenty of warning signs his tenure was going to be turbulent.

Early on, he praised a former leader of the opposite party who had a reputation for ruling with an iron fist, perhaps telegraphing his intentions. He made an embattled colleague facing allegations of sexual assault the head of a legislative committee, then lied about meeting with one of the victims. He locked the chamber doors and called for law enforcement to force dissident Democrats to return to their duties. He strong-armed his colleagues and made offers in exchange for their vote on one of the most controversial proposals in years. He had a history of using campaign money to cover an at-times lavish lifestyle, fueled by private clubs, alcohol, and the company of women. And even before his highest ascension, he had to defend himself against an allegation that he was having an extramarital affair.[1]

Casada's years-long pursuit of power, cavalier attitude in the midst of controversy, and ever-present loyalty to his closest friends were sure to catch up to him at some point. But in the end, it was a tenuous cocktail of unfettered desire, aggressive maneuvers, political paranoia, and an endless rumor mill that resulted in his brief reign and sudden downfall. When the dust settled, Casada's time in charge of the chamber would turn out to be the shortest for any state House Speaker in more than a century.[2]

And then, the FBI came calling.

## UPWARD MOMENTUM

Born in August 1959, Richard Glen Casada Jr. was perhaps best described by one of his colleagues: a political animal.[3]

A partisan to his core, Casada had the rare mix of being good at both retail politics and climbing the ladder through coalition building among various Republican factions. Through years of work and savvy political decision-making, he became a fixture around the Tennessee legislature for his affable smile, his willingness to strike a deal, an ability to bounce back from missteps, and the foresight to recognize shifting political winds before others.

Long before he established himself in the world of Tennessee politics, Casada grew up in Kentucky, where his grandfather had farmed hemp and he was a member of a 4-H youth organization. After graduating from Western Kentucky University in 1982, Casada married his wife, Jill, and lived in Bowling Green, Kentucky, before they picked up stakes and moved to the Nashville area.[4]

Casada entered the political sphere in February 1994, when he was one of six candidates seeking to represent District 4 on the Williamson County Commission in Tennessee. When the final results were tallied, Casada ended up topping the incumbent by sixteen votes (though both would go on to serve on the commission as the top two finishers in the field).

While on the commission, Casada voiced concerns over everything from school funding to what he called state interference in local affairs. "State government has put their nose in our business and all they are doing is meddling," he said while sponsoring a resolution directing the county's legislators to exempt Williamson County from a state law. Later in his career, Casada would regularly support efforts by state lawmakers to undercut local governments while decrying federal overreach in Tennessee.[5]

After serving on the County Commission for seven years, Casada decided in 2001 to run in a special election for the state legislature after a five-year Democratic incumbent resigned to take a lobbying job. To do so, Casada first had to sell his home in a neighboring district and move to the area represented by the open seat. Casada quickly resigned from the commission to focus his full attention on the campaign, which came shortly after the 9/11 terror attacks. Early voting for the general election was to get underway just before Thanksgiving and end two weeks before Christmas.[6]

A staunch opponent of a state income tax—an issue that was being pushed by Republican governor Don Sundquist at the time—Casada benefited from several local residents who expressed their support for him with letters to the editor in the *Tennessean*. One supporter noted how the attacks were a reminder of the necessity of having the "right leaders" in office, adding, "Extraordinary times like these demand extraordinary leaders like Glen Casada." In an unusual move, Casada's wife even wrote a letter to the newspaper after she said one of Casada's primary opponents put "false information" in a mailer sent to voters. Casada ended up winning the Republican nomination by more than five hundred votes.[7]

During the general election, Casada, who was forty-two at the time, squared off against fifty-seven-year-old singer songwriter Gene Cotton, a Democrat and environmental activist whose campaign was boosted by a recorded phone call on his behalf by singer and Middle Tennessee resident Naomi Judd. Casada touted endorsements from the National Rifle Association and then state senator Marsha Blackburn, who said he would help keep up the fight against "government elitists in Nashville and Memphis" who wanted to impose the income tax.[8]

Although he showed some concern that not enough Republicans would be motivated to participate in the election during the holiday season, Casada said he thought he would carry enough of the district's Democratic vote to prevail. "Southern Democrats are a different animal than the party as a whole," he said. "Tennessee Democrats are conservative."[9]

Casada's confidence was justified—he ended up winning by a more than 2–1 margin, giving Republicans forty-two seats in the state House of the ninety-nine-member chamber. Estimates indicated Casada spent about $70,000 on the race while Cotton spent roughly $15,000.[10]

At the time of the election, Williamson County still had a formidable base of Democrats, but Casada's win was an indication of the significant political shift that would soon spread through much of the state. Today, Williamson County is one of the most Republican areas in Tennessee and in recent years has produced a US senator, state House Speaker, state Senate majority leader, and governor.[11]

When he entered the statehouse, Casada joined a Williamson County delegation that included Blackburn and state representative Charles Sargent. More than twenty years later, Blackburn and Sargent would become political royalty in Williamson County, though from competing elements of the Republican Party. Blackburn seized on populist, anti-income tax sentiment to make the jump into national politics. She served eight terms in Congress before becoming Tennessee's first female Republican US senator in 2019. Sargent came from the GOP's pro-business wing and worked his way up to chair of the powerful Finance Committee over his

Rep. Charles Sargent, left, speaks with Rep. Bob Ramsey on the House floor on April 23, 2018

twenty-two years in the state House. Casada identified more with the Blackburn faction, but paid enough attention to establishment interests to keep in the good graces of his largely affluent constituency.

## THE CONDUCTOR

When he first joined the Tennessee General Assembly, Casada caroused with his fellow members as if he had been in the legislature for years. "Ignorance is bliss," he said in January 2002. "I don't feel nervous."[12]

Like the salesman that he was—a man who had sold everything from real estate to medical equipment and animal pharmaceuticals during his career—Casada exuded confidence throughout his time in the legislature, rarely showing signs of frustration even during the most trying times.

At the same time, Casada knew how to push the political envelope, leading his caucus into new territory as he became one of the more vocal conservatives in the House Republican Caucus. He sponsored a measure that would allow the sale of pro-life license plates that became law after a prolonged legal battle and touted Tennesseans' support for the Second Amendment and the "family unit." He sponsored a bill to allow pharmacists to refuse to prescribe birth control and one to rename a highway after former President Ronald Reagan. A 2006 news story noted Casada was one of the House's "most ardent and outspoken conservatives."[13] Passing his legislative proposals wasn't always the goal—so long as he could score political points. With Democrats still maintaining a majority in 2007, Casada was also known as the least successful lawmaker, having only one of his bills approved during the first year of the two-year legislative session.[14]

After President Barack Obama entered the White House in 2008, Casada jumped at the chance to support a lawsuit to force the Illinois Democrat to prove his citizenship status.[15] Although the citizenship issue was red meat for Republicans, Casada was also willing to throw the occasional bone to Democrats. In 2003, he praised Gov. Phil Bredesen, a moderate Democrat, for cutting the state budget. "The governor's doing a good job," Casada said. "I support him. I'm impressed with Governor Bredesen."[16]

In addition to his legislative efforts, Casada was seemingly unafraid to take a stand on an issue or make controversial statements. He said the state needed to stop being a "magnet for illegal immigrants" and was one of the more vocal opponents to Republican governor Bill Haslam's efforts to expand Medicaid after the passage of the Affordable Care Act. Perhaps most infamously, Casada in 2015 called for the Tennessee National Guard to be activated to "gather up" Syrian refugees living in the state.[17]

Throughout his time in the legislature, Casada often had opinion pieces published in newspapers on a variety of subjects including immigration, malpractice reform, waste in the state budget, federal "overreach," the state's taxes on food, the Affordable Care Act, and refugees.

As the Republican Party made gains in the Tennessee legislature, Casada rose in prominence. He entered the ranks of leadership in 2004 as House Republicans' whip—the legislative role dedicated to gauging support for issues among the caucus—before unsuccessfully trying to become minority leader in 2005. In 2006, he ousted his fellow Williamson County delegation member, Charles Sargent, to become Republican Caucus chair, holding the position until 2010.

In many ways, Casada's rise in the caucus was perfectly timed for his own personal benefit. His position in leadership gave him an even stronger foothold on the House Republican Caucus when the GOP surprised many by taking control of the lower chamber after the 2008 general election. For several years Republicans had been chipping away at Democrats' advantage in the House and Senate, the latter of which officially flipped to GOP control after the 2006 election thanks in large part to the efforts of East Tennessee Republican senator Ron Ramsey.

Heading into the 2008 race, few expected Republicans to secure a

The House Republican Caucus holds a procedural vote in Nashville on November 20, 2018

majority in the ninety-nine-member House. But after the results were tallied, the GOP had managed to beat Democrats by one seat, giving the Republican Party in Tennessee its first majority in both legislative chambers at the same time since Reconstruction. State representative Brian Kelsey, a Germantown Republican, credited Casada and Rep. Jason Mumpower of Bristol, who was in line to become the next House Speaker if Republicans took control of the chamber, for helping secure the GOP majority in the House. For years, Casada had been one of the legislature's most prolific fundraisers, a trait he maintained throughout his political career.[18]

Legislative maneuverings delayed the GOP's official takeover, when Republican representative Kent Williams, a northeast Tennessee restaurateur, bucked his caucus and joined with Democrats to have himself elected House Speaker for the 2009-2010 legislative session.

When Republicans took control of the House after the November 2010 election, Casada made his long-planned bid to become Speaker. He was seen as a favorite heading into the caucus election, as a host of groups supporting him blasted rival Rep. Beth Harwell of Nashville as too moderate to take the helm of the chamber. But after all the bluster, Harwell won the GOP nomination in a secret vote and went on to become the chamber's first female Speaker.

Undeterred by the loss, Casada continued to stick to his envelope-pushing ways, filing legislation to ban political candidates from receiving contributions from labor unions and moving to block a proposal under consideration by the Nashville city council that would have required companies doing business with the city to adopt antidiscrimination policies for sexual orientation and gender identity.[19]

Casada became House Republican Caucus chair once again in 2012 before being elected House majority leader in 2016.

Casada's efforts to climb the political ladder didn't come without pushback. In the lead-up to the 2016 caucus meeting in which he and Rep. Mike Carter, a former general sessions judge from Ooltewah, were vying to become the chamber's majority leader, Casada became the subject of attacks by an anonymous political blog. The blog had gained attention in previous months as the controversy around Rep. Jeremy Durham, who had been expelled from the legislature in September 2016, unfolded. The site frequently defended Durham while attacking other Republicans, including Harwell—the House Speaker—and journalists covering the story.

Days before the November 2016 caucus vote, the blog highlighted a video that featured Casada touching the leg of an unidentified woman at a Nashville bar. When Casada addressed the caucus, he said the blog was falsely suggesting he was having an extramarital affair. Speaking with passion, Casada denied the assertion and called for House Republicans to come together.

"If I'm elected, I'm going to go after these people—I'm going to stop it," Casada intoned.[20]

Despite the controversy—and maybe due to sympathy from colleagues who felt he was unfairly targeted—Casada prevailed 42–29.

Casada's ascension to majority leader gave him an opportunity to directly influence who would join the ever-growing Republican caucus through candidate recruitment efforts, campaign fundraisers, and financial or staff assistance with elections. Heading into the 2018 election, Casada took the uncommon approach of getting heavily involved in several contested primary campaigns for open legislative seats. When most of his chosen candidates won, he had cultivated a built-in core of allies in his upcoming bid for the chamber's top job.

In December 2018, Casada finally reached his political peak when the House Republican Caucus—which had grown its supermajority to seventy-three of the ninety-nine House members—picked him over two others to be the chamber's Speaker.[21]

After the election, Casada outlined his ideas for leading the House in

Republican Glen Casada said he wanted to model his Speakership on Democratic representative Jimmy Naifeh, seen here signaling his position on a vote on the House floor in May 1989 (Larry McCormack, Nashville Banner. Nashville Public Library, Special Collections)

his new role, which he equated to being a musical conductor. "You've got to give a vision so that the orchestra members know what to play and how to do it," he said.[22]

Once he was formally elected to the post when the legislature returned in January 2019, he quickly etched his mark on the chamber. He changed the House's committee system, named two conservative-leaning Democrats as committee chairs, and praised former House Speaker Jimmy Naifeh, a Democrat who had been known for his tight control of the chamber.

Casada handed another committee chairmanship to Rep. David Byrd, a Waynesboro Republican who had been facing protests because of allegations that he had inappropriately touched multiple teens decades earlier.

## BACKING BYRD

In March 2018, WSMV-TV ran a story that featured three women who accused Byrd of multiple instances of inappropriate sexual conduct when he was their high school basketball coach in the 1980s. One woman said she was fifteen years old when Byrd began assaulting her by inappropriately touching her over her clothes, kissing her multiple times while she was on school property, and pulling her hands toward his genitals. A second woman said when she was sixteen, she went to Byrd's hotel room during

Rep. David Byrd attends a House committee hearing in Nashville on March 27, 2019

a team trip and he inappropriately touched her under her clothes while they were lying on his bed. A third woman, who was fifteen at the time, said she was alone with Byrd in a swimming pool while on an out-of-town trip when he made a sexual advance toward her. A month before the TV story aired, one of the women contacted Byrd and recorded a phone call in which he acknowledged he had done something wrong, without specifying exactly what, and said he regretted his actions.[23]

After the story aired, then House Speaker Beth Harwell called for Byrd to resign. Rather than comply, Byrd issued a statement in which he said he had "done nothing wrong or inappropriate" during his time as a member of the House of Representatives. He also questioned the motives of the three former students.

Unlike Harwell, Casada offered a much more measured response. Calling the allegations shocking and out of character, Casada said, "The David Byrd I know is not the David Byrd being described in these allegations."[24] Casada refused to call for Byrd's resignation and sprang to the embattled lawmaker's defense during his re-election campaign. Casada ran digital ads likening him to Donald Trump and US Supreme Court nominee Brett Kavanaugh. All three were victims of "lies & fake news" spread by liberals, according to the ad.[25]

After Byrd was successfully re-elected to the House in November 2018—he beat his Democratic opponent by netting 77 percent of the total votes in the Republican-favored district—Casada embraced Byrd on a whole new level by naming him chair of an education subcommittee.

The move was classic Casada: welcome controversy rather than run away from it, ignore critics, and show his House Republican colleagues he would stand by its members no matter what headaches or pushback they might get from the media, Democrats, or the public. The decision to elevate Byrd from backbencher to chairman less than a year after the allegations emerged was hardly unprecedented. For years, Casada defended his former protégé, Rep. Jeremy Durham, when he was facing his own allegations of sexual misconduct that would lead to his ouster in 2016.

On multiple occasions, Casada went out of his way to defend Byrd. In February 2019, he wrote an editorial criticizing "the media's inability and unwillingness to accurately, fairly, and consistently report the facts."[26] The op-ed came in response to a news story in which he said in a video discussing the Byrd controversy, "If I was raped, I would move. . . . And hell would have no fury."

Unlike with Durham, public pressure against Byrd manifested in the form of protests that took place at the statehouse throughout the 2019 session. When a group of women attended a committee meeting led by Byrd in March and silently held up signs protesting the embattled lawmaker, Casada ordered state troopers to remove them from the room. He justified the move in a statement, saying the group was "disrupting the legislative process."[27]

The removal of the protesters was in line with other moves Casada made during the session aimed at eliminating dissent. He allowed committee chairs to ban audience members from video livestreaming committee meetings while instituting a similar prohibition when the House met in the chamber. He cut off Democrats' microphones during floor debates when they questioned the Speaker. He took aim at the media for "letting a liberal political activist drive their agenda instead of sticking to the facts," referring to a former Democratic congressional candidate who was seizing on the Byrd scandal.

In addition to the burgeoning controversy over Byrd, protesters increased a pressure campaign on the state's political leaders for yet another dispute—the presence of a statue inside the Capitol honoring Confederate general, slave trader, and early Ku Klux Klan leader Nathan Bedford Forrest.

Located on the second floor of the statehouse just outside the House and Senate chamber, the bronze Forrest bust had been the subject of protests and calls for removal since it was first put in place in 1978. Although there had been demonstrations against the statue for decades, the issue of

Demonstrators hold up signs protesting Rep. David Byrd's chairmanship of a House subcommittee in Nashville on March 5, 2019

Confederate monuments in public spaces gained greater attention after a white gunman opened fire on congregants at a South Carolina church in 2015 and following the killing of George Floyd in Minneapolis at the hands of police in 2020. Although several states moved forward on removing statues, Tennessee officials refused to budge on the Forrest bust. Republicans had been so protective of the state's Confederate-related monuments in recent years that they twice passed legislation making it more difficult to remove statues and other historical monuments.

While then governor Bill Haslam, a Republican, expressed support for relocating the bust outside of the Capitol, successor Bill Lee—who took office in January 2019—said he favored adding context to the Forrest statue rather than moving it. Lt. Gov. Randy McNally, the leader of the Senate, agreed with that step, while Casada largely shied away from making any changes. As the Byrd protests continued, Casada became the focus of the Forrest bust's opponents. In an early March incident, a protester threw a cup of liquid at Casada in a Capitol elevator. Despite the skirmish, Casada—who was called racist by protesters—eventually joined in on the call to add context to the bust.

The monument was ultimately removed in 2021, despite the work of Casada's successor to try to block its relocation to the Tennessee State Museum. Justin Jones, the man who was banned from the Capitol for throwing the cup at Casada, was elected to the House in 2022. By that time, Casada had left state government under a cloud.

Protesters stand in front of the Nathan Bedford Forrest bust in the state Capitol on March 4, 2019

The dual controversies facing Casada were building into a troubling narrative for the new Speaker. Although Capitol onlookers have always viewed the Tennessee House as the more unpredictable and animated chamber, Casada's time in charge coincided with increasing tumult.

His months-old tenure as Speaker was marked by other unusual incidents and developments. Following through on his courtship of votes in the lead-up to his race to become Speaker, Casada elevated many of the more fringe or far-right-leaning members of the Republican Caucus to leadership positions. In the preceding years, then House Speaker Beth Harwell and Gov. Bill Haslam often pumped the brakes on some of the less-measured legislative ideas being pushed by the GOP.

The Speaker dished out pay raises to legislative staffers, including his chief of staff, who went from making $68,000 the year before to nearly $200,000. He also installed white noise machines outside his legislative office, deputized "hall monitors" to listen to what was being discussed around the legislature, maintained a list of members' bills to kill, and began frequently using the state plane.[28]

Additional reporting about Casada's actions in the House further revealed how he punished members who dared to stand up to him, including moving the offices of Republicans whom he viewed as his critics to obscure locations in the legislative office building.

The slow boil of news and distractions that seemed to surround Casada continued throughout the 2019 legislative session, which lasted until early May. The Speaker seemed to grow more hardened by the day, and at one point called for the Tennessee Titans and other businesses to not "get so much involved in politics" after the groups spoke out against a slate of bills critics said would harm the LGBTQ community.[29]

One of the few times Casada relented during the session came in March, after he met with one of Byrd's accusers for a private meeting. Casada falsely claimed he had met with one of the victims, but when he was called out, he sat down with one of Byrd's accusers. After the meeting wrapped, Casada made a rare rebuke of one of his Republican colleagues by stripping the embattled lawmaker of his position as committee chair, citing bipartisan concerns. But with the move coming after Byrd's vote against a contentious school voucher bill heavily promoted by Casada, some saw that as a more likely reason for his removal. Casada's office called it an "absolute lie" to suggest a connection to the voucher vote.[30]

## VOUCHING FOR IT

The most contentious day of the 2019 legislative session for Casada came in April, when the House floor was considering the hotly contested and controversial school voucher bill. For years, school choice advocates had been pushing Tennessee's lawmakers to approve a measure that would take money away from public schools in favor of a voucher program similar to ones that had been introduced in other Republican-controlled states. With Lee's election as governor, voucher advocates were hopeful a new era was beginning after predecessor Haslam had been largely cool to the idea. Lee as a candidate had been coy about his support for a state-funded voucher program, but decided to pursue legislation to create one in his first year in office. Casada had previously not weighed in much on vouchers, but throwing his support behind the issue provided the new Speaker an opportunity to show his legislative strength—and prove his mettle to deep-pocketed school choice advocacy groups. Earlier in the year, Casada had made it clear his chamber would be asserting itself in new ways in the budget process, flexing his political muscles.[31]

As the legislation snaked its way through the committee process, Casada put his weight behind the governor's $25 million proposal, including a rare personal appearance to vote to send the measure out of a key House panel. In the lead-up to the vote, Casada made overtures to support House members' legislation or legislative initiatives, essentially pet projects for which they needed funding, in return for backing the voucher bill.[32]

When the school voucher proposal was finally up for consideration by the full House, it became evident that the Speaker's office had miscalculated its support among the full membership. When the board was opened, a screen at the Speaker's podium showed the vote was knotted at 49–49, apparently dooming the bill to failure. Opponents shouted from the floor for Casada to take the vote, but the Speaker refused. He kept the vote open forty minutes while furiously lobbying lawmakers to try to secure at least one vote to reach the fifty needed for bills to pass.[33]

Casada and staffers fanned out to put the screws to recalcitrant lawmakers, holding urgent meetings on the balcony behind the Speaker's podium (and having sergeants-at-arms block reporters from peering through the blinds to see who was being hotboxed). The stalemate ended after Rep. Jason Zachary, a Knoxville Republican, switched his vote to a yes, giving the proposal the votes it needed to pass by the slimmest of margins.[34]

Two Republican lawmakers later told the *Tennessean* about House leadership's lobbying efforts, including one member who said a Casada staffer asked what he wanted in return for his vote and another who said he was offered incentives before and during the voting process. Many of the House members who voted for the legislation ended up having their appropriation requests funded in the state budget.[35]

One of the more shocking allegations about Casada's efforts to secure votes was an assertion that the Speaker offered Rep. John Mark Windle, a conservative Democrat from Livingston, a promotion to a generalship in the Tennessee National Guard if he changed his vote. Windle, who once missed a legislative session to serve in Iraq, had recently been promoted to colonel in the guard. He told Nashville television station WTVF that another lawmaker had overheard about the alleged promotion in exchange for a yes vote.

Rep. Kent Calfee, a Kingston Republican, said he witnessed Casada corner Windle on the balcony outside the House chamber. Calfee recalled Casada saying he couldn't promote Windle to be a general in the National Guard but the governor could and that he would call him. Calfee said he spoke to the governor about it afterward, but Lee repeatedly denied any knowledge of the alleged discussion or the possibility of promoting Windle.[36]

Chief of staff Cade Cothren speaks on his phone during a meeting on the balcony outside the House chamber on April 29, 2019

Cade Cothren confers with fellow House aides and Rep. Matthew Hill on the House floor on the day of a controversial school voucher vote on April 23, 2019

Rep. John Mark Windle addresses colleagues on the House floor on January 31, 2019

Windle refused the entreaties and stayed with his vote opposing the voucher bill. Casada denied the allegation.[37]

Using strong-arm tactics, Casada ended up personally working hard to secure the outcome of the vouchers vote in the House, with his actions representing a significant departure from the man who in 2010 declared "I wouldn't want to make it look like we were twisting arms."[38] Power in politics has a funny way of changing one's mind.

As it had throughout the months-long legislative session, controversy continued when the House met on its final day of the year. A protester seated in the upstairs gallery of the House temporarily stopped the floor session as she yelled for Casada to resign. The Speaker repeatedly hammered his gavel as if to drown out her shouts, called for order, and had the woman removed by state troopers. Later in the day, Casada ordered the chamber's doors to be locked when Democrats attempted a walkout because of frustrations with the Speaker, who hinted at the possibility of sending law enforcement to force missing members to return.[39]

The chaos of the final day of session mirrored the tumultuous series of events that had occurred over the course of the five months Casada was Speaker. Unwilling to acknowledge the unusual year in governance,

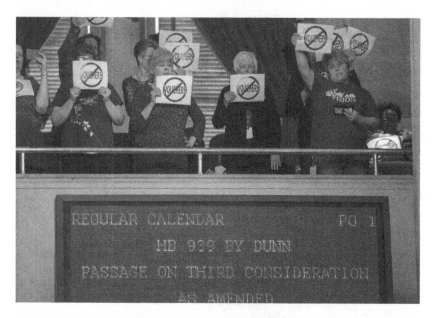

Protesters hold up signs opposing school vouchers on the day the controversial measure was up for a vote on April 23, 2019

Casada deemed the 2019 legislative session a ringing success. "The House hasn't been run better in the past 50 years," he declared.[40]

## TROUBLE IN GLEN'S HOUSE

During an end-of-session press conference, Casada was asked about a news story by WTVF-TV highlighting years-old racist text messages his chief of staff, Cade Cothren, had sent, including one in which he said "Black people are idiots." Casada pushed back, saying he had never seen "any kind of racist or bigoted action" by Cothren. Asked about the fact that he was included in one of Cothren's text messages, the Speaker said if he had received it he would "strongly scold whoever sent that to me," while raising doubts about the WTVF story.[41]

Around the Capitol, Cothren had been known to be a smooth-talker who sported a closely cropped beard and embraced the lively night-life element of politics and government in Tennessee. With an affinity for flashier outfits, Cothren played many different roles for Casada: chief of staff, spokesman, top campaign aide, and even drinking buddy.

Casada later issued a statement in which he said he had known Cothren for almost a decade and he'd never known him to "act in a manner" in which the text messages "falsely portray him." Cothren later said he didn't remember sending the text messages because they were several years old. But he acknowledged doing "things in the past that I'm not proud of," without elaborating much other than to say he was not a racist.[42]

For the time being, Casada and Cothren thought they had faced the worst of their problems. They were wrong.

Days later, the Speaker and his chief of staff faced a series of additional damning news reports. First came an admission from Cothren that he had previously used cocaine while in his legislative office before Casada became Speaker. The bombshell was followed by revelations of more text messages from 2015 and 2016 in which he bragged to a former acquaintance about his activities.[43]

Casada acknowledged he had known about Cothren's past drug use, but he was confident his thirty-two-year-old top staffer had turned his life around. As he had done so many times with his other allies, the Speaker maintained his continued support for Cothren after the initial drug use story was published.[44]

That same day, the *Tennessean* published a story highlighting how Cothren had a history of sending sexually explicit text messages and making inappropriate advances toward women. The text messages, which were obtained from a confidential source, showed Casada had participated in some of the sexually charged messages objectifying women. In the text messages, Cothren solicited oral sex and naked photos from a legislative intern, sought sex with a lobbyist, referred to another woman as a "cunt," and called Nashville police officers who had given him parking tickets "rent a cop cocksuckers."[45]

When the story broke, Casada acknowledged he needed to "reevaluate some things" while Cothren said he was "not the same guy that I was several years back." Within hours, Cothren had resigned as Casada's chief of staff.[46] It was a remarkably sudden turn of events that was a significant shift for Casada compared to the months-long defenses he mounted for Durham and Byrd, the two other embattled Republicans Casada had defended. But with the Speaker already ruffling feathers with members of his own party during the session, in part due to his heavy-handed tactics and the school vouchers bill, Casada made the expedient decision to jettison his chief of staff, a mastermind of his ascent to the Speakership.

Appearing on a Nashville-area talk radio station a few days later, Casada downplayed the text messages as "locker room talk" between two adult men—a reference to Donald Trump's defense after an infamous audio recording surfaced late in the 2016 presidential campaign. At the same time, Casada admitted he was wrong and "got caught up in the moment." Despite calls from Democrats to resign, Casada refused.[47]

Maintaining stillness in the midst of scrutiny was right out of Casada's classic political playbook.

In 2015, Casada backed one of his Republican House members who was facing pushback because of a Facebook post the lawmaker wrote that was deemed racist. In 2016, Casada held out until the bitter end when fellow Williamson County Republican representative Jeremy Durham faced allegations over his own sexually inappropriate text messages and later an attorney general's investigation that found he had engaged in sexual misconduct with at least twenty-two women. And even in the 2019 text message scandal involving Casada's chief of staff, the Speaker maintained his support for Cothren until he couldn't any longer because the revelations kept mounting.[48]

Unfortunately for Casada, the headlines and the headaches continued, putting his fellow Republicans on the defensive as they waited for further news to drop at any moment.

The *Tennessean* reported about the existence of white noise machines

Rep. Glen Casada confers with aide Cade Cothren, right, at a House Republican Caucus meeting in Nashville on November 17, 2016

outside Casada's legislative office, as well as concerns among lawmakers that their own offices and committee meeting rooms were bugged with recording devices and a system that allowed Cothren to eavesdrop on private conversations.[49]

WTVF reported that FBI agents had begun interviewing unnamed lawmakers about whether improper incentives were made in exchange for "yes" votes on the controversial school vouchers bill that was narrowly approved in April.[50]

As was the case with the Durham scandal in 2016, the text messages between Casada and Cothren once again thrust the culture of the Tennessee Capitol into the spotlight. Rep. Patsy Hazlewood, a Signal Mountain Republican, said while Cothren's resignation was a "good first step," House Republicans needed to take additional action to root out any behavior that was demeaning or denigrating.[51]

Earlier in the session, Rep. Rick Staples, a Knoxville Democrat, was found to have violated the legislature's sexual harassment policy after a woman told the *Tennessean* he made inappropriate comments about her appearance and grabbed and held onto her waist. Although the Staples allegation barely moved the needle on bolstering calls for additional change in the legislature, the Casada ordeal forced the Republican supermajority to face heightened scrutiny and look inward because of the Speaker's at-times brash moves throughout the session.[52]

While Gov. Bill Lee and Lt. Gov. Randy McNally—Casada's Senate counterpart—were initially reticent to wade too deeply into the scandal, eventually they both suggested Casada should step down. Lee, a former businessman, said if Casada worked for his company he'd ask him to re-sign. McNally was slightly more forceful, saying he thought it was in the best interest of the legislature and the state for Casada to "vacate" his office.[53]

Although Casada thought the worst of his problems were over, other members of his chamber's Republican caucus, which included many social-conservative members who were averse to Casada's antics and at-times freewheeling behavior, had other ideas.[54]

For years Casada had been known for living large. He used campaign donors' money to cover monthly membership dues and meals at a private club in Nashville known as The Standard. During a two-year period, he spent nearly $22,000 in campaign money on food and drinks and poten-tially used donors' money in 2016 to cover the bar tab at a popular Nash-ville hot chicken restaurant where Cothren claimed to have had sex with a woman in the bathroom.[55]

Casada and Cothren engaged in a back and forth that later made it difficult for the Speaker to downplay. After Cothren's text about the bath-room, Casada responded to note the brief period he had been away.

"R u a minute man???;)," Casada asked.

"Yes, I take after you. Like father like son," Cothren answered.

"Lolol! If I'm happy, then all is good," came Casada's reply.[56]

During a thirty-minute conference call with the House GOP caucus that took place less than a week after the news broke about the text mes-sages between Casada and Cothren, Rep. Bill Dunn, a Knoxville Republi-can who was in line to become the Speaker's interim successor, called on Casada to resign. Other Republicans questioned Casada's ability to sur-vive the scandal. Firebrand Rep. Jerry Sexton of Bean Station, a former pastor and Casada ally, said the caucus had to do some soul searching and called for a "vote of confidence" to determine where members stood on keeping Casada as Speaker. Several members, including the more Tea Party–aligned lawmakers, many of whom Casada had helped get elected or named to leadership, signaled continued support for him. Meanwhile, the Speaker assured the caucus that there was "nothing else" that would

Rep. Jeremy Faison, left, poses for a selfie with former governor Winfield Dunn on January 19, 2019

Gov. Bill Lee delivers his annual State of the State address in Nashville on February 3, 2020

be revealed in the media while touting the House's accomplishments for the year.[57]

After the phone call, Casada said he welcomed the idea of holding a caucus meeting to discuss his future, while Rep. Jeremy Faison, a Cocke County Republican who had called for Casada to resign days earlier, noted a "spirit of fear" had spread among House lawmakers after Casada became Speaker.[58]

"It has not been the people's house," Faison said. "It's been Glen's house."[59]

## SPEAKER IS SILENCED

To decide Casada's fate, the House Republican Caucus gathered on May 20 at a downtown Nashville hotel that doubled as a museum. Walking past modern art, including photos of nude women, a rooster inside a plexiglass container, and an image of the head of a bear on a human's body, Republicans gathered in a basement conference room without the presence of media, staff, or the public. Members were directed to put their phones and purses on a table in the back of the room to avoid distractions and keep the inner dealings of the caucus as private as possible, at least until the discussion was over.

Since Casada had entered House leadership, he had often defended the use of private caucus meetings in order to allow members to fully air out "personal matters."[60]

"People do not speak openly when they're afraid that their concerns and fears may be written as fact," Casada said in 2009, a decade before his House colleagues would determine his fate as Speaker behind closed doors. "We need people to open up and tell us where they are."[61]

Heading into the meeting, Casada privately lobbied his colleagues to stand by him, including the freshman members whom he had helped get elected less than a year earlier. When the caucus had finally gathered, Casada—who throughout his decades in the legislature could be seen with a charismatic smile on his face—appeared worn down. In the days after the scandal erupted, Casada briefly grew a scruffy beard, a notable departure for a man who had almost always previously been clean shaven. One member later recalled Casada calling the scrutiny the "most difficult thing in his life."[62]

As the meeting approached, Casada once again touted the House's work during the 2019 session while saying the news stories were the product of

Rep. Mike Carter is sworn in to his latest term on the House floor on January 8, 2019

House majority leader William Lamberth and caucus chair Cameron Sexton, bottom right, speak to reporters after a Republican vote of no confidence for House Speaker Glen Casada on May 20, 2019

a media that hated him and House Republicans, echoing the same type of defense Jeremy Durham had used in 2016.

Despite his pleas, Casada faced a new headache within the caucus after Rep. Mike Carter, a former judge and head of the House Ethics Committee, alleged in the days leading up to the caucus meeting that Casada had tried to "rig" an ethics investigation. After much internal discussion, the caucus collected votes on whether the group still had confidence in Casada's ability to lead the House. The final vote was 45–24 against the Speaker. Confidence in Casada was lost.[63]

Casada said in a statement he would "work" in the coming months to regain the GOP's confidence. But he signaled no intention to resign as Speaker, which angered several Republicans. The governor, lieutenant governor, and House majority leader—who had stood next to Casada on

Speaker Glen Casada, center, is joined by former House Speakers on January 8, 2019. From left are Bill Jenkins, Kent Williams, Beth Harwell, and Jimmy Naifeh

a stage during the news conference on the final day of the legislative session just nineteen days earlier—all swiftly called for Casada to resign. The next day, Casada acceded to the calls, indicating he would step down in the weeks ahead.[64]

He followed through on his promise on his birthday, August 2, marking the end of his tumultuous reign as Speaker.

Casada became the shortest-serving Tennessee House Speaker since Democrat Ralph Davis, who was the chamber's leader in 1893. A lawyer who was elected Speaker of the House in January, Davis was found guilty of "swindling" a client out of bail bond money. The House adopted a resolution in March calling on Davis to resign, but he refused to step down. The chamber subsequently passed a second resolution "to declare the office of Speaker vacant" and moved to elect a permanent replacement.[65]

Like Davis, Casada continued to serve in the legislature after his resignation as Speaker.

Casada briefly entertained running for his old job of caucus whip, but soon settled into a backbencher role. An audit of Casada's campaign finances later found he failed to keep receipts for about $100,000 in expenditures, making it difficult for state officials to determine whether his use of donors' money was legal. "You did wrong, but you're not Jeremy

[Durham]," registry member Tom Lawless told Casada, who was issued a $10,500 civil penalty—payable by his political action committee.[66]

Casada and two fellow Republican lawmakers had their homes and offices searched by FBI agents in January 2021. He announced he would not seek re-election in 2022, officially marking the end to his two decades as a member of the Tennessee General Assembly. Casada, who had been fired from his job as a pet pharmaceutical salesman during his fall from the Speakership, had trouble finding gainful employment following the scandal. He even had a brief stint as a delivery driver for Amazon. But he wasn't quite done with elected office, setting his sights on running for clerk in his home county, a job paying $135,000 per year. Though Casada heavily outspent his rival, voters in Williamson County appeared to have had enough. He lost by an embarrassing 3-to-1 margin.[67]

Four months after he lost his bid to become clerk, Casada and his longtime aide Cothren were arrested on bribery and kickbacks charges in a twenty-count federal indictment for their roles involving a shadowy political campaign mail vendor. If convicted, they would each face up to twenty years in prison.

Rep. Robin Smith (R-Hixson), center, attends the House floor session in which Glen Casada is elected Speaker on January 8, 2019

# SEVEN

★ ★ ★

# Trouble with Campaign Cash

PUBLIC OFFICIALS AND CAMPAIGN finances go hand in hand. Donors give money to candidates they hope can win office and later remember their support when it comes time to introducing and making new laws. But as with any complex system, the world of campaign finances can be a murky web that leads bad actors to think they can pull a fast one on the public and use money in the wrong way.

Such was the case recently in Tennessee, when Republican lawmakers in the House and one in the Senate were charged by federal investigators for illegal campaign finance activities. The legislative session was returning to a semblance of normalcy in early 2022 after two years of grappling with the COVID-19 pandemic and recovering from the chaos of the collapse of Glen Casada's Speakership in the House. Then a prominent Republican abruptly announced she was resigning from the House and a little later pleaded guilty to a federal corruption charge.

There had been little hint that Rep. Robin Smith of Hixson, a former state Republican Party chair, political consultant, and onetime congressional candidate, was going to throw in the towel on a longstanding insistence that she was not the target of an FBI investigation into campaign finance matters. As recently as the night before she quit, Smith had returned a call to a fellow Republican lawmaker to strategize about a bill coming up in one of her committees. But then federal prosecutors filed a charging document, and Smith submitted her resignation from the House. The following day, Smith agreed to plead guilty to "honest services" fraud. In other words, public corruption.

Rep. Cameron Sexton addresses GOP colleagues after being nominated to succeed Glen Casada as Speaker on July 24, 2019

Smith had been a vocal supporter of Casada even as most of the rest of the Republican caucus was prepared to jettison him from his leadership role in 2019 over his heavy-handed leadership style and a racist and sexist text messaging scandal. After Casada resigned under pressure, Smith floated her name as a successor, though she wasn't able to garner much support. She next set her sights on ousting Rep. Jeremy Faison, one of Casada's most vocal critics, as House Republican Caucus chair in late 2020. The position holds wide authority over campaign issues, and Smith touted her expertise in the field as her qualification for the job. But the caucus again demurred and returned Faison to the position.

Shortly thereafter, the earth started moving under Smith's feet. Federal agents in January 2021 descended on the homes and offices of Smith, Casada, and Todd Warner, a newly elected House member who wasn't even going to be sworn into office until the following day. Smith professed to be stunned by the raid.

"Right now, I don't even really know," Smith told reporters gathered at the end of her driveway in Hamilton County after agents went through her home. Her attorney insisted Smith was not the "target" of the investigation and that she had not done anything wrong.[1]

Things were even more embarrassing for Casada, whom TV news cameras captured answering the door to federal agents in little else than a bath robe.[2]

Smith, a former Pfizer sales representative, was elected chair of the Tennessee Republican Party in 2007 in the aftermath of the FBI's Tennessee Waltz corruption sting. She attacked majority Democrats as having conducted an "assault on legislative ethics and decency." She also gained national attention for lobbing attacks at 2008 Democratic presidential candidate Barack Obama and his wife, Michelle.

Smith denounced as "political thuggery" a move by Democrats to strip state senator Rosalind Kurita of her narrow 2008 primary win after she had cast a key vote for Sen. Ron Ramsey to become the first Republican Speaker of the Senate since Reconstruction. Smith was far less sympathetic of GOP representative Kent Williams the following year when he banded together with all forty-nine of the chamber's Democrats to have himself elected Speaker of the House. Smith declared Williams had "lied in a quest for personal power" and violated a pledge to vote for the GOP nominee. As a result, the party stripped Williams of the ability to run for re-election on the Republican ticket (he nevertheless won as an independent).[3]

Smith gave up her party leadership role in May 2009 to run for an open congressional seat in southeast Tennessee. She was endorsed by the Club for Growth and the Susan B. Anthony List but ended up losing to attorney Chuck Fleischmann by 1,049 votes. Smith's camp blamed Fleischmann's political consultant Chip Saltsman for what it considered dirty tactics. Fast-forward to 2020, and Saltsman was in the role of chief political advisor to new House Speaker Cameron Sexton. Smith's attorney tried to deflect attention from her involvement with a mysterious political vendor

Rep. Rick Tillis attends a House Republican Caucus meeting in Nashville on November 20, 2018

Rep. Matthew Hill (R-Jonesborough) speaks to reporters on the House floor on April 17, 2019

called Phoenix Solutions by saying it was the result of a "turf war" between political consultants.

Smith's attorney Ben Rose said the "name we keep hearing in our interviews with members, lobbyists, political folks and even lawyers is that of Chip Saltsman. They are telling us things like: 'This all started with Chip,' 'Chip is behind this,' 'Chip is helping fuel this,' 'We know this is all political.' Keep in mind that many of these folks are actually apolitical and don't have a dog in the fight one way or the other." Rose wouldn't identify who was purportedly making such statements.[4]

While federal prosecutors were mum about the reasons behind the probe, the subjects of the raids appeared to confirm questions a handful of reporters had been raising about shadowy campaign vendors during the previous election cycle.[5]

## SETTLING POLITICAL SCORES

The precipitous collapse of Rep. Glen Casada from the House Speakership in 2019 didn't spell the end of turmoil within the Republican caucus. While several candidates started organizing bids to become the new Speaker, a faction of members still had some vengeance to mete out. Rep.

Rick Tillis, a Lewisburg jeweler and brother of US senator Thom Tillis (R-NC), had outraged Casada loyalists by conducting an anonymous social media campaign to mock the Speaker and his backers when Casada was leading the House.

The Twitter account was called CHBmole, or Cordell Hull Building Mole, a reference to the office building that's home to Tennessee lawmakers. Rep. Andy Holt of Dresden, whom the account disparaged as a "mental child" and a member of the "Fascist Funboy Faction," outed Tillis, the House Republican whip, as being behind the attacks. Even after the account was deactivated in May 2019, House GOP political consultant Michael Lotfi boasted of collecting IP addresses, metadata, device IDs, and other electronic signatures to allegedly prove Tillis had posted under the account. "I love a good pissing contest," Lotfi tweeted at the anonymous account.

It turned out to be a poor choice of words when a chair in Tillis' office was discovered to be soaked in urine. Lotfi denied he had relieved himself on the lawmaker's furniture. One alternate theory was that an infirm visitor had an accident while awaiting a meeting with the lawmaker, though the idea of an intentional act quickly captured the imagination of the Capitol crowd.[6]

Rep. Matthew Hill of Jonesborough, a top Casada lieutenant, tried to rally the former Speaker's coalition to get elected as the chamber's new leader in his own right. But a series of revelations about Hill came to light, including that he had pushed for a $4 million slush fund for local projects to support members who voted for the controversial school voucher bill that had roiled the General Assembly during the 2019 session.[7] Also, the *Tennessean* reported Hill had failed to register or pay taxes on a Christian magic business he owned.[8] And there were still a lot of hurt feelings for Hill's power over so-called "kill bill" lists to decide which pieces of legislation would advance—or be defeated—in committees. Hill denied any such authority, but there was enough ill will generated among Republicans that his colleagues couldn't fathom placing him in the chamber's highest position of power.

The House GOP instead picked Cameron Sexton, a Crossville banker, as its nominee to succeed Casada. Despite the Casada faction now being thoroughly on the outs, the group still mobilized to go after Tillis for the anonymous Twitter attacks. After a heated closed-door discussion, a red-faced Tillis was seen storming out of the room, and he subsequently

FBI agents leave with items from Kent Calfee's office, heading to Glen Casada's office next, at the Cordell Hull State Office Building in Nashville, January 8, 2021. It's unknown what they are searching for (Stephanie Amador - USA TODAY NETWORK)

submitted his resignation as whip, the chamber's No. 4 Republican leadership position responsible for incumbent re-election efforts.

While the position was vacant, House Republican leader William Lamberth of Portland named a seven-member campaign committee to guide election matters. A majority of its membership was made up of Casada loyalists like Timothy Hill (Matthew Hill's brother), Tim Rudd, and Mary Littleton. Another was Robin Smith, who had once served as a private political consultant to the caucus.

Despite a long political career in the state that included her controversial stint as Republican Party chair, it was Smith's first term in office. She soon began lobbying her colleagues to make use of a mail vendor called Phoenix Solutions out of Santa Fe, New Mexico.[9] The outfit would soon gain work designing and mailing constituent surveys and other taxpayer-funded correspondence. It would also be linked to a nasty primary campaign to defeat Tillis.

Starting in early June 2020, a digital ad campaign began to attack Tillis, and a mailer soon followed. The theme of several of the ads was Tillis' role in the anonymous Twitter account—certainly a hot topic among Capitol insiders, but hardly a matter likely to come up among voters in the local hardware store or diner.[10] The ads were paid for by a shadowy political action committee called the Faith Family Freedom Fund, or FFFF. Tillis' chief rival was Todd Warner, a local businessman who poured $154,100 of his own money into the race.

Tillis' supporters noticed something amiss during the race: The FFFF and Warner's campaign vendor, a hitherto unheard of outfit called Dixieland Strategies out of Rainbow City, Alabama, were using the same presorted mail code out of Chattanooga. So was a campaign mailer for Republican representative Paul Sherrell of Sparta, whose vendor was none other than Phoenix Solutions.

A complaint filed with the state Registry of Election Finance was met with little interest and the issue appeared to be poised to quickly fade away after Warner won both the primary and the general election. But on the eve of the legislative session in January 2021, federal agents descended on the homes and offices of Casada, Smith, Warner, and former top legislative aide Cade Cothren, launching speculation into overdrive about what the investigators could be looking for. Reporters began connecting the dots between the intense Tillis-Warner race and the suddenly prominent campaign vendor Phoenix Solutions.

Established in New Mexico in November 2019, where its owners were hidden behind anonymous registration records, the company filed paperwork four days later to do business in Tennessee. Within a month, Phoenix Solutions was getting approved to handle taxpayer-funded constituent correspondence for GOP lawmakers. It then moved on to the more lucrative role of designing and sending out campaign mail for candidates. Following the 2020 primaries, the House GOP placed Phoenix Solutions on its approved vendors list, driving even more business to the mysterious outfit. The company ended up pulling in more than $230,000 from Republicans in a little more than a year in business. Once the feds started sniffing around, the bottom fell out.[11]

Casada and Smith declined to say whether they held a personal stake in the new company, and nobody could locate Matthew Phoenix, the man who signed a W-9 IRS form submitted to the General Assembly and who purportedly spoke with GOP leaders about doing work on behalf of the caucus. At least one vendor confirmed to reporters he had done work at Cothren's behest for both the FFFF and Phoenix Solutions.[12]

"I had zero indication that I was talking with anyone other than Matthew Phoenix with Phoenix Solutions," said Rep. Johnny Garrett, a Goodlettsville attorney who succeeded Tillis as GOP whip. "I know that that is out there that maybe this person doesn't exist. I had no inclination even during the call or after the call that I was with anyone but a legitimate person, a legitimate company."[13]

Garrett also confirmed Smith had defended Phoenix Solutions' bona fides after the questions were raised about links to the attacks on Tillis. Lawmakers don't take kindly to any whiff of incumbents being targeted by their own caucus, so it's unlikely Phoenix Solutions would have received further business had a formal link to the Tillis attacks been established.

## DEFEAT FROM THE JAWS OF VICTORY

While sporadic reports of FBI activity percolated around the General Assembly, no charges were forthcoming for several months. Members of the state Registry of Election Finance on several occasions appeared ready to wash their hands of lingering complaints about the Faith Family Freedom Fund's activities in the Warner-Tillis race, with panel members at one point browbeating the complainant about the basis of his suspicions that Warner had coordinated his campaign activities with the PAC.

The case appeared on the verge of being dismissed when Warner's attorney, Peter Strianse, got into a testy exchange with registry member Hank Fincher, a Harvard-educated attorney and former Democratic state lawmaker, about whether the panel had the authority to seek more details about Warner's arrangement with vendor Dixieland. Fincher responded by requesting an audit of both Warner's campaign account and the FFFF PAC.[14] The former didn't reveal much, but the latter would lead to a bombshell.

In earlier correspondence with the registry, FFFF treasurer Sydney Friedopfer had dismissed allegations of coordination between the PAC and the Warner campaign as chasing down "rabbit holes." When the registry tried to reach her again as part of the audit, the efforts were met with radio silence. The audit's outlook changed drastically when the registry was finally able to locate and contact Friedopfer in Utah.

Testifying under oath in January 2022, Friedopfer explained that she had been a twenty-two- or twenty-three-year-old student at Vanderbilt University in Nashville when Cade Cothren asked her to open the PAC for him.[15]

"He said he just couldn't have a name on it, considering everything he had gone through, which I'm sure everyone's aware," she said. "But yeah, he resigned from his position as chief of staff to Glen Casada. And he

Rep. Todd Warner is sworn in to the House on January 13, 2021

didn't want his name on the political action committees."

Cothren had been drummed out of his $200,000-per-year job as Casada's chief of staff in 2019 following revelations of racist and sexist text messages and boasts of taking cocaine in his legislative office.

While Friedopfer said she wasn't well versed in political matters, she pressed Cothren about whether it was OK for her to register the group for someone else. "I asked him if it was illegal to open it for him," she recalled. "And he said no."

In retrospect, she said, it might not have been the best move.

"At the time, I thought I loved him, I guess," she said. "But I was young and he's 10 years older than me. And I trusted him. And so I opened the political action committee for him."

Friedopfer said she filled out the paperwork, signed her name, and submitted the document to the registry. She then photographed the e-filing confirmation and sent it to Cothren. "He took over from there," she told the panel.

Friedopfer said she was unaware of the PAC's activities until she started getting calls from reporters about the Tillis-Warner race and later when the registry came calling. So she got in touch with Cothren about what she should do.

"He told me that you don't have any authority over me and that nothing can happen," she told the registry. "He said that no action could be taken against me in a court of law."

As for previous written correspondence with the registry, Friedopfer said she was not the author. "That was not me," she said.

The registry responded to Friedopfer's testimony by issuing subpoenas to Cothren, Casada, Warner, and several others about their roles with the PAC and the race against Tillis. With federal prosecutors yet to reveal what they had been searching for in their raids and interviews of the previous year, the state campaign finance panel's probe appeared to become the most promising avenue for shedding light on any potential misdeeds.

Casada, meanwhile, said he was surprised and hurt by his inclusion in the subpoenas.

"I feel like a kid sitting on the side of the road, and someone's just come and punched me in the nose for no reason," Casada said at a chamber meeting in his home county. "I have no knowledge of this PAC, I have no association, and there's no reason to think that I do."[16]

Casada said his previously close ties with Cothren were a thing of the past.

"It's been three years ago when he was employed by me," he said. "And I feel like you're exhibiting biases by just assuming because he once worked for me three years ago, you know, that somehow I'm involved."

Cothren's attorney wrote a letter to the registry saying her client would refuse to testify, citing his Fifth Amendment rights against self-incrimination. The panel decided against pursuing the matter itself, instead referring the investigation to the district attorney in Williamson County.[17]

## PHOENIX, WE HAVE A PROBLEM

The registry's decision to finally get state law enforcement involved in the probe came a week after Smith was charged with participating in a scheme to make money from the secretive political vendor Phoenix Solutions. Her plea agreement detailed the steps she took to establish and promote the vendor with an unnamed former state House Speaker from January through August 2019 and his former chief of staff who had been forced out in May of that year after published allegations of "inappropriate and illegal conduct"—descriptions that could only describe Casada and Cothren.

The company was founded in New Mexico in 2019 with Smith's "knowledge and support," and Cothren's and the lawmakers' roles were concealed because of an expectation the outfit would be denied business by

Reporters follow and ask questions of Speaker Glen Casada regarding a school voucher bill during a session in Nashville on May 1, 2019 (Shelley Mays - USA TODAY NETWORK)

the General Assembly and House Republican Caucus if colleagues knew who was behind it. Smith and Casada allegedly received kickbacks from Cothren in exchange for directing business to the outfit. Smith acknowledged in her plea that she knew the company had been created by Cothren under the alias of Matthew Phoenix. When Smith was told by the office of legislative administration that a phone conversation might be necessary in order to receive a mailing list, she wrote to Cothren that he "may have to assume the role of Matthew again." Cothren's answer was, "Matthew, reporting for duty!" He accompanied his reply with a meme of actor Harrison Ford giving a salute as Han Solo from *Star Wars*.

Smith kept up the Matthew Phoenix charade in conversations with other officials. She wrote to Holt Whitt, the acting chief of staff to Casada successor Cameron Sexton, that Phoenix had been a political operative with Washington firm Jamestown Associates, but that he had become "tired of doing the DC/Trump stuff." Smith then forwarded the exchange to Cothren with an accompanying message: "Shhhhhhhhhh."[18]

According to the charging document, Smith assured the Speaker's office and fellow Republican caucus members she didn't make any money from Phoenix Solutions. But an email from Cothren to Smith and Casada the previous month included a breakdown of how the profits were to be shared (30 percent for Cothren and 25 percent each for Casada and Smith.). "Let me know what is best for you and I will cut checks for each of you," Cothren wrote.[19]

Between its founding in late 2019 and the end of the 2020 election cycle, Phoenix Solutions collected $231,000 from House Republicans, including more than $74,000 funneled through Smith's campaign account and her political action committee called Leadership Pioneers.[20] In essence, Smith was able to launder campaign donations through Phoenix Solutions and pocket a share of the profits. Federal prosecutors described it as a classic kickback scheme.[21]

While Phoenix Solutions' haul wasn't massive, it was only the beginning for what was planned to be a much larger operation. Had Smith succeeded in her bid to topple Casada critic Faison as caucus chair, she could have exerted vast authority over campaign-spending decisions in key House races. And with both Smith and Casada still maintaining strong ties to the former Speaker's faction in the chamber, they could have persuaded more members to place their money with Phoenix Solutions, all the while collecting larger payouts on the back end.

Not everyone was surprised by Smith's guilty plea. Faison, the caucus chair she had tried to topple in 2020, said he suspected from the start that something was amiss with Phoenix Solutions.

"I knew something was wrong, and I've maintained since Day 1 that Matthew Phoenix was bullshit and that the whole thing was a lie, and the whole thing was her and Glen Casada," Faison said.[22]

In August 2022, Casada and Cothren were arrested on public corruption charges for their roles in Phoenix Solutions. In a twenty-count indictment, federal prosecutors detailed efforts in what was described as an elaborate bribery and kickback scheme the two had formed after Casada was no longer Speaker of the House.

According to the indictment, Casada, Cothren, and Smith engaged in a "conspiracy to steal from the state and its citizens" by directing taxpayer dollars to Phoenix Solutions. The indictment made clear that Cothren was hiding his involvement by using the name Matthew Phoenix, in part because the former legislative staffer had fallen out of favor with Republican lawmakers for the way he managed Casada's office.

The indictment noted a host of text messages between Cothren and Casada, as well as Smith, that helped prosecutors connect the dots. The formation of Phoenix Solutions was necessary in part because of an internal rule among House Republicans prohibiting political campaign companies owned by members like Casada and Smith from being named caucus vendors.

"How do we get around that to do [caucus] mail?" Casada asked in a text message to Cothren. "No one needs to know whose company it is," Cothren replied, adding he would disguise his voice if he was asked to address caucus officials.[23]

Although he made efforts to conceal his involvement, Cothren was sloppy in other ways. He opened a bank account in the name of Phoenix Solutions and listed himself as the company's president and chief manager. Any mail sent to the New Mexico–based postal address for Phoenix Solutions was forwarded to Cothren's home address in Nashville. And in endorsing the General Assembly's checks written to the vendor, Cothren allegedly signed his own name.[24]

After Cothren started the new company in fall 2019, Casada and Smith touted Phoenix Solutions to their colleagues. By January 2020, business began flowing toward the vendor. According to the indictment, a lawmaker—known as Individual 4 but clearly a reference to Smith—submitted an invoice to the state for $3,400 from Phoenix Solutions for material produced for the lawmaker's mailer program. The state issued a check a month later. Similarly, Casada submitted an invoice to the state for work done by Phoenix Solutions.[25]

Around the same time, House Speaker Cameron Sexton's office told Smith they needed to work directly with Phoenix Solutions due to a change in the mailer program's guidelines. After the conversation with the Speaker's office, Smith told Cothren the state could not pay Phoenix Solutions without a W-9 from the Internal Revenue Service. Cothren signed a W-9 with the name Matthew Phoenix and sent it via email to the Tennessee House Majority Caucus.

In subsequent months, Casada, Smith, and Cothren worked their way through a series of delays in issuing additional payments to Phoenix Solutions. Eventually, the vendor began receiving more payments. In total, Phoenix Solutions and companies owned by Casada and Smith received nearly $52,000 from the state in 2020. As had become clear in Smith's indictment, the trio had devised a plan to split the proceeds among themselves.

Cothren provided a summary of the total profit earned from each client that had used the vendor and noted that 20 percent of the profit was to be "left in [the] business."

As a result of the scheme, Casada and Cothren were ultimately charged

Former top House staffer Cade Cothren ducks into a waiting vehicle after pleading not guilty to federal charges in Nashville on August 23, 2022 (John Partipilo, *Tennessee Lookout*)

with conspiracy, theft concerning programs receiving federal funds, bribery and kickbacks, honest services wire fraud, using a fictitious name to carry out a fraud, and money laundering.

Not named in the indictment was Rep. Todd Warner, who had also had his home, office, and business searched by federal agents.

When Casada and Cothren appeared in court after their arrests, each entered pleas of not guilty. Casada and his attorneys declined to offer comment to reporters outside the courtroom while Cothren simply said, "The truth will come out."

The presiding judge in the cases against Casada, Cothren, and Smith was Eli Richardson, a former FBI agent and assistant US attorney who had prosecuted former senator John Ford in 2008. Casada had served just two terms when five former lawmakers were ensnared in the FBI's Tennessee Waltz bribery case, but he was more than willing to try to score political points against the then dominant Democrats.

"Sometimes fear is a good motivator," Casada told the Associated Press in 2006. "Maybe fear of getting caught will change things as they have been done in the past."

And Casada was philosophical about former representative Chris Newton, the lone Republican ensnared in the case, getting sentenced to a year in prison after pleading guilty.

Sen. Brian Kelsey (R-Germantown), right, confers with Rep. Matthew Hill (R-Jonesborough) on the House floor in Nashville on April 30, 2019

"I think it will make him a better man when it's all said and done," Casada said.[26]

## THE STUNTBABY COMETH

The investigation into Phoenix Solutions and its ties to Casada, Smith, and Cothren wasn't the only campaign finance probe rocking the state Capitol. The other involved state senator Brian Kelsey, an ambitious Republican attorney from the affluent Germantown community outside Memphis.

Kelsey, who served three terms in the state House before joining the Senate in 2009, was indicted by federal prosecutors in 2021 for his role in an unusual money scheme that dated back to a failed bid for Congress from a few years before.

In his early days in the legislature, Kelsey's attention-seeking antics earned him the nickname "Stuntbaby of Germantown." In 2007, he theatrically placed bacon in an envelope during a House floor debate over what he called a pork-barrel spending scheme by Democrats—never mind that most Republican colleagues were eager to participate. GOP members were outraged two years later when backbencher Kent Williams banded together with all forty-nine of the chamber's Democrats to have himself elected Speaker. Kelsey, who filed a sexual harassment complaint on a female colleague's behalf against Williams after his election, was later exposed for having sent a text message offering to dial back his attacks in exchange for personal advancement. "Tell Kent I'm willing to talk about reconciliation if he's willing to talk about chairman of the full [judiciary] committee," Kelsey acknowledged telling an aide.[27]

Kelsey ascended to the upper chamber after Sen. Paul Stanley's resignation following an affair with a legislative intern. While in the Senate, Kelsey served stints as chair of the chamber's judiciary and education committees. But Kelsey's ambition didn't stop there. The state Senate was holding a floor session in 2016 when Republican US representative Stephen Fincher made his surprise announcement that he wouldn't seek another term representing a West Tennessee congressional district. Before state lawmakers had even adjourned for the day, Kelsey sent out a tweet saying "Yes, I'm in," along with a campaign logo.[28]

Kelsey was thought to have a strong chance at winning the seat, drawing endorsements from former US senator Rick Santorum of Pennsylvania (who had won Tennessee's presidential primary in 2012), anti-abortion groups, and several fellow members of the General Assembly. But his campaign never caught on. When the ballots were counted in August, Kelsey received just 13 percent to finish in an embarrassing fourth place.

Months after the GOP race had wrapped up, the *Tennessean* published stories questioning financial transactions that occurred during Kelsey's congressional bid. The paper explored the financial dealings of a political action committee for a Nashville restaurant called The Standard, which had a private upstairs area where members could smoke cigars and sip bourbon in overstuffed leather chairs. The story noted an unusual arrangement that occurred with several lawmakers: the Standard Club PAC gave money to lawmakers, who then spent almost the same amount of money at the restaurant that they later reported as covering "dues/subscriptions."[29]

Kelsey, who was one of the lawmakers highlighted in the story, gave $106,000 from his state campaign committee to the Standard's PAC in July 2016. Within days, the PAC reported sending $97,000 to a federal PAC known as Citizens for Ethics in Government. Federal filings, however, did not indicate the latter had been formally registered.[30]

The newspaper noted the name of the PAC was similar to one previously started by controversial Tennessee Republican donor Andy Miller, who had ties dating back to 2011 with The Standard and its owner, Josh Smith, who had started the PAC in the restaurant's name. Campaign finance records for Miller's Citizens 4 Ethics in Government indicated it received $37,000 from the Standard Club PAC in July 2016.[31]

That same month, the restaurant's PAC contributed $30,000 to the federal PAC of the American Conservative Union, a national political group that advocates for conservative policies and runs CPAC conferences. Miller's PAC also gave $36,000 to the American Conservative Union.

The same day Miller's PAC gave money to the American Conservative Union, the organization announced it had created a radio ad supporting Kelsey's bid for Congress. The ads, which cost $80,000, ran in Memphis and Jackson, according to federal and local radio disclosures. The series of transactions, while complex, were problematic for Kelsey because they appeared to suggest coordination between Kelsey and the group purportedly making independent expenditures, which is prohibited by law.[32]

In June 2017, the Campaign Legal Center, a Washington, DC–based watchdog, filed a complaint with the Federal Election Commission over the transactions, alleging Kelsey created an "illegal scheme to pass the money through a dark money daisy chain and straw donor reimbursement scheme."[33] Kelsey dismissed the group's complaint as a "frivolous attack" by an organization funded by liberals who were focused on defeating conservative lawmakers.[34] The Campaign Legal Center, which was founded by a Republican, has filed complaints against members of both parties.[35]

Kelsey's rejection of any wrongdoing was right out of the playbook of his political predecessors: blame the opposition and the media rather than address the core allegations.

For a few years, the issue faded into the background, as often happens in cases of alleged campaign finance violations. But persistent rumors worked their way around the legislative office complex that federal investigators were interviewing lawmakers who had given contributions to Kelsey's congressional bid. The *Tennessean* in late 2019 confirmed three people, including former lieutenant governor Ron Ramsey, an East Tennessee Republican, had been questioned by federal investigators and that Kelsey was the subject of a grand jury probe. Once again, Kelsey rejected the notion he had done any wrong, saying he welcomed any investigations.[36]

But with the five-year statute of limitations on most federal crimes approaching, Kelsey appeared to have run out the clock on any charges. Then in October 2021, federal prosecutors in Nashville filed an indictment naming Kelsey and restaurateur Josh Smith on conspiracy and campaign finance charges. Kelsey's longtime friend Jeremy Durham, the former lawmaker who was ousted from the House in 2016 over serial sexual misconduct allegations, and Miller, the longtime GOP donor, also featured in the charging document. While they were described as un-named co-conspirators, their identities were easily deduced. For exam-ple, only Durham meets the description of a "member of the Tennessee House of Representatives from in or around January 2013 to in or around September 2016, when he was expelled." And only Miller was "a Tennessee businessman and prominent political fundraiser" who had given $30,000 to Smith's PAC in July 2016.

In the indictment, federal prosecutors alleged that between February and October 2016 Kelsey and Smith were involved in a "conspiracy to un-lawfully and secretly funnel" money from the lawmaker's state campaign committee to benefit his federal campaign. Further, the feds alleged Kelsey and Smith made excessive contributions that were illegal and filed false campaign finance reports. Much of the indictment noted the financial transactions highlighted by the *Tennessean* years earlier.

According to the charging document, Kelsey, Smith, and Durham met for a dinner at The Standard about three weeks before the 2016 pri-mary election (and three days before a state attorney general's report on Durham's alleged sexual misconduct that would lead him to suspend his re-election campaign). Prosecutors say Kelsey handed a check for $106,341 to Smith with instructions to give $37,000 to Miller's PAC. Around the same time the American Conservative Union's political director, Amanda Bunning, emailed Smith to coordinate contributions to her organization. And Kelsey sent Bunning an email touting his legislative record to get him a better score in the group's ratings.[37]

Bunning was a former aide to US Senate Republican leader Mitch Mc-Connell and the daughter of baseball hall of famer and US senator Jim Bunning. She later left the ACU for a job with the Ingram Group, a Nash-ville lobbying firm. She also married Kelsey.[38]

In a hastily announced video conference call with reporters, Kelsey de-nounced the indictment as "nothing but a political witch hunt," noting the charges were brought after Republican president Donald Trump had been succeeded by Democrat Joe Biden. The new administration was "trying to take me out" because he had only narrowly been re-elected in 2018 and Democrats thought they could pick up the seat in the 2022 election.[39] The idea that a new president would be directing federal prosecutions based on a state Senate race in Tennessee was widely belittled.

In subsequent remarks on the Senate floor, Kelsey lamented the di-visiveness of national politics and urged both sides to "come together again in the peace, strength, and unity that defines our great state and

Sen. Brian Kelsey, right, and Rep. Jeremy Durham hold a press conference in Nashville on February 2, 2015

nation."[40] For longtime observers of Kelsey's brand of extreme partisanship, the comments rang particularly hollow. For example, in the middle of his 2016 campaign, Kelsey published an op-ed in the *Jackson Sun* in which he said, "If you are looking for a candidate who will sit idly by as liberals tear away at the conservative foundations of our country, I am not your candidate. I have stood up to Democrats and to Republicans, and I have won."[41]

While Kelsey beseeched his colleagues to reserve judgment until he could present his case in court, he was far less patient as a freshman lawmaker in 2005, when he called for members arrested in the Tennessee Waltz bribery sting to be immediately expelled from the General Assembly. "Innocent until proven guilty beyond a reasonable doubt is the standard we use for putting someone in jail—not the standard for allowing him to serve in public office," he said at the time.[42]

In an odd twist, Kelsey said in his floor comments following the indictment that the *Tennessee Journal* had reported that the attorney for the government's lead witness had said his client secured immunity from prosecution. No such development had appeared in the pages of the newsletter. The item most closely matching Kelsey's description detailed Durham's attorney announcing in an unrelated court case that his client recently learned he was no longer facing criminal charges. The lawyer didn't say anything about Kelsey or immunity for testifying.[43]

If it was true that Durham had flipped on Kelsey, it would have signaled a major break between the longtime friends. Kelsey served as best man at Durham's wedding and stood by him even after he was ousted from the House. Shortly after Durham's expulsion from the General Assembly, Kelsey joined him at a University of Tennessee football game, where the former lawmaker got thrown out for getting into a fight with other fans. Kelsey claimed not to have seen the scuffle.[44]

Kelsey pledged to promptly prove he was "totally innocent" after he was first charged, but his legal team eventually settled on a more deliberate approach, getting the judge to agree to a yearlong delay for his trial and then being granted several further postponements. Meanwhile, Kelsey announced he would step aside as chair of the Senate Education Committee while trying to clear his name in court. At first, he tried to plow ahead with his re-election bid, even joining other lawmakers in holding a fundraiser before the in-session ban on campaign donations began. On the eve of the candidate-filing deadline, Kelsey announced he wouldn't run again due to an "exciting change" in his personal life.[45] The Senate proceeded to celebrate the retiring lawmaker in a resolution as "a public-spirited citizen of the highest order."

The laudatory measure passed 29–0.

In October 2022, restaurateur Josh Smith threw in the towel and pleaded guilty to one count of aiding and abetting the illegal transfer of $67,000 in "soft money" from Kelsey's state campaign account. The following month, just weeks after the expiration of his final term in the General Assembly, Kelsey followed suit and struck a deal to admit guilt on two of five counts levied against him: conspiracy to defraud the federal government and accepting excessive campaign contributions.[46]

But less than two weeks before he was scheduled to be sentenced in the case, Kelsey's new attorneys filed a legal motion seeking to withdraw his guilty plea and asking for the case to be dismissed on the basis that "the facts do not actually constitute a crime." According to court documents, Kelsey had been forced to make a decision on a plea deal within forty-eight hours of the offer being made by prosecutors. He had agreed to the deal with "unsure heart and confused mind" because he was grappling with his father's terminal cancer diagnosis and suffering sleepless nights following the birth of twin sons.

Kelsey submitted a sworn declaration saying he didn't fully understand the consequences of pleading guilty, which included losing access to the banking system, his legislative health and pension benefits, and his job. "Other than speeding tickets, I have no experience with the criminal justice system as a defendant," Kelsey wrote. The statement garnered much eye-rolling among the Capitol crowd who recalled his imperious six years as chair of the Senate Judiciary Committee.[47] Kelsey's motion was rejected.

Before the about-face on the guilty plea, longtime ethics champion Randy McNally—who had worn a wire for the FBI during a corruption probe of state lawmakers in the 1980s—wrote to the judge urging him to exercise leniency for Kelsey. The lieutenant governor's letter, which had been requested by Kelsey's wife, Amanda, was never submitted to the court.

Former senator Katrina Robinson speaks to reporters after the Senate votes to oust her from the chamber on February 2, 2022

# EPILOGUE
# The Same Old Song

NO COLLECTION OF CORRUPTION STORIES is ever truly complete, as new allegations and cases can arise at any given moment.

Several Republicans had gotten into hot water since their party gained control of the General Assembly. That's not necessarily because Democrats haven't been bad actors, too, but because the minority party tends to get far less scrutiny from the public and press. One exception was Democratic state senator Katrina Robinson of Memphis, who was ousted from the upper chamber in 2022 after she was convicted in one federal fraud case and agreed to pretrial diversion in another.

Robinson was charged in 2020 with misspending federal grant money intended for her nursing school on items ranging from her wedding to a designer purse. Most of the charges were thrown out in court, but a jury still convicted her of two counts in September 2021. Robinson's supporters argued she shouldn't become ineligible to serve until she was sentenced. But Lt. Gov. Randy McNally, a key figure in the Operation Rocky Top probe of the 1980s, pressed colleagues to act promptly and decisively. Robinson took to the well of the chamber to denounce what she called a "procedural lynching." She was still expelled on a partisan vote of 27–5 in February 2022, becoming the first sitting state senator to be ousted since the Civil War.[1]

In early 2023 three other Democrats faced expulsion after they had the audacity to lead anti-gun protests inside the House chamber following a mass shooting at a Nashville school that left six dead, including three nine-year-olds. With protesters calling for gun control inside and around the statehouse, Rep. Justin Jones of Nashville, Rep. Justin Pearson

Justin Pearson of Memphis speaks on the House floor on April 3, 2023. Pearson and Justin Jones of Nashville, seated, were later expelled for leading a gun protest from the well of the chamber

of Memphis, and Rep. Gloria Johnson of Knoxville took to the well of the chamber and led protesters who were gathered inside the House gallery in chants. Jones and Pearson took turns speaking into a bullhorn while Republican leaders huddled in a frenzy. In the following days, Republican leaders, including House Speaker Cameron Sexton, criticized the three Democrats as "left-wing protesters" and equated their actions to the January 6, 2021, insurrection in the US Capitol. With tempers still high, Republicans hastily filed resolutions to expel Jones, Pearson, and Johnson—who became known as the Tennessee Three on social media. Critics argued the punishment didn't fit the crime—the House had only ejected members three other times since Reconstruction. Despite the national media attention, Republicans plowed ahead in their ouster efforts, ultimately expelling Jones and Pearson, who are both Black. The effort to oust Johnson, who is white, fell short by a single vote. The chamber's actions were met with widespread criticism, including from president Joe Biden, former vice president Al Gore, and former Republican National Committee chair Michael Steele. Less than a week after their expulsions, Jones and Pearson were reappointed to their old seats by their respective county legislative bodies.

While in the national spotlight, Tennessee Democrats highlighted the heavy-handed tactics of Republicans as evidence of anti-democratic leanings and argued the majority was more focused on cultural issues than matters affecting everyday residents. The entire ordeal was largely on brand for a Republican Party that for years had managed to score points with their base by playing partisan politics while minimizing or ignoring Democrats' attempts to shift the conversation and influence their agenda.

Every scandal tends to bring a course correction on ethics rules as lawmakers come to grips with the fact that they can't just rely on their good intentions to avoid problems. Following the Tennessee Waltz arrests of 2005, the General Assembly held a special session to address the circumstances that had made for such a fertile hunting ground for undercover agents. With Democrats' numerical advantage slipping, Republicans, including McNally, pushed for a stricter set of rules and a standalone Ethics Commission.

But once Republicans took over control of both chambers, they began chipping away at the oversight. Senate Republican Caucus chair Bill Ketron of Murfreesboro, along with Rep. Glen Casada, led the charge on merging the Ethics Commission back under the same umbrella as the Registry of Election Finance. Ketron was elected Rutherford County mayor in 2018 but left a mess of campaign finance filings related to his Senate and political action committee accounts behind. A 2020 audit found Ketron couldn't account for a combined $241,000 in contributions. The mayor explained he had given his daughter, Kelsey Ketron, control over the accounts when he was undergoing cancer treatments. Kelsey Ketron had pleaded no contest to fifteen counts of fraud and forgery related to her work for her father's insurance agency.[2]

After much back-and-forth, Ketron in October 2021 paid a $135,000 civil penalty to the registry, a necessary step for him to qualify to run for re-election as mayor. But he ended up finishing third in the Republican primary.

The latest rounds of FBI activity and federal charges generated increased campaign finance reporting requirements and other ethics rules changes in Tennessee. But if the past is any guide, any move toward greater oversight will be followed by a gradual easing of the rules—and of vigilance and self-awareness. Until the next scandal hits.

Reflecting on five decades of corrupt and questionable activity in Tennessee government and politics raises questions about whether any grand conclusions can be drawn or who may be the next to fall.

The preceding pages illustrate that corruption is not limited to one party or another. It has no geographic boundaries or statute of limitations. Devious actions by politicians are as old as the state and as current as tomorrow's headlines.

A familiar pattern can be detected from this chronicle of corruption and scandal: when faced with scrutiny or criticism, officials tend to deflect and deny wrongdoing at all costs while blaming others until they can no longer prevent their downfall. Grasping onto power is an understandable human instinct, yet ill-advised for most of those described here as any good deeds will be outweighed by their mistakes.

As we previously stated, not all of Tennessee's elected officials are on the take, bending the rules, or making decisions they hope never see the light of day. Far from it. There have been and there will continue to be plenty of good actors who head to the Capitol with the hope of introducing and enacting new laws that make their home state a better place.

And yet it is important to keep an arm's-length distance and healthy skepticism about any public official or candidate promising the moon. Watchdogs—be they reporters, competing candidates, or government agencies—are vitally important at a time when trust in government across the country has hit record lows.

In the current environment of shrinking newsrooms, hyper partisanship, and no-holds-barred campaign tactics, the need to scrutinize government and elected officials is more important than ever to promote good governance. The pursuit of power can have a way of turning well-intended public officials toward a level of self-importance that can justify almost any bending of the rules.

It may be impossible to stop someone with ill intentions before they act. But without proper guardrails, lawmakers can go off the rails. One-party control, be it led by Democrats or Republicans, can be an intoxicating elixir that gives members of the majority an unfettered belief that they can do no wrong. As a result, it can often take a crisis of leadership or breakdown of ethics before any overhaul is considered, let alone enacted. And if history is any indication, reforms can take years to enact, with the passage of time clouding the public's collective memory of corruption in their government and keeping the status quo intact. Maintaining a vigilant skepticism of elected officials, no matter their party, always serves the interest of the public.

# APPENDIX
# Tennessee Lawmakers Behaving Badly

*Not every scandal could fit in this book but here's a recap of some Tennessee lawmakers who have run into trouble in recent decades.*

**1970** **Rep. Bryan Elder and Rep. Hugh Dixon,** BOTH DEMOCRATS
Charged with violating the state's conflict of interest law after companies owned by Dixon and Elder entered contracts with the state. Elder resigned before the indictment, after he said he had become aware of the conflict of interest. A criminal court judge ruled the state's conflict of interest law did not apply to members of the legislature and dismissed the charges against Elder while the charges against Dixon never went to trial. When the Elder case was appealed to the state supreme court, the high court sustained the rulings of two lower courts, affirming the conflict of interest law was never intended to apply to state lawmakers.[1]

**1979** **Rep. Robert Fisher,** REPUBLICAN
Charged with soliciting a $1,000 bribe from a sheriff to defeat a bill in the legislature. After being found guilty, he was given a thirty-day suspended sentence and fined $500. When the legislature returned to Nashville in January 1980, the House voted 92–1 to expel Fisher, making him the first member to be ousted since Reconstruction.[2]

**1980** **Rep. Emmitt Ford,** DEMOCRAT
Convicted of federal insurance fraud charges in 1980, Ford at first refused to step down from his seat in the state House. It wasn't until the eve of the 1981 session that the brother of state senator John Ford and US representative Harold Ford Sr. agreed to resign, averting formal ouster proceedings.[3]

**1982   Sen. Edgar Gillock, DEMOCRAT**

Twice beat federal bribery and racketeering charges in the 1970s, only to be convicted in 1982 of using his elected office to obtain $130,365 from executives of Honeywell Inc. to help land computer contracts worth $2.5 million with the Tennessee Department of Employment Security and $2 million with Shelby County.

**1982   Rep. Tommy Burnett, DEMOCRAT**

Considered a rising star in the General Assembly, Burnett pleaded guilty in 1982 of failing to file income taxes. Because the offense was considered a misdemeanor, Burnett was eligible to run for re-election from prison and won. In 1990, he was convicted in the FBI's Rocky Top public corruption investigation.[4]

**1989–1991 Operation Rocky Top**

In a wide-ranging investigation that led to dozens of indictments stemming from a federal investigation into illegal gambling in Tennessee, current and former lawmakers were charged. Among them were House majority leader Tommy Burnett, former state Reps. Jack Burnett and Landon Colvard, in addition to lobbyists, state regulators, and bingo operators. Rep. Ted Ray Miller, a Democrat, killed himself with a shotgun the day he was expected to be indicted for extortion. Secretary of State Gentry Crowell, who had repeatedly appeared before a grand jury, fatally shot himself before he was indicted.

**1995   Rep. Joe Bell, DEMOCRAT**

Accused of violating the legislature's sexual harassment policy after a statehouse secretary recorded a conversation with Bell in which he solicited sex. He was removed as chairman of the House Agriculture Committee and did not seek re-election.[5]

**1996   Sen. Carl Koella, REPUBLICAN**

Charged with leaving the scene of a fatal accident involving a motorcycle after spending the day campaigning with Republican governor Don Sundquist. After being re-elected, he pleaded guilty to a misdemeanor and was sentenced to community service.[6]

**2002 Rep. Keith Westmoreland,** REPUBLICAN

The northeast Tennessee lawmaker was arrested in Sandestin, Florida, on seven counts of indecent exposure following repeated incidents at a hotel pool and hot tub. Westmoreland, who had been investigated for similar cases in Nashville earlier in the year, returned to his Kingsport home and took his own life.[7]

**2002 Rep. Ronnie Davis,** REPUBLICAN

Charged with federal conspiracy, money laundering, and extortion for attempting to get diplomatic passports for two people who did not qualify for them. Prosecutors alleged Davis and an accomplice created fake stationery from the offices of Vice President Al Gore, Gov. Don Sundquist, and others to obtain the passports. He was defeated in the 2002 general election by a Democrat and later sentenced to two years in prison.[8]

**2005 Operation Tennessee Waltz**

An FBI bribery sting involving a fake electronics recycling company led to the conviction of five former lawmakers: Sen. Ward Crutchfield (Democrat), Sen. John Ford (Democrat), Sen. Kathryn Bowers (Democrat), Rep. Chris Newton (Republican) and former Sen. Roscoe Dixon (Democrat).

Sen. Jeff Miller, who served as chairman of the Senate Republican Caucus, resigned from his leadership position and did not seek re-election after he acknowledged that he accepted $1,000 in cash as part of the sting operation. Miller, who said he considered the money to be a campaign contribution, was not ultimately charged with a crime.[9]

**2006 Sen. Jerry Cooper,** DEMOCRAT

Charged with conspiracy to commit bank and mail fraud for his efforts to defraud a bank co-owned by Lt. Gov. John Wilder. A federal jury acquitted him of all charges in June 2007. That same year state election finance officials fined Cooper $120,000 after a complaint alleged Cooper had funneled thousands of dollars from his campaign into his personal account.[10]

**2007**  Rep. Rob Briley, DEMOCRAT

In one of the state's first social media–driven scandals, a YouTube video of House Judiciary chairman Rob Briley's drunken driving arrest went viral. The video showed Briley berating Watertown police officers, calling one a Nazi and singing "Springtime for Hitler" from the Mel Brooks movie and musical *The Producers*. When he was booked into jail, Briley listed the name of a lobbyist for the state trial lawyers' association, which had an extensive agenda before his committee, as his main contact. He didn't seek re-election after going to rehab.[11]

**2009**  Sen. Paul Stanley, REPUBLICAN

The boyfriend of a twenty-two-year-old legislative intern who was having an affair with Stanley attempted to extort $10,000 from the lawmaker. When the plot was made public, Stanley, under pressure from Republican leadership, resigned from his post as chairman of the Commerce Committee and later from the Senate.[12]

**2015**  Rep. Joe Armstrong, DEMOCRAT

Charged with fraud and income tax evasion for a scheme in which he and a wholesaler attempted to turn a $500,000 profit for buying state tobacco tax stamps before a tax increase, which Armstrong had supported and voted for, took effect. After a jury convicted him of filing a false income tax return, Armstrong was given three years' probation.[13]

**2016**  Rep. Jeremy Durham, REPUBLICAN

An investigation by Attorney General Herbert Slatery accused Durham of inappropriate sexual conduct with twenty-two women. As a result, the House in September 2016 voted 70–2 to expel him from the body, the first expulsion since Robert Fisher in 1980. He was separately issued a $465,000 penalty for hundreds of state campaign finance violations.

**2016**  Rep. Curry Todd, REPUBLICAN

The sponsor of Tennessee's controversial law to allow handgun carry permit holders to be armed in bars and restaurants that serve alcohol, Todd was arrested in 2011 after failing a roadside sobriety test. Police found a loaded handgun stuffed into the center console of Todd's car. The lawmaker was also arrested on misdemeanor charges the day of the 2016 primary for removing campaign signs of his opponent, Mark Lovell, who later posted bond for his rival. Lovell won the nomination.[14]

**2017  Rep. Mark Lovell,** REPUBLICAN
Accused of sexual harassment after he attended a series of receptions in
Nashville during the legislative session. After a formal complaint was
filed and an investigation determined he was guilty of misconduct, Lovell
resigned.

**2018  Rep. David Byrd,** REPUBLICAN
Accused of sexual misconduct by three women who alleged Byrd inappropriately touched them as teenagers when he was their high school
basketball coach in the 1980s. Byrd was recorded apologizing to one of
the women, but never admitted any specific sexual misconduct. Byrd
was never charged.[15]

**2019  Rep. Rick Staples,** DEMOCRAT
After multiple complaints were filed against him, Staples was found
to have violated the legislature's sexual harassment policy. One of the
women who filed a complaint told the *Tennessean* how Staples had inappropriately touched her and commented on her appearance during a
visit to the legislature. In 2020, state officials fined Staples $26,000 for
unrelated campaign finance violations.[16]

**2021  Sen. Katrina Robinson,** DEMOCRAT
Robinson was charged with misspending federal grant money meant
for her for-profit nursing school in Memphis. While most of the charges
were thrown out in federal court, she was convicted on two counts and
struck a pretrial diversion deal on another case alleging she had tried to
cheat a man out of $14,470 by falsely claiming the money was needed to
cover tuition for a student at her healthcare school. The Senate ousted
her from the seat in February 2022.

**2021  Sen. Brian Kelsey,** REPUBLICAN
Charged with federal campaign finance crimes related to his unsuccessful
bid for Congress in 2016. Prosecutors alleged Kelsey had directed money
from his state account to the federal independent expenditure arm of the
American Conservative Union. Kelsey agreed to a deal with prosecutors,
but then sought to withdraw his guilty plea before he was scheduled to
be sentenced in early 2023.

**2022**  Rep. Robin Smith and Rep. Glen Casada, BOTH REPUBLICANS
Smith pleaded guilty to federal charges related to her promotion of a
shadowy political vendor called Phoenix Solutions. Prosecutors said
Smith had conspired with former House Speaker Glen Casada and his
onetime chief of staff Cade Cothren to direct taxpayer and donor money
to the outfit they controlled and profited from. Casada and Cothren were
scheduled to go on trial in late 2023.

**2022**  Rep. Torrey Harris, DEMOCRAT
Harris was arrested on felony theft and misdemeanor domestic assault
charges in Nashville after an ex-boyfriend accused him of domestic assault and stealing his dog, computer, and gaming console. Harris overwhelmingly won his primary election the following month. The case was
later retired provided Harris didn't face any charges over the next six
months.[17]

**2023**  Rep. Scotty Campbell, REPUBLICAN
Found to have violated the legislature's harassment policy after at least
one legislative intern filed a complaint over inappropriate communications with the lawmaker. Campbell initially defended himself, saying his
"private conversations" were "consensual" and between adults. Although
House leadership had been aware of the issue for several weeks and apparently made arrangements to accommodate the victim, it wasn't until
a WTVF "NewsChannel 5 Investigates" report was released that Campbell resigned.[18]

# NOTES

**FOREWORD**

Bill Haslam was governor of Tennessee from 2011 to 2019.

**INTRODUCTION**

1. "Tennessee Notes," *Tennessee Journal* 4, no. 12 (March 20, 1978): 4.
2. Associated Press, "Gillock Bribery Trial Delayed for Appeal of Evidence Ruling," *Johnson City Press*, Dec. 4, 1976, 6. https://www.newspapers.com/image/590517227.
3. *United States v. Gillock*, 445 U.S. 360 (1980).
4. "Bribes and Bribery," *Knoxville Journal and Tribune*, Nov. 13, 1887, https://www.newspapers.com/image/584432119.
5. "Bribery Charged," *Journal and Tribune*, May 5, 1895, https://www.newspapers.com/image/584236916; J. Eugene Lewis, "The Tennessee Gubernatorial Campaign and Election of 1894," *Tennessee Historical Quarterly* 13, no. 4 (Dec. 1954): 301–28
6. Carl Manning and Associated Press, "1910 Pardon Caused Outcry," in *Leaf Chronicle*, Oct. 18, 1978, https://www.newspapers.com/image/367091121; *Pittsburgh Gazette* quoted in "Editorial Expressions on Governor's Pardon," *Nashville Banner*, April 18, 1910, https://www.newspapers.com/image/604375897; *Richmond Virginian* quoted in "Gov. Patterson Pardons D. B. Cooper," *Chattanooga News*, April 13, 1910, https://www.newspapers.com/image/603022387; "Scarcely Less Than Treason to State," *Chattanooga Daily Times*, April 17, 1910, https://www.newspapers.com/image/605600731.
7. "Attempt to Bribe Two Republicans in Legislature," *Knoxville News Sentinel*, Jan. 2, 1911, https://www.newspapers.com/image/586491843.
8. "Senator Clabo Held for Accepting Bribe to Change His Vote," *Bristol Courier Herald*, April 7, 1921, https://www.newspapers.com/image/584769959.
9. "Jury Acquits Senator Clabo," *Chattanooga Daily Times*, Jan. 11, 1922, https://www.newspapers.com/image/605497726.

10. "Alleged Corruption at Nashville," *Bristol Herald Courier*, April 11, 1921, https://www.newspapers.com/image/584770460.

11. David D. Lee and David L. Lee, "The Attempt to Impeach Governor Horton," *Tennessee Historical Quarterly* 34, no. 2 (Summer 1975): 189. https://www.jstor.org/stable/42623518.

12. "'Trust People,' Says Ed Crump, Telling How He Plays Politics," *Chattanooga Daily Times*, Jan. 7, 1931, 1, https://www.newspapers.com/image/604318611.

13. J. U. Snyder, "Eleventh-Hour Defense Ill-Timed; Crump Held Up as Discredited," *Knoxville Journal*, May 26, 1931, 16, https://www.newspapers.com/image/586392302.

14. Lee and Lee, "Attempt to Impeach," 195, 201.

15. Fred Hixson, "Indictments Are Promised if Quiz Shows Bribe Offer," *Chattanooga Daily Times*, Oct. 21, 1937, https://www.newspapers.com/image/604474858.

16. Fred Hixson, "Bribes for Lawmakers," *Chattanooga Daily Times*, Dec. 1, 1946, https://www.newspapers.com/image/604671906.

17. Larry Daughtrey, "Provides Free Liquor: Hensley," *Tennessean*, April 15, 1975, https://www.newspapers.com/image/112006581; John Parish, "Fair-Trade Law on Liquor Axed by State Senate," *Jackson Sun*, April 3, 1975, https://www.newspapers.com/image/282982498.

18. Jim O'Hara and James Pratt, "McWherter, in 1st Veto, Slaps Bingo," *Tennessean*, April 22, 1987, https://www.newspapers.com/image/112351994.

19. M. Lee Smith, "Capitol Commentary: Stage Now Set for Gillock Trial," *Johnson City Press*, March 25, 1980, 4, https://www.newspapers.com/image/590619615. 4; "Tennessee Notes," *Tennessee Journal* 4, no. 12 (March 20, 1978): 4.

20. Robert Sherborne, "Neal Not Disheartened by Gillock Ruling," *Tennessean*, March 20, 1980, 1, https://www.newspapers.com/image/111982418.

21. Louis Graham, "Gillock Convicted of Extortion; Tax Evasion, Fraud also Bring 'Guilty,'" *Memphis Commercial Appeal*, Nov. 11, 1982, A1, https://www.newspapers.com/image/772472406.

22. "Notes & Quotes," *Tennessee Journal* 26, no. 15 (April 10, 2000): 4.

## CHAPTER 1

1. William Bennett, "Baker and Kuykendall Win; Pop Charter Gets Approval," *Commercial Appeal*, Nov. 9, 1966, https://www.newspapers.com/image/770538020.

2. Larry Daughtrey, "Dunn, Brock Victorious," *Tennessean*, Nov. 4, 1970, https://www.newspapers.com/image/111932754.

3. Tom Sharp and Associated Press, "Republicans Take Control of State Senate," *Jackson Sun*, Nov. 3, 2004, https://www.newspapers.com/image/284141601.

4. Sharp, "Republicans Take Control."

5. "Blanton the Man," *Tennessee Journal* 3, no. 2 (Jan. 10, 1977).

6. Sarah Grace Taylor and Patrick Filbin, "Hamilton County Cold Case Unit Solves Murder with Ties to Former Tennessee Gov. Ray Blanton," *Chattanooga Times Free Press*, June 9, 2021, https://www.timesfreepress.com/news/2021/jun/09/hamiltcounty-cold-case-unit-solves-murder-tie.

7. John Hale, "Long Way from Eggs under Porch," *Tennessean*, Nov. 6, 1974, https://www.newspapers.com/image/111574594.

8. John Parish, "'I'm Not Afraid of Hard Work,'" *Jackson Sun*, Dec. 21, 1966, https://www.newspapers.com/image/282929957.

9. United Press International, "Blanton Lived in Controversy," *Times News*, June 10, 1981, https://www.newspapers.com/image/594215609.

10. "Adamsville Election Results Are Given," *Jackson Sun*, Oct. 11, 1961, https://www.newspapers.com/image/282796865; John Parish, "Blanton Wins Governorship, Promises 'Period of Progress,'" *Jackson Sun*, Nov. 6, 1974, https://www.newspapers.com/image/283169152; Robert Kollar, "Ray Blanton: A Vote Getter," *Tennessean*, Aug. 14, 1966, https://www.newspapers.com/image/116608469.

11. Associated Press, "Murray Concedes Defeat," *Leaf Chronicle*, Aug. 10, 1966, https://www.newspapers.com/image/353462068; "GOP Scores Gains across the Nation; Blanton Is Victor," *Jackson Sun*, Nov. 9, 1966, https://www.newspapers.com/image/282917168; Joe Hatcher, "Politics: Blanton Becomes 'Miracle Man' for Tennessee Democrats," *Tennessean*, Nov. 10, 1966, https://www.newspapers.com/image/113232293.

12. Associated Press, "Sen. Baker Takes Oath of Office," *Jackson Sun*, Jan. 10, 1967, https://www.newspapers.com/image/282965481; "Ray Blanton FBI FOIA No. 1483477-000 Document 1," p. 2, uploaded to Scribd by TNScandalsBook, April 14, 2023, https://www.scribd.com/document/638336547/Ray-Blanton-FBI-FOIA-No-1483477-000-Document-1.

13. William Collins and Robert Margo, "The Economic Aftermath of the 1960s Riots in American Cities: Evidence from Property Values," *Journal of Economic History* 67, no. 4 (Dec. 2007): 853. https://www.jstor.org/stable/40056402.

14. "Ray Blanton FBI FOIA No. 1483477-000 Document 1," p. 3.

15. William Bennett, "Bruce Upset Unseats Pipkin; Willis and Sugarmon Defeated; Ray Blanton, Irwin Win Easily," *Commercial Appeal*, Aug. 2, 1968, https://www.newspapers.com/image/770829436; Parish, "'I'm Not Afraid of Hard Work.'"

16. John Parish, "Blanton Endorses Johnson, Sees First Ballot Victory," *Jackson Sun*, March 25, 1968, https://www.newspapers.com/image/282100117; "Presidential Veto Draws Objection from Rep. Blanton," *Jackson Sun*, Aug. 18, 1968, https://www.newspapers.com/image/283200425.

17. Joe Hatcher, "Politics: Congressional Delegation Avoiding Chicago Like Plague," *Tennessean*, Aug. 22, 1968, https://www.newspapers.com/image/112207582; Bob Gilbert, "Mrs. HHH Is Given Roses at Nashville," *Jackson Sun*, Sept. 20, 1968, https://www.newspapers.com/image/283128694.

18. "GOP Challenges Rep. Blanton in 7th District," *Jackson Sun*, Nov. 3, 1968, https://www.newspapers.com/image/283110681; "Blanton Raps Forced Busing of Students," *Jackson Sun*, Sept. 16, 1968, https://www.newspapers.com/image/283120867.

19. William Street, "Blanton Political Base Rally Raises Point of Diplomacy," *Commercial Appeal*, Oct. 6, 1968, https://www.newspapers.com/image/770868420.

20. Kent Gardner, "Blanton View Gives 'Twist' to Campaign," *Commercial Appeal*, Oct. 30, 1968, https://www.newspapers.com/image/770871554.

21. Joe C. Carr, *Tennessee Blue Book, 1969–1970* (Nashville: State of Tennessee, 1969), 245; "Blanton Is Big Winner," *Jackson Sun*, Nov. 6, 1968, https://www.newspapers.com/image/283116607.

22. Lee Stillwell, "Blanton in Race for Baker's Seat in the Senate," *Knoxville News Sentinel*, April 16, 1972, https://www.newspapers.com/image/773782396; Jim Squires, "Blanton, Baker Crush Foes, Eye November," *Tennessean*, Aug. 4, 1972, https://www.newspapers.com/image/111983843.

23. "Blanton, Baker Exchange Barbs," *Knoxville News Sentinel*, Sept. 20, 1972, https://www.newspapers.com/image/773862499; "Blanton Says Baker Is Self-Promoter," *Knoxville News Sentinel*, Sept. 11, 1972, https://www.newspapers.com/image/773856759; "Blanton Criticizes Baker Absenteeism," *Commercial Appeal*, Sept. 17, 1972, https://www.newspapers.com/image/771391154; "Blanton Asks: Why Can't Baker Talk for Himself?" *Leaf Chronicle*, Sept. 24, 1972, https://www.newspapers.com/image/353410081; "Blanton Raps Baker over Campaign $," *Johnson City Press*, Sept. 27, 1972, https://www.newspapers.com/image/590026616.

24. Jim Squires, "Palmer Claims Blanton Getting 'Outside' Funds," *Tennessean*, July 29, 1972, https://www.newspapers.com/image/112038144.

25. "Blanton Denies Nepotism," *Tennessean*, July 17, 1971, https://www.newspapers.com/image/111760350.

26. Chris French, "Howard Baker Wants to Become First Re-elected Tennessee GOP Senator," June 8, 1972, https://www.newspapers.com/image/284240129; Chris French and Associated Press, "Baker Re-election Try First for a Republican," *Johnson City Press*, Oct. 19, 1972, https://www.newspapers.com/image/589892186.

27. "Wallace Offers Support to Blanton's Campaign," *Johnson City Press*, Nov. 3, 1972, https://www.newspapers.com/image/589964252.

28. "Baker to Open Four-Day 'Whistle Stop' Train Trip," *Tennessean*, Oct. 30, 1972, https://www.newspapers.com/image/112040894; "Baker Denies Bribe Assertion," *Johnson City Press*, Nov. 1, 1972, https://www.newspapers.com/image/589963292.

29. "Senate Candidates Audits Due Study," *Knoxville News Sentinel*, May 31, 1974, https://www.newspapers.com/image/773860158; "State Tallies Unofficial, but Final," *Tennessean*, Nov. 9, 1972, https://www.newspapers.com/image/112136582; Tim Wyngaard, "Baker, Beard Campaigns among Costliest," *Knoxville News Sentinel*, Sept. 14, 1973, https://www.newspapers.com/image/773913572.

30. John Parish, "That's Politics," *Jackson Sun*, March 9, 1973, https://www.newspapers.com/image/284355336; William Street, "Traditional Coon Supper Serves as Blanton 'Coming-Out' Party," *Commercial Appeal*, April 27, 1973, https://www.newspapers.com/image/771383116.

31. Bill Rawlins and Associated Press, "3 More Due to Announce," *Knoxville News Sentinel*, May 5, 1974, https://www.newspapers.com/image/774096514; "Blanton Backs Funds Review," *Knoxville News Sentinel*, May 7, 1974, https://www.newspapers.com/image/774098220.

32. United Press International, "Mental Health, Election Reform Talked," *Kingsport Times*, June 25, 1974, https://www.newspapers.com/image/592725338; "Blanton

Urges 3 Campaign-Related Law Changes," *Commercial Appeal*, June 26, 1974, https://www.newspapers.com/image/771436896.

33. Associated Press, "15 Politicians Sign Unity Pledge," *Johnson City Press*, Sept. 27, 1973, https://www.newspapers.com/image/589980894.

34. Keel Hunt, "Blanton Calls Corporate Gift Issue 'Dead,'" *Tennessean*, July 27, 1974, https://www.newspapers.com/image/111542113.

35. Larry Daughtrey, "Democrats' Task Tough in November," *Tennessean*, Aug. 2, 1974, https://www.newspapers.com/image/111523622.

36. John Parish, "Campaigns Get Boost," *Jackson Sun*, June 25, 1974, https://www.newspapers.com/image/283773050.

37. United Press International, "Blanton: Watergate Will Be Issue," *Jackson Sun*, Aug. 5, 1974, https://www.newspapers.com/image/283557957; "Alexander Announces for Governor," *Knoxville News Sentinel*, Feb. 7, 1974, https://www.newspapers.com/image/773937125; United Press International, "November Campaign One of Issues: Alexander," *Kingsport Times*, Aug. 16, 1974, https://www.newspapers.com/image/592642281; Associated Press, "Lamar Alexander: Governor's Race Made More Positive," *Johnson City Press*, Aug. 13, 1974, https://www.newspapers.com/image/590024026.

38. Associated Press, "Pre-Watergate Role of Foe Questioned," *Johnson City Press*, Aug. 6, 1974, https://www.newspapers.com/image/590004903; Robert Shaw, "Candidates Swap Gibes at Table," *Knoxville News Sentinel*, Sept. 13, 1974, https://www.newspapers.com/image/773900225; Duren Cheek, "Dunn Says He's 'Emotionally Drained,'" *Knoxville News Sentinel*, Aug. 9, 1974, https://www.newspapers.com/image/773944209; Associated Press, "Alexander Likes New Look," *Commercial Appeal*, Aug. 13, 1974, https://www.newspapers.com/image/771445387.

39. Ellis Binkley, "Blanton and Unity," *Times News*, Aug. 25, 1974, https://www.newspapers.com/image/592626274; United Press International, "Hooker Takes Swipe at Alexander," *Kingsport Times*, Aug. 19, 1974, https://www.newspapers.com/image/592643121.

40. Associated Press, "Dunn's New Jet 'Economy Move for the People,'" *Johnson City Press*, July 12, 1973, https://www.newspapers.com/image/589909216; Larry Daughtrey, "Dunn Took Bowl Trip in Plane," *Tennessean*, Sept. 5, 1973, https://www.newspapers.com/image/111582602; Associated Press, "Dunn 'Repaid State for Plane Use,'" *Knoxville News Sentinel*, Oct. 3, 1974, https://www.newspapers.com/image/773905018; Dwight Lewis, "Reason for Dunn Jet Clear: Blanton," *Tennessean*, July 5, 1974, https://www.newspapers.com/image/111519949.

41. "'Absurd,' Fulton Says of Blanton Charges," *Tennessean*, Oct. 18, 1974, https://www.newspapers.com/image/111490410; "Alleged 1972 Blanton Campaign Abuses Issue Snowballs," *Commercial Appeal*, Oct. 20, 1974, https://www.newspapers.com/image/771486539; Duren Cheek, "Blanton Answers Brown's Charges," *Daily News Journal*, Oct. 31, 1974, https://www.newspapers.com/image/368463073.

42. Larry Daughtrey, "Turned Down Milk Money: Alexander," *Tennessean*, Oct. 29, 1974, https://www.newspapers.com/image/111512774; United Press International,

"John Connally Is Indicted," *El Paso Herald-Post*, July 29, 1974, https://www.newspapers.com/image/799092066.

43. "Record Hit by Alexander," *Knoxville News Sentinel*, Nov. 1, 1974, https://www.newspapers.com/image/774093594.

44. Thomas Jordan, "Blanton Promises Effort as a 'People's Lobbyist,'" *Commercial Appeal*, Oct. 22, 1974, https://www.newspapers.com/image/771486882; "Singing for Ray," *Tennessean*, Oct. 28, 1974, https://www.newspapers.com/image/111511569.

45. "Alexander, Blanton Predict Win," *Knoxville News Sentinel*, Nov. 5, 1974, https://www.newspapers.com/image/774095315.

46. Joe C. Carr, *Tennessee Blue Book, 1975–1976* (Nashville, TN: State of Tennessee, 1975), 269; Larry Daughtrey, "Blanton Wins in Sweep," *Tennessean*, Nov. 6, 1974, https://www.newspapers.com/image/111574397.

47. Larry Daughtrey, "Blanton Says Austerity a Must," *Tennessean*, Jan. 19, 1979, https://www.newspapers.com/image/108987313.

48. Larry Daughtrey, "Blanton May Ask Pay Raise Restudy," *Tennessean*, Jan. 14, 1975, https://www.newspapers.com/image/109003138.

49. William Bennett, "$26,000 Raise Awaits Blanton," *Commercial Appeal*, Jan. 16, 1975, https://www.newspapers.com/image/771508934; "3 Oppose Blanton Hike," *Knoxville News Sentinel*, Jan. 22, 1975, https://www.newspapers.com/image/774053731; William Bennett, "Blanton Crimps Butler Jobs," *Commercial Appeal*, Jan. 22, 1975, https://www.newspapers.com/image/771517837; United Press International, "'Escalator' Ruling Is Asked," *Times News*, Feb. 8, 1975, https://www.newspapers.com/image/592623498.

50. Henry Samples, "City Man Named to Blanton Cabinet," *Johnson City Press*, Jan. 21, 1975, https://www.newspapers.com/image/589921297; John Haile, "Blanton Appointees Due Challenge?" *Tennessean*, Jan. 22, 1975, https://www.newspapers.com/image/108992343.

51. Associated Press, "Blanton's 'Unpaid' Aide Gets $21,000 Contract," *Jackson Sun*, March 21, 1975, https://www.newspapers.com/image/283187513; "'Unpaid' Aide's Hiring Defended by Blanton," *Knoxville News Sentinel*, March 22, 1975, https://www.newspapers.com/image/773975485.

52. Larry Daughtrey, "Blanton's Budget Target of Jibes," *Tennessean*, March 28, 1975, https://www.newspapers.com/image/109003448.

53. "Blanton Declares Faith in State," *Commercial Appeal*, March 5, 1975, https://www.newspapers.com/image/771513459.

54. United Press International, "Pie-Thrower Finds Joke Is a 'Lemon,'" *Knoxville News Sentinel*, April 18, 1975, https://www.newspapers.com/image/774053454.

55. Tim Wyngaard, "Blanton Ex-Aide Charges 'Tricks,'" *Knoxville News Sentinel*, Oct. 16, 1974, https://www.newspapers.com/image/773933152.

56. Morris Cunningham, "FBI to Investigate '72 Blanton Race," *Commercial Appeal*, April 25, 1975, https://www.newspapers.com/image/771523312; Tim Wyngaard, "Blanton Bid for Brock Aid 'Considered,'" *Knoxville News Sentinel*, April 26, 1975, https://www.newspapers.com/image/774054533; Tim Wyngaard, "Blanton Got $4000 from Truckers," *Knoxville News Sentinel*, April 27, 1975, https://www.

newspapers.com/image/774054570; United Press International, "Blanton Accused of Trying to Build Political Empire," *Kingsport Times*, April 28, 1975, https://www.newspapers.com/image/592746691.

57. Associated Press, "Gov. Blanton Won't Discuss Testimony," *Johnson City Press*, Oct. 23, 1975, https://www.newspapers.com/image/590342195; Hank Hillin, "Investigation of a Government," *Commercial Appeal*, Dec. 22, 1985, https://www.newspapers.com/image/773087183; Associated Press, "Judge Places Memphis Corporation on Probation for Illegal Donations," *Commercial Appeal*, Dec. 5, 1975, https://www.newspapers.com/image/771515782; Associated Press, "Federal Probe of Blanton Closes," *Johnson City Press*, Jan. 15, 1976, https://www.newspapers.com/image/590321376.

58. John Parish, "A Conflict of Interest?" *Jackson Sun*, Sept. 4, 1975, https://www.newspapers.com/image/283125600; Larry Daughtrey, "Blanton Names Panel to Guide Transition," *Tennessean*, Nov. 8, 1974, https://www.newspapers.com/image/111581926.

59. Joseph Weiler, "Blanton Family's Firm Hired without Bidding," *Commercial Appeal*, Nov. 22, 1975, https://www.newspapers.com/image/771520734.

60. "Tennessee Today: Nashville," *Kingsport Times*, Nov. 24, 1975, https://www.newspapers.com/image/592687902; "Job Granted Blanton's Kin Sparks Audit," *Commercial Appeal*, Nov. 25, 1975, https://www.newspapers.com/image/771527102; "Bid on Courts Said Submitted," *Tennessean*, Nov. 27, 1975, https://www.newspapers.com/image/112146269; Frank Sutherland, "Halt Ordered in Emergency State Buying," *Tennessean*, Nov. 26, 1975, https://www.newspapers.com/image/112146214; Joseph Weiler and Leon Munday, "Blanton Family Affair Found in Paving Bids; Single Typewriter Used," *Commercial Appeal*, Dec. 4, 1975, https://www.newspapers.com/image/771512378; Frank Sutherland, "Probe of Possible Collusion Ordered," *Tennessean*, Dec. 5, 1975, https://www.newspapers.com/image/112026237.

61. Bill Roberts, "Blanton Back at Home," *Jackson Sun*, Dec. 5, 1975, https://www.newspapers.com/image/283045220.

62. Frank Sutherland, "Plummer Blasts DA Charges of Purchasing Probe Interference," *Tennessean*, Dec. 7, 1975, https://www.newspapers.com/image/112027805.

63. Associated Press, "Only 4 Blanton Bills Passed In 1st 100 Days," *Jackson Sun*, April 27, 1975, https://www.newspapers.com/image/283021248; John Parish, "The 'Short' Session," *Jackson Sun*, May 30, 1975, https://www.newspapers.com/image/282946061; John Parish, "Blanton Appeals for Gas-Tax Support," *Jackson Sun*, June 10, 1975, https://www.newspapers.com/image/283013924.

64. John Haile, "General Assembly Convenes Tomorrow," *Tennessean*, Jan. 5, 1975, https://www.newspapers.com/image/108990556. Associated Press, "State Legislature Will Convene Facing Possible Tax Raises," *Johnson City Press*, Dec. 30, 1975, https://www.newspapers.com/image/590329623; John Parish, "Murray: 'Little Time Wasted,'" *Jackson Sun*, June 29, 1975, https://www.newspapers.com/image/283046178.

65. United Press International, "Lawmakers Give Blanton Low Marks in UPI Survey," *Kingsport Times*, Dec. 22, 1975, https://www.newspapers.com/image/592748888; Associated Press, "State Legislature Will Convene."

66. United Press International, "Blanton Says Charges Won't Drive Him Out," *Kingsport Times*, Dec. 5, 1975, https://www.newspapers.com/image/592735868.

67. Erik Schelzig and Associated Press, "Williams' Path to Speaker's Seat Full of Twists," *Jackson Sun*, Jan. 18, 2009, 4B, https://www.newspapers.com/image/284138079.

68. John Haile, "Blanton Forms Patronage Plan," *Tennessean*, Dec. 12, 1974, https://www.newspapers.com/image/111705262; Larry Daughtrey, "Former State Employees Tell GOP Legislators of 'Political Firings,'" *Tennessean*, Aug. 6, 1975, https://www.newspapers.com/image/112105303; Erik Schelzig and Associated Press, "Williams' Path to Speaker's Seat Full of Twists," *Jackson Sun*, Jan. 18, 2009, https://www.newspapers.com/image/284138079; Larry Daughtrey, "Big Trouble Is A-Brewing," *Tennessean*, March 9, 1975, https://www.newspapers.com/image/109020485.

69. "Liquor Licenses," *Tennessee Journal* 2, no. 18 (May 3, 1976).

70. United Press International, "Traveling Governor Hits Back," *Daily News Journal*, Dec. 12, 1977, https://www.newspapers.com/image/367693240; "Blanton," *Tennessee Journal* 4, no. 1 (Jan. 2, 1978); "Tennessee Notes," *Tennessee Journal* 4, no. 47 (Nov. 21, 1977).

71. John Triplett and A. B. Albritton, "Blanton, Aides Spare No Travel Cost," *Commercial Appeal*, Dec. 18, 1977, https://www.newspapers.com/image/771868441; John Triplett and A. B. Albritton, "Data Shows Blanton Takes a Flight Averaging Every Other Working Day," *Commercial Appeal*, Dec. 19, 1977, https://www.newspapers.com/image/771873142; Mark McNeely, "Blanton Pays for Use of Jet," *Knoxville News Sentinel*, May 20, 1978, https://www.newspapers.com/image/774156524.

72. John Triplett and A. B. Albritton, "Blanton Won't Allow 'Negative' Challenges by Press," *Commercial Appeal*, Dec. 20, 1977, https://www.newspapers.com/image/771874997.

73. John Haile, "From Start There Was Controversy," *Tennessean*, Dec. 24, 1978, https://www.newspapers.com/image/112179126

74. United Press International "Court Upholds Conviction in License Test Extortion," *Tennessean*, Sept. 30, 1977, https://www.newspapers.com/image/111496933.

75. John Haile and Patricia Welch, "State Clemency, Pardon Files Seized," *Tennessean*, Oct. 23, 1976, https://www.newspapers.com/image/111686066.

76. Associated Press, "FBI Seizes Blanton Legal Office Records," *Johnson City Press*, Oct. 23, 1976, https://www.newspapers.com/image/590244980; Associated Press, "FBI Checks Possibility of Payoffs for Easing Prisoners' Sentences," *Commercial Appeal*, Oct. 24, 1976, https://www.newspapers.com/image/771654058.

77. Associated Press, "FBI Checks Possibility of Payoffs"; Nancy Varley, "Blanton Aide Denies Pardon-Parole Payoff," *Tennessean*, Oct. 24, 1976, https://www.newspapers.com/image/111686426; Kenneth Jost, "Bar Has Recording of Alleged Peebles

Bribe Talk: Sources," *Tennessean*, April 25, 1975, https://www.newspapers.com/image/112042216.

78. Hank Hillin, "The Scheme Becomes Clear," *Commercial Appeal*, Dec. 23, 1985, https://www.newspapers.com/image/773088095.

79. United Press International, "Blanton Urges Levi to Enter Paroles Probe," *Commercial Appeal*, Oct. 27, 1976, https://www.newspapers.com/image/771654356.

80. Doug Hall and Marsha Vande Berg, "'Timing' of Files Seizure Denied by U.S. Attorney," *Tennessean*, Oct. 28, 1976, https://www.newspapers.com/image/111703014; United Press International, "Anderson Links Probe to 'Politics,'" *Commercial Appeal*, Oct. 28, 1976, https://www.newspapers.com/image/771654412.

81. Marsha Vande Berg, "Lebanon Mayor Recounts Day of Pardon Talk," *Tennessean*, Oct. 30, 1976, https://www.newspapers.com/image/111709781.

82. Larry Daughtrey and Marsha Vande Berg, "Official Taped Extradition 'Deal' for FBI," *Tennessean*, April 28, 1977, https://www.newspapers.com/image/112478060; Associated Press, "State to Probe Bribe as Fairness Measure," *Commercial Appeal*, April 28, 1977, https://www.newspapers.com/image/771676059.

83. "Ray Blanton FBI FOIA No. 1483477-000 Document 1," p. 10.

84. "Ray Blanton FBI FOIA No. 1483477-000 Document 1," pp. 10, 12.

85. "Ray Blanton FBI FOIA No. 1483477-000 Document 1," p. 9.

86. "Blanton Takes Hearing Power for Extradition," *Tennessean*, May 19, 1977, https://www.newspapers.com/image/111892271.

87. *Humphreys v. State of Tennessee*, Court of Criminal Appeals. Aug. 29, 1975, https://law.justia.com/cases/tennessee/court-of-criminal-appeals/1975/531-s-w-2d-127-0.html.

88. Keel Hunt, *Coup: The Day the Democrats Ousted Their Governor, Put Republican Lamar Alexander in Office Early, and Stopped a Pardon Scandal* (Nashville, TN: Vanderbilt University Press, 2017).

89. John Parish, "'Cronyism' Rep. Beard Decries Blanton's 'Mockery,'" *Jackson Sun*, Sept. 13, 1977, https://www.newspapers.com/image/283158356; William Bennett, "Panel Planning Study of Prisoner's Outside Job," *Commercial Appeal*, Sept. 14, 1977, https://www.newspapers.com/image/771939908; "Humphreys Developments," *Tennessee Journal* 3, no. 41 (Oct. 10, 1977).

90. "Tennessee Notes," *Tennessee Journal* 3, no. 36 (Sept. 5, 1975).

91. Bennett, "Panel Planning Study."

92. Doug Hall, "To Pardon Humphreys before Leaving Office, Blanton Says," *Tennessean*, Sept. 16, 1977, https://www.newspapers.com/image/111470936.

93. Nashville Bar Association, "Blanton CLE Blanton CLE | November 2016 | Blanton/Marin Full Interview (9-15-1977)," YouTube, posted November 2016, 13:50 to 13:59, https://www.youtube.com/watch?v=BaqfzM5gSPA.

94. "Parents Of Murder Victim Demand Pardon Be Dropped," *Times News*, Oct. 2, 1977, https://www.newspapers.com/image/592933087; Bill Rawlins and Associated Press, "GOP Has Store of Targets in Blanton-Humphreys Issue," *Knoxville News Sentinel*, Oct. 2, 1977, https://www.newspapers.com/image/774253802. United

Press International, "Alexander Urges Demos To Nix Blanton," *Times News*, Nov. 24, 1977, https://www.newspapers.com/image/68797087.

95. Doug Hall, "'Brash' Blanton Defends Pardon For Humphreys," *Tennessean*, Oct. 4, 1977, https://www.newspapers.com/image/112168354.

96. Doug Hall, "Tell 'Positive' News Also, Blanton Says," *Tennessean*, Dec. 20, 1977, https://www.newspapers.com/image/111569308.

97. Doug Hall, "Restrained Blanton 'Reminds' Press of Responsibility," *Tennessean*, Dec. 27, 1977, https://www.newspapers.com/image/111590891.

98. United Press International, "'More You Hit, Harder I Get,' Says Governor," *Commercial Appeal*, Jan. 2, 1978, https://www.newspapers.com/image/771681716.

99. United Press International, "Blanton Levels New Blast at Nation's News Media," *Times News*, April 14, 1978, https://www.newspapers.com/image/70757664.

100. Associated Press, "Blanton View of Media Is 'Slight Improvement,'" *Commercial Appeal*, April 30, 1978, https://www.newspapers.com/image/771865008.

101. United Press International, "Blanton Takes a Fall, Blames the News Media," *Kingsport Times*, Sept. 21, 1978, https://www.newspapers.com/image/592938787; "Tennessee Notes," *Tennessee Journal* 4, no. 46 (Nov. 13, 1978).

102. "Convention Opens Today," *Tennessean*, Aug. 1, 1977, https://www.newspapers.com/image/111783517.

103. Tre Hargett, *Tennessee Blue Book, 2021–20022* (Nashville, TN: State of Tennessee, 2021), https://publications.tnsosfiles.com/pub/blue_book/21-22/21-22tnpastgovs.pdf.

104. Larry Daughtrey, "Some Resist Ray Transfer: Blanton," *Tennessean*, July 2, 1977, https://www.newspapers.com/image/111800849; "Blanton Repeats Vow to Retire from Public Office," *Knoxville News Sentinel*, July 2, 1977, https://www.newspapers.com/image/774297687.

105. Associated Press, "Vote Is Viewed as Endorsement," *Commercial Appeal*, March 9, 1978, https://www.newspapers.com/image/771856734.

106. Associated Press, "Petitions for Blanton Circulating," *Johnson City Press*, April 28, 1978, https://www.newspapers.com/image/590450247; Doug Hall, "Official Admits UT Blanton Poll Data Withheld," *Tennessean*, April 21, 1978, https://www.newspapers.com/image/111101872; Duren Cheek, "Blanton: 'I Can Win 2nd Term If I Want It,'" *Times News*, May 7, 1978, https://www.newspapers.com/image/593054144.

107. Larry Daughtrey, "'I'll Not Run': Blanton—Emotional Speech Proudly Defends Administration," *Tennessean*, May 28, 1978, https://www.newspapers.com/image/112425998.

108. Daughtrey, "'I'll Not Run.'"

109. Kathleen Gallagher, "Pardons Probe End Seen Today," *Tennessean*, April 12, 1978, https://www.newspapers.com/image/112111294. "No Indictments Expected In Pardons-Paroles Probe," *Tennessean*, April 13, 1978, https://www.newspapers.com/image/112111593.

110. Carolyn Shoulders, "Pardons Board Votes Said Changed: Henry," *Tennessean*, June 29, 1978, https://www.newspapers.com/image/112205314.

111. Shoulders, "Pardons Board Votes."

112. United Press International, "Signed False Claims, Ex-Pardon Chief Says," *Kingsport Times*, June 30, 1978, https://www.newspapers.com/image/593064513; Kirk Loggins, "Sisk: Saw No Need for Probe of 'Solicitation,'" *Tennessean*, July 4, 1978, https://www.newspapers.com/image/111289427; Associated Press, "Ousted Parole Official Is Ordered Reinstated," *Commercial Appeal*, July 7, 1978, https://www.newspapers.com/image/772208297.

113. Linda Wallace and Dan Henderson, "Blanton Again Pledges Pardon," *Commercial Appeal*, Sept. 7, 1978, https://www.newspapers.com/image/772210009; Mark McNeely, "'Opposed to Humphreys Pardon, Will Sign Petition against It,' Butcher Says," *Knoxville News Sentinel*, Sept. 17, 1978, https://www.newspapers.com/image/774244511.

114. John Parish, "Stop-Pardon Drive Aimed at Blanton," *Jackson Sun*, Sept. 15, 1978, https://www.newspapers.com/image/284485328.

115. "Governor Turns 'Iffy' on Humphreys Pardon," *Knoxville News Sentinel*, Oct. 24, 1978, https://www.newspapers.com/image/774279861; "Blanton Decides against Pardon for Humphreys," *Knoxville News Sentinel*, Oct. 31, 1978, https://www.newspapers.com/image/774281871.

116. "Local Reaction Guarded on Blanton Pardon Move," *Kingsport Times*, Nov. 1, 1978, https://www.newspapers.com/image/595541750.

117. Charles Fontenay, "Democrats Mulling Alexander's Landslide," *Tennessean*, Nov. 9, 1978, https://www.newspapers.com/image/112170972; Larry Daughtrey, "It's Baker, Alexander! Democrats Aid in Easy Victory for Alexander," *Tennessean*, Nov. 8, 1978, https://www.newspapers.com/image/112170880.

118. John Parish, "Blanton Blamed for Landslide," *Jackson Sun*, Nov. 10, 1978, https://www.newspapers.com/image/284480527.

119. Larry Daughtrey, "It's Baker, Alexander!".

120. Doug Hall, "Alexander to Bring Cool Control to Job," *Tennessean*, Nov. 8, 1978, https://www.newspapers.com/image/112170543.

121. Larry Daughtrey and Jim O'Hara, "Blanton, Alexander Take Stands on Issues," *Tennessean*, Nov. 3, 1974, https://www.newspapers.com/image/111562017; Hall, "Alexander to Bring Cool Control."

122. United Press International, "Alexander Meets 'Gracious' Blanton, Talks Transition," *Kingsport Times*, Nov. 9, 1978, https://www.newspapers.com/image/595543597.

123. Kirk Loggins, "Some in Clerk-Office Quiz Said to Have Legal Woes," *Tennessean*, Nov. 9, 1978, https://www.newspapers.com/image/112170972.

124. United Press International, "Blanton May Still Free Humphreys," *Kingsport Times*, Nov. 17, 1978, https://www.newspapers.com/image/595544942

125. Associated Press, "Hooker Asks Censure Move, if Humphreys Freed," *Johnson City Press*, Nov. 21, 1978, https://www.newspapers.com/image/590345621.

126. Alan Bostick, "No Dillydallying: Fate Jailed," *Tennessean*, Sept. 28, 1990, https://www.newspapers.com/image/112780498; Ted Riggs, "Glenn, Vols' No. 14, Was Once Inmate 81177," *Knoxville News Sentinel*, Dec. 5, 1978, https://www.newspapers.com/image/774246015.

127. Larry Daughtrey and Doug Hall, "FBI Nabs Blanton Aides," *Tennessean*, Dec. 16, 1978, https://www.newspapers.com/image/112175037.

128. Alan Carmichael, "State Leaders Ask Accused Aides to Quit," *Tennessean*, Dec. 17, 1978, https://www.newspapers.com/image/112175202; Associated Press, "Ray Escapes from State Prison," *Johnson City Press*, June 11, 1977, https://www.newspapers.com/image/590277751.

129. "FBI Says State Pardons Probe May Be 'Only Tip of Iceberg,'" *Commercial Appeal*, Dec. 17, 1978, https://www.newspapers.com/image/772193714.

130. United Press International, "Blanton's Pardons Set Record, More Likely," *Knoxville News Sentinel*, Dec. 23, 1978, https://www.newspapers.com/image/774248193.

131. Associated Press, "Blanton Testifies in Parole Scandal," *Johnson City Press*, Dec. 23, 1978, https://www.newspapers.com/image/590375470.

132. Hank Hillin, "The Scheme Becomes Clear," *Commercial Appeal*, Dec. 23, 1985, https://www.newspapers.com/image/773088095.

133. Kirk Loggins, "Hooker Asks Blanton to Resign, Brandt to Govern Clemencies," *Tennessean*, Dec. 20, 1978, https://www.newspapers.com/image/112177953.

134. Kirk Loggins, "Brand Asked to 'Be Governor' in Executive Clemency Matters," *Tennessean*, Dec. 20, 1978, https://www.newspapers.com/image/112177558.

135. Larry Daughtrey and Doug Hall, "Blanton: 'I'm A Target,'" *Tennessean*, Jan. 6, 1979, https://www.newspapers.com/image/111490665.

136. William Bennett, "Emotional Blanton Emphasizes Progress," *Commercial Appeal*, Jan. 11, 1979, https://www.newspapers.com/image/772115572.

137. John Haile, "Blanton: 'Proud of Record, Never Willingly Hurt State,'" *Tennessean*, Jan. 11, 1979, https://www.newspapers.com/image/111705262.

138. Doug Hall and Carolyn Shoulders, "Blanton Asks Humphreys, Denton Files," *Tennessean*, Jan. 12, 1979, https://www.newspapers.com/image/111501518; United Press International, "Blanton's Legal Counsel Prepares Clemency Papers," *Times News*, Jan. 13, 1979, https://www.newspapers.com/image/593624344.

139. United Press International, "Commutation Papers Prepared for All 16 Convicts Working for Governor," *Knoxville News Sentinel*, Jan. 13, 1979, https://www.newspapers.com/image/774130804.

140. "Vast Clemency Move May Up Inaugural Date," *Tennessean*, Jan. 14, 1979, https://www.newspapers.com/image/111503065.

141. "No Early Inaugural Plans Being Made," *Knoxville News Sentinel*, Jan. 15, 1979, https://www.newspapers.com/image/774131153.

142. Doug Hall, "Blanton Frees Humphreys; Clemency for 51 Others," *Tennessean*, Jan. 16, 1979, https://www.newspapers.com/image/111834461.

143. Doug Hall, "More Guts Than Brains, Responds Crowell," *Tennessean*, Jan. 17, 1979, https://www.newspapers.com/image/111835417.

144. Hall, "Blanton Frees Humphreys."

145. Hall, "Blanton Frees Humphreys."

146. Alan Carmichael, "'Sickening,' Alexander's Reaction," *Tennessean*, Jan. 16, 1979, https://www.newspapers.com/image/111834461; "Reaction to Blanton's Action Is Overwhelmingly Negative," Jan. 16, 1979, https://www.newspapers.com/

image/774131238; Jim Dykes, "Superlatives Used in Condemnation of Blanton's Action," *Knoxville News Sentinel*, Jan. 16, 1979, https://www.newspapers.com/image/774131241; United Press International, "Blanton May Add 18 More to Clemency List," *Kingsport Times*, Jan. 17, 1979, https://www.newspapers.com/image/593628473.

147. John Haile and Dwight Lewis, "Convicts Start Exodus, Revoke Move Studied." *Tennessean*. Jan. 17, 1979, https://www.newspapers.com/image/111835004; "Blanton Grants Clemency To 52 Tennessee Convicts," *New York Times*, Jan. 17, 1979, https://www.nytimes.com/1979/01/17/archives/blanton-grants-clemency-to-52-tennessee-convicts-commutations.html.

148. Larry Daughtrey, "'Inappropriate' Oath Rejected by Alexander," *Tennessean*, Jan. 16, 1979, https://www.newspapers.com/image/111834461.

149. Doug Hall, "Blanton Frees Humphreys; Clemency for 51 Others," *Tennessean*, Jan. 16, 1979, https://www.newspapers.com/image/111834461.

150. Joel Ebert, "A Coup in Tennessee," *Tennessean*, Jan. 17, 2019, https://www.newspapers.com/image/591276736.

151. Ebert interview with Alexander, November 2018.

152. Ebert interview with Alexander, November 2018.

153. Ebert interview with Alexander, November 2018.

154. Ebert interview with Hal Hardin, November 2018.

155. Hunt, *Coup*, 187.

156. Ebert interview with David Fox, November 2018.

157. Hunt, *Coup*, 192–93. Ebert interview with Bill Koch, November 2018.

158. Larry Daughtrey and Doug Hall, "Alexander Sworn In; Blanton Pushed Out," *Tennessean*, Jan. 18, 1979, https://www.newspapers.com/image/111835703.

159. Delores Ballard, "'Pardon Me, Ray,'" *Jackson Sun*, Jan. 23, 1979, https://www.newspapers.com/image/284489248.

160. Ballard, "'Pardon Me, Ray.'"

161. "Johnny's Gibes," *Tennessean*, Jan. 20, 1979, 4, https://www.newspapers.com/image/111837908.

162. United Press International, "Pardon Probe Report Due Today Or Friday," *Kingsport Times*, March 15, 1979, https://www.newspapers.com/image/592821795. Kathleen Gallagher, "Pardons Jury Indicts 6," *Tennessean*, March 16, 1979, https://www.newspapers.com/image/111479657.

163. Gallagher, "Pardons Jury Indicts 6." https://www.newspapers.com/image/111479657.

164. United Press International, "New Clemency Trial Ordered," *Tennessean*, Sept. 5, 1979, https://www.newspapers.com/image/772158706.

165. Associated Press, "Plea Bargain Brings Testimony against Sisk in Clemency Case," *Johnson City Press*, Feb. 7, 1981, https://www.newspapers.com/image/590924425.

166. United Press International, "Blanton Aide, Trooper Plead Guilty in Scandal," *Times News*, March 12, 1981, https://www.newspapers.com/image/594235639; Carol Clurman, "My Spirit Broken, Tearful Sisk Says as 5 Years Meted," *Tennessean*, July 2, 1981, https://www.newspapers.com/image/112246068.

167. Adell Crowe, "Benson Smile Tells Blanton: 'I'm Innocent,'" *Tennessean*, May 2, 1981, https://www.newspapers.com/image/112212948.

168. "Murrell Receives 2 Years In Prison Plus $7,500 Fine," *Tennessean*, Oct. 11, 1979, https://www.newspapers.com/image/112239596.

169. United Press International, "Blanton Sentence Climax to Five Years of Probes," *Knoxville News Sentinel*, Aug. 16, 1981, https://www.newspapers.com/image/774495297.

170. Associated Press, "'Most Investigated Governor' Boasted of Non-Indictments," *Knoxville News Sentinel*, Oct. 30, 1980, https://www.newspapers.com/image/774499147.

171. David Lyons, "Blanton Indicted on Federal Tax, Liquor License Charges," *Knoxville News Sentinel*, Oct. 30, 1980, https://www.newspapers.com/image/774499144; Carol Clurman, "Blanton Indicted," *Tennessean*, Oct. 30, 1980, https://www.newspapers.com/image/111986687.

172. United Press International, "Jury Finds Blanton guilty," *Times News*, June 10, 1981, https://www.newspapers.com/image/594214697.

173. "A Black Mark on Tennessee," *Knoxville News Sentinel*, Nov. 1, 1980, https://www.newspapers.com/image/774256056; Joel Kaplan, "Gene Blanton Requests Trial Site Change," *Tennessean*, June 12, 1981, https://www.newspapers.com/image/112230891; United Press International, "Jury Finds Blanton Guilty"; Carol Clurman and Joel Kaplan, "Blanton Guilty," *Tennessean*, June 10, 1981, https://www.newspapers.com/image/112225304.

174. Carol Clurman, "Blanton Receives 3-Year Terms in Silence," *Tennessean*, Aug. 15, 1981, https://www.newspapers.com/image/112216116; United Press International, "Ray Blanton Draws 3-Year Prison Term," *Knoxville News Sentinel*, Aug. 15, 1981, https://www.newspapers.com/image/774495183.

175. Dwight Lewis, "Halfway House the Next Stop for Ray Blanton," *Tennessean*, May 14, 1986, https://www.newspapers.com/image/112445671; Alan Bostick, "9 Blanton Mail Fraud Convictions Set Aside," *Tennessean.* Jan. 29, 1988, A1, https://www.newspapers.com/image/112358519.

176. Woody Baird, "Ex-Gov. Ray Blanton Running for Congress," *Knoxville News Sentinel*, May 22, 1988, https://www.newspapers.com/image/774799008.

177. Jim O'Hara and Dwight Lewis, "Tanner Swamps Blanton's Hopes," *Tennessean*, Aug. 5, 1988, https://www.newspapers.com/image/112459830.

178. Richard Locker, "Blanton Still Paying Dues," *Commercial Appeal*, April 2, 1989, https://www.newspapers.com/image/773632915; Terry Keeter, "From Governor to New-Car Salesman, Blanton Survives Seesaw Existence," *Commercial Appeal*, Nov. 17, 1990, https://www.newspapers.com/image/773721378; "Alimony Problem Lands Blanton Back behind Bars," *Jackson Sun*, Feb. 9, 1991, https://www.newspapers.com/image/284035448.

179. Phil Williams, "Even Despicable Governors Deserve a Fair Trial," *Tennessean*, Jan. 12, 1992, https://www.newspapers.com/image/112513761; Paula Wade, "Ray Blanton Loses Bid to Clear Name of Federal Convictions," *Commercial Appeal*, Nov. 17,

1993, https://www.newspapers.com/image/774324572; Associated Press, "Blanton Fails to Get Convictions Erased," *Commercial Appeal*, Aug. 29, 1996, https://www. newspapers.com/image/774555702.

180. W. Matt Meyer, "Blanton: A Legacy of Service, scandal," *Jackson Sun*, Nov. 23, 1996, https://www.newspapers.com/image/282247819.

181. In re: Chattanooga Police Complaint No. 79-8071, Criminal Court of Hamilton County, Case No. 311550, June 7, 2021, https://www.courthousenews.com/wp-content/uploads/2021/06/William-Edward-Alley.pdf.

182. Associated Press, "Two Charged in 1979 Murder of Crime Figure," *Johnson City Press*, Oct. 28, 1992, https://www.newspapers.com/image/590791483; In re: Chattanooga Police Complaint No. 79-8071.

183. In re: Chattanooga Police Complaint No. 79-8071; Kathleen Gallagher, "Two More Called in Pardons, Paroles Probe," *Tennessean*, July 22, 1977, https://www. newspapers.com/image/111793323.

184. In re: Chattanooga Police Complaint No. 79-8071.

185. Hank Hillin, *FBI Codename TennPar* (Nashville, TN: Pine Hall Press), 411.


CHAPTER 2

1. Don Doyle, "Tennessee Centennial Exposition," Tennessee Encyclopedia, last updated March 1, 2018, https://tennesseeencyclopedia.net/entries/ tennessee-centennial-exposition.

2. "Fair Article Surprises Bankers, Mayor Say," *Knoxville News Sentinel*, Dec. 31, 1980, A1, https://www.newspapers.com/image/774458919.

3. Charles Siler, "Go Up, Up and Around on Fair's Giant Wheel," *Knoxville News Sentinel*, April 2, 1982, https://www.newspapers.com/image/774345673; Jennifer Bradley, "(Re)imagining an Urban Identity: Knoxville and Its 1982 International Energy Exposition," Master's Thesis, University of Tennessee, 2003, https://trace. tennessee.edu/utk_gradthes/5197 https://trace.tennessee.edu/cgi/viewcontent. cgi?article=6605&context=utk_gradthes; Wendell Rawls Jr, "Pomp and Festivity Prevail as Knoxville Opens World's Fair," *New York Times*, May 2, 1982, https:// www.nytimes.com/1982/05/02/us/pomp-and-festivity-prevail-as-knoxville-opens-world-s-fair.html.

4. Jan Maxwell Avent, "City Population Figure Corrected; It's 175,045," *Knoxville News Sentinel*, Sept. 9, 1982, https://www.newspapers.com/image/774343591.

5. Richard Powelson, "Reagan Opens Fair with Plea for Peace," *Knoxville News Sentinel*, May 2, 1982, https://www.newspapers.com/image/774327188; Ronald Reagan, "Remarks at the Opening Ceremonies for the Knoxville International Energy Exposition (World's Fair) in Tennessee," Ronald Reagan Presidential Library and Museum, May 1, 1982, https://www.reaganlibrary.gov/archives/speech/ remarks-opening-ceremonies-knoxville-international-energy-exposition-worlds-fair.

6. Tom Zito, "The World's Fair: In Search of Energy," *Washington Post*, May 3, 1982, https://www.washingtonpost.com/archive/lifestyle/1982/05/03/

the-worlds-fair-in-search-of-energy/58d8ca21-bf02-475e-9447-40cc57a59ff6; Avent, "City Population Figure Corrected"; Powelson, "Reagan Opens Fair"; Reagan, "Remarks at the Opening Ceremonies"; Zito, "The World's Fair."

7. "Basic & Fun Facts Regarding the Fair," City of Knoxville, accessed Feb. 23, 2023, https://knoxvilletn.gov/visitors/knoxville_info/1982_worlds_fair.

8. Frank Sutherland, "Butcher Said Eyed for Commerce Post," *Tennessean*, Dec. 1, 1976, https://www.newspapers.com/image/111687965.

9. Associated Press, "Reaganomics 'a Failure All Around': Carter" *Daily News Journal*, Oct. 10, 1982, https://www.newspapers.com/image/393604828; Joel Kaplan and Bob Hetherington, "Jake's Fair and Notell Motel Ltd.," *Tennessean*, Nov. 10, 1983, https://www.newspapers.com/image/112392691.

10. "'Scruffy Little City' Did It; Fair Hits Goal," *Tennessean*, Nov. 1, 1982, https://www.newspapers.com/image/112452144; "Basic & Fun Facts Regarding the Fair."

11. "'Scruffy Little City' Did It."

12. James Coates and Andy Knott, "Financing of 'Jake's Fair' a Web of Many Strands," *Tennessean*, April 4, 1982, https://www.newspapers.com/image/112258377.

13. Larry Daughtrey and Thomas Chester, "1982 Was the Year of the Peak," *Tennessean*, Oct. 24, 1983, https://www.newspapers.com/image/112387690.

14. Alan Hall, "Cozy Ties, Examination Warnings," *Tennessean*, Nov. 8, 1983, https://www.newspapers.com/image/112386904; Daughtrey and Chester, "1982 Was the Year of the Peak."

15. Daughtrey and Chester, "1982 Was the Year of the Peak"; Jim Balloch, "Butcher Dies after Falling," *Knoxville News Sentinel*, May 1, 2002, https://www.newspapers.com/image/776117908.

16. Sandra Roberts, "Patriarch Stays Put in Union," *Tennessean*, Nov. 1, 1983, https://www.newspapers.com/image/112359672.

17. Daughtrey and Chester, "1982 Was the Year of the Peak."

18. Daughtrey and Chester, "1982 Was the Year of the Peak."

19. Larry Daughtrey, "Showdown Coming Up," *Tennessean*, Jan. 10, 1971, https://www.newspapers.com/image/111893288.

20. "Jake Butcher Is Candidate," *Leaf Chronicle*, May 2, 1974, https://www.newspapers.com/image/353500066.

21. Associated Press, "Jake Butcher May Seek Seat," *Memphis Press-Scimitar*, Aug. 26, 1974, https://www.newspapers.com/image/800233866.

22. William Bennett, "Butcher Takes Primary Offensive as Clement Retreats Some," *Commercial Appeal*, July 14, 1978, https://www.newspapers.com/image/772218721.

23. Bennett, "Butcher Takes Primary Offensive."

24. "Tennessee Notes," *Tennessee Journal* 4, no. 44 (Oct. 30, 1978): 4.

25. Jake Butcher, "Butcher Seeks Unity," *Daily News Journal*, Nov. 30, 1978, https://www.newspapers.com/image/367684872.

26. Butcher, "Butcher Seeks Unity."

27. Daughtrey and Chester, "1982 Was the Year of the Peak."

28. Associated Press, "A Climb from Hay Bales to Millions Tumbled in '83," *Jackson Sun*, Nov. 14, 1984, https://www.newspapers.com/image/283619912.

29. "Butcher Named to Inaugural Finance Unit, 'Has Discussed' Cabinet Post," *Knoxville News Sentinel*, Dec. 1, 1976, https://www.newspapers.com/image/774117893.

30. James Pratt and Joel Kaplan, "State Deposits Flowed to Banks," *Tennessean*, Nov. 3, 1983, https://www.newspapers.com/image/112365068.

31. Hall, "Cozy Ties, Examination Warnings."

32. Bob Hetherington, "Regulators Bring Down the Giant," *Tennessean*, Nov. 7, 1983, https://www.newspapers.com/image/112384756.

33. "Jake Butcher's Knox Bank Undergoing Federal Audit," *Tennessean*, Nov. 6, 1982, https://www.newspapers.com/image/112464101.

34. "Jake Butcher's Knox Bank."

35. Larry Daughtrey and Thomas Chester, "Chamber of Horrors," *Tennessean*, Nov. 9, 1983, https://www.newspapers.com/image/112389257.

36. Daughtrey and Chester, "1982 Was the Year of the Peak."

37. "$2.2 Million Loss for '82 Reported by Butcher Bank." *Commercial Appeal*, Jan. 29, 1983, https://www.newspapers.com/image/772593751.

38. Advertisement, "At United American Bank, There Are Two Ways of Looking at Money Market Accounts," *Knoxville News Sentinel*, Feb. 6, 1983, https://www.newspapers.com/image/774352095. Advertisement, "United American Bank," *Knoxville News Sentinel*, Feb. 13, 1983, https://www.newspapers.com/image/774354754.

39. Jack Maltby, "United American Files Petition against FDIC," *Times News*, Feb. 10, 1983, https://www.newspapers.com/image/594216398.

40. Jane Gibbs DuBose and Charles Siler, "Insolvent UAB Closed," *Knoxville News Sentinel*, Feb. 14, 1983, https://www.newspapers.com/image/774355773.

41. Tom Eblen, "UAB Open after Its Merger," *Daily News Journal*, Feb 15, 1983, https://www.newspapers.com/image/393731270.

42. "Jake Butcher Wins Award," *Commercial Appeal*, Feb. 26, 1983, https://www.newspapers.com/image/766888583.

43. United Press International, "Congressional Panel to Probe Butcher Banks," *Times News*, June 2, 1983, https://www.newspapers.com/image/595652400.

44. James Pratt, "Butcher, Associate Bankrupt," *Tennessean*, Aug. 23, 1983, https://www.newspapers.com/image/111792653; Lois Reagan Thomas, "C. H. Butcher Jr. Bankrupt; Assets to Be Liquidated," *Knoxville News Sentinel*, July 15, 1983 https://www.newspapers.com/image/774342586.

45. Associated Press, "Jake Butcher's Llamas Auctioned for $4,100," *Johnson City Press*, Dec. 29, 1983, https://www.newspapers.com/image/591152954; "Jake Butcher Moves to Luxury Home in Orlando," *Miami Herald*, June 20, 1983, https://www.newspapers.com/image/623329979.

46. Larry Daughtrey and James Pratt, "Butcher, Aides Indicted," *Tennessean*, Nov. 14, 1984, https://www.newspapers.com/image/111531001.

47. Ike Flores, "2 Bankers' Releases Not Likely," *Johnson City Press*, March 22, 1990, https://www.newspapers.com/image/591771162.

48. Jim Balloch, "No Bail for C. H. Butcher Jr," *Knoxville News Sentinel*, Feb. 6, 1986, https://www.newspapers.com/image/774608487; Jim Balloch, "Butcher Clan

Arrested," *Knoxville News Sentinel*, Feb. 14, 1986, https://www.newspapers.com/image/774610730; "C. H. Butcher Jr. Chronology," *Knoxville News Sentinel*, Sept. 1, 1986, https://www.newspapers.com/image/774825575.

49. "C. H. Butcher Jr. Chronology"; James Pratt, "State Gives Butcher Jr. 5 Years," *Tennessean*, April 29, 1987, https://www.newspapers.com/image/112392983.

50. Kristi Umbreit, "Butcher, 2 Others Indicted, Including Rep. Duncan's Son," *Tennessean*, June 19, 1986, https://www.newspapers.com/image/112339843; Jim Balloch, "Butcher, Steiner Not Guilty," *Knoxville News Sentinel*, Aug. 31, 1986, https://www.newspapers.com/image/774914040.

51. Steve Baker, "Rep. Ford, Butcher Indicted," *Johnson City Press*, April 25, 1987, https://www.newspapers.com/image/591021156.

52. Pratt, "State Gives Butcher Jr. 5 Years"; Shirley Downing, "Judge Declares Ford Mistrial after Second Juror Dismissed," *Commercial Appeal*, April 28, 1990, https://www.newspapers.com/image/773839535; Woody Baird, "Congressman Cleared of Corruption Charges," Associated Press, April 9, 1993, https://apnews.com/article/6b1f63d7570b612ed4245907b1481f6c.

53. "C. H. Butcher Jr. to Serve Sentence in Florida," *Knoxville News Sentinel*, July 16, 1987, https://www.newspapers.com/image/774820208; "C. H. Butcher Jr. Freed after 7 Years of 20-Year Term," *Tennessean*, Feb. 4, 1983, https://www.newspapers.com/image/113041912; Elizabeth Davis, "C. H. Butcher Dies after Apparent Fall," *Tennessean*, May 1, 2002, https://www.newspapers.com/image/112709778.

54. Jim Balloch, "Jake Butcher Quietly Paroled," *Knoxville News Sentinel*, May 1, 1992, https://www.newspapers.com/image/775194167; Barbara Aston-Wash, "Butcher Surveys Decade: Devastation and Healing," *Knoxville News Sentinel*, May 10, 1992, https://www.newspapers.com/image/775199289.

55. Matt Lakin, "Jake Butcher, Disgraced Banking Kingpin, Dies," *Knoxville News Sentinel*, July 20, 2017, https://www.newspapers.com/image/319671823.

## CHAPTER 3

1. Joel Ebert, "Randy McNally Set to Fill Large Boots," *Tennessean*, January 1, 2017, https://www.tennessean.com/story/news/politics/2017/01/07/randy-mcnally-set-fill-large-boots-tennessees-next-lieutenant-governor/96105922.

2. Joel Ebert interview with Randy McNally, Dec 9, 2016.

3. Joel Ebert interview with Randy McNally, Dec 9, 2016.

4. John Haile, "Despite GOP Gains Assembly Remains Democratic," *Tennessean*, Nov. 8, 1978 https://www.newspapers.com/image/112170535.

5. Woody Register, "No State Law to Stop False Drug Sales," *Tennessean*, April 8, 1981, https://www.newspapers.com/image/112279670; Marsha Vande Berg and Joel Kaplan, "House Approves Congress' Seats Revamp Plan," *Tennessean*, June 18, 1981, https://www.newspapers.com/image/112199024.

6. Jim O'Hara, "Burnett's Post May Be Left Unoccupied, *Tennessean*, Dec. 16, 1982, https://www.newspapers.com/image/113489163; "Building with Brock Abandoned by GOP," *Johnson City Press-Chronicle*, Nov. 11, 1982, https://www.newspapers.

com/image/590795806; "GOP Names Scruggs, Henry in House," *Tennessean*, Nov. 29, 1984, https://www.newspapers.com/image/112213761.

7. Ed Cromer, "Heart Attack Kills Lawmaker," *Tennessean*, May 8, 1984, https://www.newspapers.com/image/112330038.

8. Joel Ebert interview with Phil Williams, July 2019; "Starring Undercover Role Pulls a Senator from Obscurity," *Tennessean*, Dec. 3, 1989, https://www.newspapers.com/image/112466666.

9. Jacob D. Baggett, "Federal Program Bribery, New Federalism, and the Missing Federal Interest," *Lincoln Memorial University Law Review* 4, no. 1 (2016), https://digitalcommons.lmunet.edu/lmulrev/vol4/iss1/5.

10. Lewis L. Laska, "Lotteries," *Tennessee Encyclopedia*, accessed Aug. 28, 2021 https://tennesseeencyclopedia.net/entries/lotteries.

11. Laska, "Lotteries."

12. Case Law Access Project, https://cite.case.law/tenn/10/272; Timothy S. Huebner, "John Catron," *Tennessee Encyclopedia*, accessed Aug. 28, 2021 https://tennesseeencyclopedia.net/entries/john-catron; State v. Smith (1829), Case Law Access Project, https://cite.case.law/tenn/10/272.

13. *State v. Smith* (1829), Case Law Access Project, https://cite.case.law/tenn/10/272.

14. Huebner, "John Catron"; "Events Related to Betting in Tennessee," *Johnson City Press*, July 6, 1998, https://www.newspapers.com/image/284462197.

15. Huebner, "John Catron."

16. Chris French, "Memphis Legislator Pockets Busing Bill," *Jackson Sun*, March 5, 1972, https://www.newspapers.com/image/284462197.

17. "Pinball Gambling," *Tennessee Journal* 3, no. 11 (March 14, 1977): 3.

18. Larry Daughtrey, "Pinball, Bingo Games Illegal In June 1982," *Tennessean*, May 18, 1979, https://www.newspapers.com/image/111471561.

19. Jim O'Hara, "Yearly Reform Efforts Seem to Cloud Bingo Law More," *Tennessean*, May 22, 1987, https://www.newspapers.com/image/112952353; Dwight Lewis, "Bingo Games Get at Least 30-Day Reprieve," *Tennessean*, Jan. 19, 1980, https://www.newspapers.com/image/112132906.

20. "Alexander Signs Legal Bingo Law," *Tennessean*, March 28, 1980, https://www.newspapers.com/image/111991345; "Estimated 800 Organizations Rushing to Gain Bingo Permits," *Tennessean*, June 11, 1980, https://www.newspapers.com/image/111909847.

21. Joel Kaplan, "Bingo Expenses Ruled at Only 25% of Receipts," *Tennessean*, Oct. 28, 1981, https://www.newspapers.com/image/111829289.

22. Kaplan, "Bingo Expenses Ruled."

23. Kaplan, "Bingo Expenses Ruled."

24. Associated Press, "Bingo Law Could Cast Wider Net," *Commercial Appeal*, June 3, 1982, https://www.newspapers.com/image/772460134; Fred Travis, "Legalized Horse, Dog Racing Bites the Dust Again," *Johnson City Press*, April 22, 1982, https://www.newspapers.com/image/590627748.

25. Joel Kaplan, "Racing Bill on Fast Track; for Bingo: Shaky Reprieve," *Tennessean*, April 26, 1984, https://www.newspapers.com/image/112344769; Joel Kaplan,

"Crowell Says Permits Soon to Be Revoked," *Tennessean*, April 27, 1984, https://www.newspapers.com/image/112349525.

26. Kaplan, "Crowell Says Permits"; Kirk Loggins, "Churches File Suit to Retain Bingo Permits," *Tennessean*, May 25, 1984 https://www.newspapers.com/image/112347957; "Bingo Is Ruled Constitutional," *Knoxville News Sentinel*, Oct. 4, 1984, https://www.newspapers.com/image/774618709.

27. Jim O'Hara, "Tentative Lift Given to Bingo," *Tennessean*, Jan. 30, 1985, https://www.newspapers.com/image/109007542; Jim O'Hara, "Bingo Bill Awaits Governor's Action," *Tennessean*, March 12, 1985, https://www.newspapers.com/image/109006060; "Alexander Won't Sign Snow Days Bill," *Tennessean*, March 27, 1985, https://www.newspapers.com/image/109008553.

28. Associated Press, "Bingo Law Appeal Ended; Statute Revision Cited," *Tennessean*, April 5, 1985, https://www.newspapers.com/image/112577674.

29. Kirk Loggins, "2 'Church' Groups Probed on Bingo," *Tennessean*, Feb. 27, 1985, https://www.newspapers.com/image/109004328; "Church Bingo Operations Reportedly Under Probe," *Tennessean*, March 19, 1985, https://www.newspapers.com/image/108997192; "State, U.S. Officials Eying Bingo Industry," *Leaf Chronicle*, April 9, 1985, https://www.newspapers.com/image/367123055.

30. "Bingo Probed in Memphis, Paper Says," *Jackson Sun*, May 22, 1985, https://www.newspapers.com/image/283993519; Joel Kaplan, "Sitting Judge Memphis Bingo Probe Subject," *Tennessean*, June 21, 1985, https://www.newspapers.com/image/112739101.

31. Joel Ebert interview with Randy McNally, Dec 9, 2016.

32. Joel Ebert interview with Randy McNally, Dec 9, 2016.

33. Joel Ebert interview with Jim O'Hara and Tom Humphrey, July 2019.

34. Joel Ebert interview with Jim O'Hara and Tom Humphrey, July 2019. Joel Ebert interview with Phil Williams, July 2019.

35. Joel Ebert interview with Phil Williams, July 2019.

36. Joel Ebert interview with Randy McNally, Dec. 9, 2016.

37. "Celebrating 100 Years of Women's Suffrage," The Hermitage Hotel, accessed March 17, 2023, https://www.thehermitagehotel.com/historic-hotel-nashville/womens-suffrage; "The History of The Hermitage Hotel," The Hermitage Hotel, accessed Aug. 27, 2021, https://www.thehermitagehotel.com/our-history.htm.

38. Joel Ebert interview with Randy McNally, Dec 9, 2016

39. Joel Ebert interview with Richard Knudsen, July 2019

40. "History," The Regas Building, accessed Aug. 27, 2021, https://theregasbuilding.org/history.

41. Joel Ebert interview with Randy McNally, July 2019.

42. Dave Boucher and Joel Ebert, "Power Opens Door to Abuse," *Tennessean*, Aug. 22, 2016, https://www.newspapers.com/image/217923123.

43. Joel Ebert interview with Jim O'Hara, July 2019.

44. Jacob D. Baggett, "Federal Program Bribery, New Federalism, and the Missing Federal Interest," *Lincoln Memorial University Law Review* 4, no. 1 (Fall 2016),

https://digitalcommons.lmunet.edu/cgi/viewcontent.cgi?article=1069&context =lmulrev; Joel Ebert interview with Randy McNally, Dec. 9, 2016.

45. Patrick Reardon and Ray Gibson, "Raymond's Tale Is One of Take and Give," *Chicago Tribune*, Jan. 20, 1986, https://www.newspapers.com/image/388920569; Joseph Fried, "Michael Burnett, 67, Criminal who Exposed City Corruption," *New York Times*, Nov. 2, 1996, https://www.nytimes.com/1996/11/02/nyregion/michael-burnett-67-criminal-who-exposed-city-corruption.html.

46. Joel Ebert interview with Richard Knudsen, July 2019.

47. Jim O'Hara, "FBI Agent Gave Money to Parties," *Tennessean*, Oct. 30, 1989, https://www.newspapers.com/image/112512616; "A 'Rather Brilliant Fellow' Infiltrated the Bingo Brass," *Tennessean*, Dec. 3, 1989, https://www.newspapers.com/ image/112466666; Phil Williams, "FBI in Lawmakers' Midst," *Tennessean*, July 30, 1989, https://www.newspapers.com/image/112505245.

48. O'Hara, "FBI Agent Gave Money"; "A 'Rather Brilliant Fellow'"; Williams, "FBI in Lawmakers' Midst."

49. Baggett, "Federal Program Bribery, New Federalism."

50. Phil Williams, "FBI Put a Judas in Bingo Crowd's Midst," *Tennessean*, Aug. 6, 1989, https://www.newspapers.com/image/112333333.

51. Jim O'Hara, "4 of 5 New Senators Oppose Racing Here," *Tennessean*, March 15, 1987, https://www.newspapers.com/image/112519825.

52. Jim O'Hara, "Lottery Resolution Sidesteps Panel Vote," *Tennessean*, March 11, 1987, https://www.newspapers.com/image/112508359.

53. Larry Daughtrey and Jim O'Hara, "Betting Bill Appears Shaky in Senate," *Tennessean*, March 19, 1987, https://www.newspapers.com/image/112402147.

54. Associated Press, "Bingo Bill Sails Through Committee," *Leaf Chronicle*, March 11, 1987, https://www.newspapers.com/image/367706330.

55. Jim O'Hara, "Cody Opinion Puts Cloud on Bingo," *Tennessean*, April 16, 1987, https://www.newspapers.com/image/112325603.

56. Bill Rawlins, "Counsel to study Bingo Bill Opinion," *Johnson City Press*, April 17, 1987, https://www.newspapers.com/image/591019232.

57. O'Hara, "Cody Opinion puts Cloud on Bingo."

58. Jim O'Hara and James Pratt, "McWherter, in 1st Veto, Slaps Bingo," *Tennessean*, April 22, 1987, https://www.newspapers.com/image/112351952.

59. Kevin Ellis, "FBI Probes State Bingo Regulators," *Tennessean*, Feb 11, 1986, https:// www.newspapers.com/image/112390794.

60. Phil Williams, "Bingo Vital to Life of Private Club 13," *Tennessean*, May 12, 1987, https://www.newspapers.com/image/112322373.

61. Joel Ebert interview with Jim O'Hara, July 2019; Joel Ebert interview with Phil Williams, July 2019.

62. David Burnham, "Paper in Nashville Dismisses Writer Linked to the FBI," *New York Times*, May 7, 1976, https://www.nytimes.com/1976/05/08/archives/paper-in-nashville-dismisses-writer-linked-to-the-fbi-newspaper-in.html.

63. Joel Ebert interview with Phil Williams, July 2019.

64. Joel Ebert interview with Richard Knudsen, July 2019; LaCrisha Butler, "Players Come Early, Stay Late," *Tennessean*, May 14, 1987, https://www.newspapers.com/image/112328440.
65. Butler, "Players Come Early, Stay Late."
66. Joel Ebert interview with Richard Knudsen, July 2019.
67. Phil Williams and LaCrisha Butler, "Illegal Paper Games, Video Poker Rampant," *Tennessean*, May 11, 1987, https://www.newspapers.com/image/112319990.
68. "Notes & Quotes," *Tennessee Journal* 13, no. 20 (May 18, 1987): 4.
69. Phil Williams, "Bingo Operator Apparently Used Fraud in Charter," *Tennessean*, June 1, 1987; Phil Williams, "Operator Uses Charities," *Tennessean*, May 31, 1987; Phil Williams, "Bingo Offers Temptation to Skim Cash," *Tennessean*, June 28, 1987, https://www.newspapers.com/image/112348997; LaCrisha Butler, Jim O'Hara, Phil Williams, Bridget Kelley, and Teresa Wasson, "Illegal Gambling Rampant at Halls," *Tennessean*, June 7, 1987, https://www.newspapers.com/image/112424205.
70. Phil Williams, "Pastor Hopes Probe to End Bingo Woes," *Tennessean*, Nov. 10, 1987, https://www.newspapers.com/image/112396427.
71. "Bingo," *Tennessee Journal* 14, no 4. (Jan. 25, 1988): 3; "General Assembly Passes Gas Bill, Bingo, Campaign Laws as Lackluster Session Ends," *Tennessee Journal* 14, no. 18 (May 2, 1988): 1.
72. Phil Williams, "IRS Begins Bingo Probe," *Tennessean*, May 29, 1988, https://www.newspapers.com/image/112435358; Phil Williams, "Grand Jury Examines Bingo," *Tennessean*, June 8, 1988, https://www.newspapers.com/image/112451580 https://www.newspapers.com/image/112451580.
73. "Notes & Quotes," *Tennessee Journal* 14, no. 33 (Aug. 15, 1988): 4; Phil Williams, "Bingo Figure Helped Senator Get Bank Loan," *Tennessean*, Aug. 21, 1988, https://www.newspapers.com/image/112970174; Phil Williams, "Third Federal Grand Jury Probes Bingo Industry," *Tennessean*, Nov. 8, 1988, https://www.newspapers.com/image/112991643.
74. Phil Williams and Jim O'Hara, "Reported Threats Fuel Bingo Industry's Woes," *Tennessean*, Jan. 8, 1989, https://www.newspapers.com/image/112971562; Phil Williams, "2 May Plead Guilty in Bingo Fraud Case," *Tennessean*, Jan. 9, 1989, https://www.newspapers.com/image/112972215; Phil Williams, "Men Admit Abducting Bingo Hall Operator," *Tennessean*, Jan. 12, 1989, https://www.newspapers.com/image/112972620.
75. Phil Williams, Jim O'Hara, and James Pratt, "Probe Explodes beyond Bingo," *Tennessean*, Jan. 27, 1989, https://www.newspapers.com/image/112976405.
76. Williams, O'Hara, and Pratt, "Probe Explodes Beyond Bingo."
77. Jim O'Hara, "Guarded Conversations in Capitol Center on the Question: 'Who Else?'" *Tennessean*, Jan. 27, 1989, https://www.newspapers.com/image/112976411.
78. Joel Ebert interview with Jim O'Hara, July 2019.
79. Joel Ebert interview with Tom Humphrey, July 2019.
80. O'Hara, "Guarded Conversations in Capitol."
81. Phil Williams, "Tennessee's Losing Gamble," *Tennessean*, Dec. 3, 1989, https://www.newspapers.com/image/112466451.

82. Jim O'Hara, "Re-Elected Tommy Burnett Now Candidate for Parole," *Tennessean*, Nov. 10, 1984, https://www.newspapers.com/image/111505460.

83. Phil Williams, "Rep. Miller kills Himself," *Tennessean*, July 18, 1989, https://www.newspapers.com/image/112457131.

84. Jim O'Hara, "Money Returned on Conditions," *Tennessean*, Oct. 20, 1989, https://www.newspapers.com/image/112458444.

85. O'Hara, "Money Returned on Conditions."

86. Joel Ebert interview with Phil Williams, July 2019.

87. John Gill, 1989–1990 submissions to the Department of Justice of major prosecutions in the Eastern District of Tennessee, "Former US Attorney John Gill summary of major prosecutions," uploaded to Scribd by TNScandalsBook, April 18, 2023, https://www.scribd.com/document/639038739/Former-US-Attorney-John-Gill-summary-of-major-prosecutions.

88. Phil Williams, "Burnett's Bingo Conviction Stands," *Tennessean*, Dec. 14, 1991, https://www.newspapers.com/image/112729878.

89. Phil Williams and Jim O'Hara, "Bingo's Number Up, High Court Rules," *Tennessean*, Feb. 28, 1989, https://www.newspapers.com/image/112982721.

90. Richard Locker, "Tenn. Officials Fill Board Overseeing Disclosure," *Commercial Appeal*, Oct. 3, 1989, https://www.newspapers.com/image/773828283; Amy Todd Geisel, "Scandal Spurred Lawmakers' Gallop," *Knoxville News Sentinel*, May 28, 1989, https://www.newspapers.com/image/775084341.

91. Larry Daughtrey, Gail McKnight, and Phil Williams, "Ethics Reform, Taxes Greet 97th," *Tennessean*, Jan. 9, 1991, https://www.newspapers.com/image/113001599; "Failure on Ethics Bills Stymies Legislature," *Tennessean*, June, 1991, https://www.newspapers.com/image/112497803.

92. Larry Daughtrey," Lawmakers Cleaning Up Their Own Act," *Tennessean*, May 27, 1995, https://www.newspapers.com/image/112523596.

93. "Rocky Top Redux: Haslam Pardons Former Lawmaker Who Once Offered Bribe to McNally," *Tennessee Journal* 45, no. 33 (Jan. 18, 2019): 3.

## CHAPTER 4

1. Richard Locker, "Ford Runs at High Speed on Track of Controversy." *Commercial Appeal*, October 5, 1990: A8, https://www.newspapers.com/image/773719738.

2. Philip Ashford, "John Ford: The Flamboyance Remains, but Shows Signs of Mellowing," *Commercial Appeal*, April 12, 1987, E1, https://www.newspapers.com/image/773186290.

3. Susan Adler Thorp, "Foul Tirade at Reporter Was Vintage John Ford," *Commercial Appeal*, May 17, 2000, A17, https://www.newspapers.com/image/774865343.

4. Charles Bernsen, "Ford Team Scored Big in 1974," *Commercial Appeal*, July 2, 1990, A1, https://www.newspapers.com/image/773723986.

5. Charles Bernsen, "Voters Back Fords Despite Foibles," *Commercial Appeal*, July 3, 1990, A5, https://www.newspapers.com/image/773724816.

6. Trent Seibert, "Operation Tennessee Waltz: John Ford," *Tennessean*, June 8, 2005, A1, https://www.newspapers.com/image/275822275.

7. "Interstate 40 Truckers Claim Sen. Ford Fired Shots at Them," *Jackson Sun*, Oct. 4, 1990, 1. https://www.newspapers.com/image/284043311.

8. Jerry Markon, "Sen. Ford Wins 5th Term in Easy Race, No Campaign by Opponent in District 29," *Commercial Appeal*, Nov. 7, 1990, A20. https://www.newspapers.com/image/773724022.

9. Brad Schmitt, "Ford to Turn Self In," *Tennessean*, Oct. 5, 1990, 10, https://www.newspapers.com/image/112433325.

10. Karanja Ajanaku, "Trucker Claims John Ford Took a Shot at Him on I-40," *Commercial Appeal*, Oct. 5, 1990, A1, https://www.newspapers.com/image/773720664.

11. Bernsen, "Voters Back Fords."

12. Ajanaku, "Trucker Claims John Ford Took a Shot."

13. Associated Press, "Sen. John Ford Accused of Firing Gun at Trucks," *Daily News Journal*, Oct. 4, 1990, 2, https://www.newspapers.com/image/422709582.

14. Associated Press, "Senator Denies Shooting Pistol," *Daily News Journal*, Oct. 5, 1990, 20, https://www.newspapers.com/image/422710612.

15. Associated Press, "Pistol Confiscated in Ford Investigation," *Leaf Chronicle*, Oct. 7, 1990, 12, https://www.newspapers.com/image/467775030; Larry Daughtrey, "Truck Had No Bullet Marks: FBI," *Tennessean*, June 7, 1991, 1, https://www.newspapers.com/image/112488792.

16. Paula Wade, "Ethics Rules Could Force Sen. Ford Out of Post," *Commercial Appeal*, Feb. 8, 1991, A1, https://www.newspapers.com/image/773652397.

17. "Notes & Quotes," *Tennessee Journal* 17, no. 10 (March 11, 1991): 4.

18. "Notes & Quotes," *Tennessee Journal* 17, no. 6 (Feb. 11, 1991): 4.

19. Daughtrey, "Truck Had No Bullet Marks," 9.

20. Associated Press, "Senate Panel Fails to Demote Ford," *Leaf Chronicle*, March 5, 1991, 11, https://www.newspapers.com/image/467601489.

21. Associated Press, "Reception to Benefit John Ford," *Jackson Sun*, May 21, 1991, 14; Larry Daughtrey, "Reports Show Lobbyists Lavish with Lawmakers," *Tennessean*, Aug 2, 1991, 21, https://www.newspapers.com/image/112455462.

22. Patricia Merritta, "Ford Verdict Could Hinge on Windshield," *Jackson Sun*, June 7, 1991, 1, https://www.newspapers.com/image/283571843.

23. Daughtrey, "Truck Had No Bullet Marks."

24. Jeffrey Fleming, "John Ford Wants Trial Moved from Lexington," *Commercial Appeal*, April 27, 1991, A8, https://www.newspapers.com/image/773978260.

25. Jeffrey Fleming, "John Ford Indicted in I-40 Flap, Senator Denies Shooting at Truck," *Commercial Appeal*, Feb. 5, 1991, A1, https://www.newspapers.com/image/773651832.

26. Michael Kelley, "Ford Fired Pistol, Trucker Testifies; Senator Rebuts View," *Commercial Appeal*, June 8, 1991, A1, https://www.newspapers.com/image/773967543.

27. Daughtrey, "Truck Had No Bullet Marks."

28. Larry Daughtrey, "Ford Disputes 'Lies' at Trial," *Tennessean*, June 8, 1991, 1. https://www.newspapers.com/image/112495028.

29. Larry Daughtrey, "Never Lost Faith Ford Says after Acquittal," *Tennessean*, June 9, 1991, 1, https://www.newspapers.com/image/112495387.

30. Daughtrey, "Ford Disputes 'Lies' at Trial."

31. Patricia Merritt, "'Hammer' Could Not Nail Ford," *Jackson Sun*, June 9, 1991, 2, https://www.newspapers.com/image/283572827.

32. Daughtrey, "Never Lost Faith Ford Says."

33. Associated Press, "Sen. Ford's Acquittal Rested on Lack of Physical Evidence," *Leaf Chronicle*, June 10, 1991, 8.

34. Sandy Hodson, "Sen. Ford Seeking $10 Million from Truckers," *Jackson Sun*, Oct. 8, 1991, 2, https://www.newspapers.com/image/283680528; Associated Press, "Trucker Pleads Guilty in Ford Incident," *Tennessean*, Oct 26, 1991, 19.

35. Paula Wade and Quintin Robinson, "Harold Ford Alleges Plot by Officials, Newspaper," *Commercial Appeal*, June 9, 1991, A10, https://www.newspapers.com/image/773971161.

36. Wade and Robinson, "Harold Ford Alleges Plot."

37. Richard Locker, "Sen. Ford Used Postage Fund to Buy Luxury Pens," *Commercial Appeal*, July 3, 1991, B1, https://www.newspapers.com/image/773957158.

38. Beverly Stewart, "Ford Admits Being Stopped on I-40, Denies Speeding," *Commercial Appeal*, April 15, 1992, B1, https://www.newspapers.com/image/774031795.

39. Richard Locker, "Campaign Funds Pay 'Personal Expenses' John Ford Cites $14,843 in Report," *Commercial Appeal*, April 28, 1992, A1, https://www.newspapers.com/image/773989274.

40. Reed Branson and Paula Wade, "Legislature Oks Ethics Bill; Much Left to Iron Out," *Commercial Appeal*, May 1, 1992, A1, https://www.newspapers.com/image/774014508.

41. Charles Tuthill, "Tennessee General Assembly: Votes by West Tennessee Legislators," *Commercial Appeal*, May 10, 1992, A10, https://www.newspapers.com/image/774034487; Charles Bernsen, "John Ford Wins Court Clerk Office; Incumbent Goldsby Locked Out," *Commercial Appeal*, August 7, 1992, A1.

42. Bartholomew Sullivan, "John Ford Told UAB He'd Be Reimbursed, Backs Bill to Grant Car Allowances," *Commercial Appeal*, Feb. 11, 1993, A1, https://www.newspapers.com/image/774023933.

43. Paula Wade, "John Ford Shoves TV Reporter," *Commercial Appeal*, Feb. 25, 1993, A14, https://www.newspapers.com/image/774002721.

44. Wade, "John Ford Shoves TV Reporter."

45. Susan Adler Thorp, "John Ford Loses Monopoly Hold on Free Tickets," *Commercial Appeal*, Nov. 22, 1992, B12, https://www.newspapers.com/image/774017124.

46. Richard Locker, "Inquiry Says Trooper Ticketing Ford Needs Courtesy Counseling," *Commercial Appeal*, March 3, 1994, A15, https://www.newspapers.com/image/773988956.

47. "State Senate: Dixon, Ford," *Commercial Appeal*, Aug. 1, 1994, A6, https://www. newspapers.com/image/774377996.

48. John Beifuss, "GOP Vows to Unseat John Ford in 1996," *Commercial Appeal*, Oct. 15, 1995, B1, https://www.newspapers.com/image/774559004.

49. Marc Perrusquia, "John Ford Gives $48,000 Court Job to Mother of Child He Fathered in '87," *Commercial Appeal*, Nov. 30, 1995, A1, https://www.newspapers. com/image/774571262.

50. Marc Perrusquia, "'It's Devastated Me' Wife Speaks on John Ford Controversies," *Commercial Appeal*, Dec. 4, 1995, A1, https://www.newspapers.com/ image/774537441.

51. Marc Perrusquia, "John Ford: Stories on Me Racist, Political," *Commercial Appeal*, Dec. 7, 1995, A1, https://www.newspapers.com/image/774540933.

52. "'I Am Not Perfect,' John Ford Says in Statement," *Commercial Appeal*, Dec. 9, 1995, B2, https://www.newspapers.com/image/774547657.

53. Marc Perrusquia, "John Ford Approves Deal for Support of 2 Kids," *Commercial Appeal*, Dec. 16, 1995, A15, https://www.newspapers.com/image/774529034.

54. Marc Perrusquia, "Ford Sired Ex-worker's Daughter, Court Rules," *Commercial Appeal*, Dec. 29, 1995, B1, https://www.newspapers.com/image/774556139.

55. Rob Johnson, "GOP's Turner Bumps John Ford from Court Clerk's Office," *Commercial Appeal*, Aug. 2, 1996, A1, https://www.newspapers.com/image/774572193.

56. Marc Perrusquia, "Ford Harassed Employee, Jury Decides—3 of 4 Counts Dismissed," *Commercial Appeal*, Nov. 8, 1996, A1, https://www.newspapers.com/ image/774689422.

57. Lawrence Buser, "Ford Can Get Dismissal in LG&W Case Without Plea," *Commercial Appeal*, April 26, 1997, A1, https://www.newspapers.com/image/774671986.

58. John Yates, "Ford Apologizes after Kick Shown on TV," *Tennessean*, April 24, 1997, 6B.

59. Richard Locker, "Ford's Shipping Bills under Review," *Commercial Appeal*, Dec. 6, 2003, B1, https://www.newspapers.com/image/775600474.

60. Richard Locker, "Ford Apologizes, Offers Payback," *Commercial Appeal*, Dec. 13, 2003. A1, https://www.newspapers.com/image/775616024.

61. Richard Locker, "I Live in District, Says Sen. Ford—Visits Children at 2 Homes, but 'Domicile' on South Parkway," *Commercial Appeal*, Jan. 28, 2005, B1, https:// www.newspapers.com/image/775554119.

62. Richard Locker, "Ford Criticizes 'White Media'—NAACP Sidesteps Request to Support His Position," *Commercial Appeal*, Feb. 9, 2005, B1, https://www. newspapers.com/image/775696668.

63. "Ford's Troubles Mount as Complaints Are Lodged about Income Disclosure," *Tennessee Journal* 31, no. 8 (Feb. 21, 2005): 1.

64. Marc Perrusquia, "Rare Subpoena Due on Ford Tax Returns," *Commercial Appeal*, Feb. 18, 2005: A1, https://www.newspapers.com/image/775615175.

65. Marc Perrusquia, "Ford Sought Contracts for Firm, Says Source—Senator Wanted $50,000 for Time, Ex-worker Says," *Commercial Appeal*, March 13, 2005, A1, https://www.newspapers.com/image/775663315.

66. Perrusquia, "Ford Sought Contracts for Firm."

67. Richard Locker and Mark Perrusquia, "Agency Says Ford Worked for Firm—As Consultant for AC Business, He Discussed Bids, Regents Confirms," *Commercial Appeal*, March 15, 2005, A1, https://www.newspapers.com/image/775679119.

68. Marc Perrusquia, "Ford Asks for Relief on His Child Support—His Income Is Lower since Doral Dental Contract Days," *Commercial Appeal*, March 18, 2005, A1, https://www.newspapers.com/image/775688187.

69. Richard Locker, "'An Innocent Omission'—Sen. Ford Says His Integrity Has Been Impugned by False Accusations," *Commercial Appeal*, March 17, 2005, A1, https://www.newspapers.com/image/775682394.

70. Richard Locker, "Broader Ford Look Possible—Ethics Members See 'Veiled Threat' in Senator's Letter," *Commercial Appeal*, March 19, 2005, A1, https://www.newspapers.com/image/775692151.

71. Richard Locker, "Ford: Yes on Ethics—Senator Defends Own Work in the Chamber Senate Approves Ban on Accepting Consulting and Lobbying Income," *Commercial Appeal*, April 15, 2005, A1, https://www.newspapers.com/image/775717113; Richard Locker, "House Votes Reform—Approves Tough Limits on Income, Consulting on 92-3-1 Vote; Critics Cry It's a Bad Bill—Three from Shelby County Vote against It; Senate Votes Monday," *Commercial Appeal*, April 22, 2005, A1, https://www.newspapers.com/image/775631552.

72. Jackson Baker, "Waiting for Godot with John Ford," *Memphis: The City Magazine*, May 1, 2014, https://memphismagazine.com/features/waiting-for-godot-with-john-ford.

73. Richard Locker, "Registry Fines Ford $10,000—Used Campaign Fund to Pay for Daughter's Wedding Reception," *Commercial Appeal*, May 12, 2005, A1, https://www.newspapers.com/image/775672509.

74. Trent Seibert, "30-Year Career Ends as Troubles Escalate," *Tennessean*, May 29, 2005, A1, https://www.newspapers.com/image/275865051.

75. "FBI TN Waltz FOIA No. 138294," p. 11, uploaded to Scribd by TNScandalsBook, April 20, 2023, https://www.scribd.com/document/639641433/FBI-TN-Waltz-FOIA-No-138294.

76. Lucas L. Johnson II, "Lois DeBerry, 68; Longtime Tenn. Lawmaker," Associated Press, Aug. 2, 2013.

77. "FBI TN Waltz FOIA No. 138294," p. 12.

78. "FBI TN Waltz FOIA No. 138294," p. 37, 44.

79. "FBI TN Waltz FOIA No. 138294," p. 55.

80. Lawrence Buser, "Guilty, All Counts—Jury of 7 Whites, 5 Blacks Rejects Dixon Defense of Entrapment and Racism in First Local Waltz Bribery Trial," *Commercial Appeal*, June 9, 2006, A1.

81. "Lois DeBerry FBI FOIA No. 1265667-0," p. 15, uploaded to Scribd by TNScandalsBook, April 16, 2023, https://www.scribd.com/document/638678778/Lois-DeBerry-FBI-FOIA-No-1265667-0.

82. Marc Perrusquia, "John Ford Verdict—CONVICTED—Tapes Show Ex-senator as Profane Power Broker with Influence for Sale," *Commercial Appeal*, April 28, 2007, A1, https://www.newspapers.com/image/776077327.

83. Trevor Aaronson, "Bowers Lured Ford into Waltz Sting by Accident—FBI: Legislature's Chiefs Expected at Meeting," *Commercial Appeal*, April 12, 2007, A6.

84. Marc Perrusquia, "Ford Slaps FBI with Own Tapes—This time Out, He Appears Tepid to Agents' Entreaties," *Commercial Appeal*, April 17, 2007, B1, https://www.newspapers.com/image/776083735.

85. Marc Perrusquia, "Promise, Then $10K in Pocket—Ford Exchange with FBI Agent Emerges on One of 20 Tapes," *Commercial Appeal*, April 13, 2007, A1, https://www.newspapers.com/image/776075116.

86. Perrusquia, "Promise, Then $10K in Pocket."

87. Ken Whitehouse, "Waltz Informant Speaks Out: What Kind of Man?" *Nashville Post*, Dec. 15, 2005, https://www.nashvillepost.com/waltz-informant-speaks-out-what-kind-of-man/article_7da8bc77-4c7b-5867-978c-c2b48ca9d6dd.html.

88. Whitehouse, "Waltz Informant Speaks Out."

89. Marc Perrusquia, "Fraud Led Willis into Role in Waltz—FBI Paid Felon Well to Aid Effort to Snare Lawmakers," *Commercial Appeal*, June 19, 2005, A1, https://www.newspapers.com/image/775703524.

90. Whitehouse, "Waltz Informant Speaks Out."

91. Perrusquia, "Fraud Led Willis into Role in Waltz."

92. Marc Perrusquia, "Elected Official Aided Kickbacks, Agent Testifies—Waltz Trial Fleshing Out Details of Juvenile Court Plot," *Commercial Appeal*, June 1, 2006, B1; Marc Perrusquia, "Opening Statements: The John Ford Trial - A Clash over Cash," *Commercial Appeal*, April 11, 2007, A1. https://www.newspapers.com/image/776069723.

93. Author's interview with Ken Whitehouse, Jan. 6, 2022.

94. Ken Whitehouse, "Waltz Informant Speaks Out: A Full Dance-Card," *Nashville Post*, Dec. 16, 2005, https://www.nashvillepost.com/business/legal/waltz-informant-speaks-out-a-full-dance-card/article_72b7aa84-943e-5986-952e-5b1e8b48ffc3.html.

95. Perrusquia, "Fraud Led Willis into Role in Waltz."

96. Perrusquia, "Fraud Led Willis into Role in Waltz."

97. "Lois DeBerry FBI FOIA No. 1265667-0," p. 18.

98. John Branston, "The Day Tim Willis Earned His Money," *Memphis Flyer*, April 18, 2007, https://www.memphisflyer.com/the-day-tim-willis-earned-his-money.

99. Branston, "The Day Tim Willis Earned His Money."

100. "John Ford on Tape," *Commercial Appeal*, May 28, 2005, A10, https://www.newspapers.com/image/775662975.

101. Chris Conley and Aimee Edmondson, "Sting on Tape—Captures Ford Taking $10,000 across His Desk," *Commercial Appeal*, May 28, 2005, A1, https://www.newspapers.com/image/775662642.

102. Lawrence Buser, "Willis Accuses Dixon—Says Former Senator Was 'Happy to See' Bribe Money," *Commercial Appeal*, June 3, 2006, A1, https://www.newspapers.com/image/775636415.

103. Bonna de la Cruz, "Ford Says He Didn't Quit over Charges," *Tennessean*, June 1, 2005, A1, https://www.newspapers.com/image/275790794.

104. Bonna de la Cruz, "Ford Calls FBI the 'Villain,' Hints at Deception Defense," *Tennessean*, June 9, 2005, A1, https://www.newspapers.com/image/303990102.

105. Perrusquia, "Opening Statements."

106. Trevor Aaronson, "Sizzler at Finish—Feds Torch 'Smoke, Mirrors' Approach: 2 Hours, 3 Testify," *Commercial Appeal*, April 25, 2007, A1, https://www.newspapers.com/image/776068947.

107. Trent Seibert and Michael Cass, "Senate Leader Castigates FBI, but Some Urge Stricter Ethics," *Tennessean*, May 28, 2005, A1, https://www.newspapers.com/image/275858837.

108. Richard Locker, "Wilder Clarifies Reaction to Legislative Sting—Says He Wasn't Criticizing Investigators, Just 'Entrapment,'" *Commercial Appeal*, June 4, 2005, A1, https://www.newspapers.com/image/775677753.

109. Locker, "Wilder Clarifies Reaction."

110. Jay Hamburg and Associated Press, "Ethics Rules Changing," *Tennessean*, May 5, 2005, A17, https://www.newspapers.com/image/27572524.

111. "Lobbyist Reporting Law a Joke," *Tennessean*, July 26, 1985, A14, https://www.newspapers.com/image/112493170.

112. Richard Locker, "Senate Code Discourages Indictees," *Commercial Appeal*, May 5, 1989, B1, https://www.newspapers.com/image/773638953.

113. Richard Locker, "John Ford's Lobby-Paid Dining Tabs Topped State," *Commercial Appeal*, Aug. 2, 1990, B1, https://www.newspapers.com/image/773653494.

114. Richard Locker, "4-Year Push to Beef Up Disclosure Rules Fails," *Commercial Appeal*, reprinted in *Tennessean*, Feb. 22, 2005, B4, https://www.newspapers.com/image/276061896.

115. Richard Locker, "4-Year Push."

116. Larry Daughtrey, "'Tennessee Waltz' Captures Some State Lawmakers in a Dirty Dance," *Tennessean*, May 29, 2005, A21, https://www.newspapers.com/image/275862727.

117. Daughtrey, "'Tennessee Waltz' Captures."

118. Erik Schelzig and Associated Press, "Tenn. Democrat Makes Push for Senate," *Miami Herald*, Oct. 11, 2006, 5A, https://www.newspapers.com/image/654976745.

119. Bonna de la Cruz, "Big Political Names Give Corker, Ford Backing," *Tennessean*, Oct. 24, 2006, A1, https://www.newspapers.com/image/277512503.

120. Jackson Baker, "John Ford's J'Accuse!" *Memphis Flyer*, March 22, 2014, https://www.memphisflyer.com/john-fords-jaccuse.

121. Katherine Burgess, "John Ford, Convicted of Bribery, Ineligible to Run for Elected Office, State Says. He's Filed Anyway," *Commercial Appeal*, Nov. 20, 2019, https://www.commercialappeal.com/story/news/2019/11/20/john-ford-ineligible-elected-office-state-says-hes-filed-anyway/4250576002.

122. "Lois DeBerry FBI FOIA No. 1265667-0," p. 27.

123. Marc Perrusquia, "DeBerry Took E-Cycle $200—Agent in Tennessee Waltz Sting Gave Money at Casino," *Commercial Appeal*, July 27, 2005, A1.

124. Trent Seibert, "Naifeh Defends Lawmaker Who Took E-Cycle Cash," *Tennessean*, July 28, 2005, A1, https://www.newspapers.com/image/775552321.

125. "Lois DeBerry FBI FOIA No. 1265667-0," p. 48.

126. "Lois DeBerry FBI FOIA No. 1265667-0," p. 48.

## CHAPTER 5

1. Dave Boucher, "GOP Nominates Harwell, Ramsey to Keep Leadership Posts," *Tennessean*, Dec. 10, 2014, https://www.tennessean.com/story/news/politics/2014/12/10/gop-nominates-harwell-ramsey-keep-leadership-posts/20218387.

2. Andy Meek, "Paul Stanley's Fall from Grace," *Memphis Daily News*, Aug. 17, 2009, https://www.memphisdailynews.com/news/2009/aug/17/paul-stanleys-fall-from-grace.

3. Dave Boucher, Jill Cowan, and Stacey Barchenger, "With Jeremy Durham, Ambition, Anger Collide," *Tennessean*, Sept. 21, 2016, https://www.tennessean.com/story/news/politics/2016/01/09/jeremy-durham-ambition-anger-collide/78500466.

4. Jill Cowan, "Rep. Durham Not Indicted in Prescription Fraud Probe," *Tennessean*, Dec. 9, 2015, https://www.tennessean.com/story/news/2015/12/09/rep-durham-not-indicted-prescription-fraud-probe/77069498.

5. Todd South, "Former Tennessee Pastor Gets Break in Child Porn Sentence," *Chattanooga Times Free Press*, July 22, 2014, https://www.timesfreepress.com/news/local/story/2014/jul/22/ex-pastor-gets-break0010in-porn-sentence/262375.

6. Jill Cowan, "Ramsey: Durham Letter in Porn Case Showed 'Poor Judgment,'" *Tennessean*, Dec. 11, 2015, https://www.tennessean.com/story/news/politics/2015/12/11/ramsey-says-durham-letter-shows-poor-judgment/77151368.

7. Cowan, "Ramsey: Durham Letter in Porn Case."

8. Joel Ebert, "Harwell, Casada Survive Challenges," *Tennessean*, Nov. 18, 2016, https://www.newspapers.com/image/246526744.

9. Jill Cowan and Holly Meyer, "HR Issues with Lawmakers Can Be Thorny," *Tennessean*, Dec. 29, 2015, https://www.tennessean.com/story/news/politics/2015/12/29/hr-issues-lawmakers-can-thorny/77746812.

10. Dave Boucher, Joel Ebert, and Jill Cowan, "Republican Caucus Keeps Jeremy Durham as Leader," *Tennessean*, Jan. 12, 2016, https://www.tennessean.com/story/news/politics/2016/01/12/gop-caucus-meeting-durham-open/78632540.

11. Erik Schelzig and Associated Press, "Durham Goes Back and Forth on GOP Leadership Resignation," *Greeneville Sun*, Jan. 25, 2016.

12. Dave Boucher and Jill Cowan, "Sexual Harassment Concerns on the Hill," *Tennessean*, Jan. 24, 2016, https://www.newspapers.com/image/150681456.

13. Jill Cowan and Dave Boucher, "Tennessee Sexual Harassment Policy Mired in Secrecy, Experts Say," *Tennessean*, Jan. 24, 2016, https://www.tennessean.com/story/news/politics/2016/01/24/tennessee-sexual-harassment-policy-mired-secrecy-experts-say/79130160.

14. Dave Boucher and Jill Cowan, "Tennessean Investigation Finds Inappropriate Text Messages," *Tennessean*, Jan. 24, 2016, https://www.tennessean.com/story/news/politics/2016/01/24/tennessean-investigation-finds-inappropriate-text-messages/79130066.

15. Dave Boucher, Jill Cowan, and Joel Ebert, "GOP Leaders Knew Durham Allegations for Months," *Tennessean*, Jan. 27, 2016, https://www.tennessean.com/story/news/politics/2016/01/27/durham-leaves-caucus-gop-leaders-acknowledge-knowing-more/79427250.

16. Dave Boucher and Jill Cowan, "Jeremy Durham Confirms Resignation as Whip," *Tennessean*, Jan. 24, 2016, http://www.tennessean.com/story/news/politics/2016/01/24/durham-resigns-whip-after-tennessean-investigation/79267590.

17. Schelzig and Associated Press, "Durham Goes Back and Forth."

18. Joel Ebert, "Haslam Questions Durham's Ability to Continue Serving," *Tennessean*, Jan. 26, 2016, https://www.tennessean.com/story/news/politics/2016/01/26/haslam-questions-durhams-ability-continue-serving/79345678.

19. Dave Boucher, "Speaker Harwell: Expel Durham from Legislature," *Tennessean*, Jan. 27, 2016, https://www.tennessean.com/story/news/politics/2016/01/27/speaker-harwell-expel-durham-legislature/79434102.

20. Boucher, "Speaker Harwell: Expel Durham."

21. Joel Ebert and Natalie Allison, "The Tennessee House Expelled a Member by Resolution in 1980. Will They Do It Again?" *Tennessean*, Aug. 20, 2019, https://www.tennessean.com/story/news/politics/2019/08/21/rep-david-byrd-tennessee-house-expelled-robert-fisher-1980/1960692001.

22. Dave Boucher, Joel Ebert, and Jill Cowan, "Harwell Calls for AG Investigation into Durham's 'Situation.'" *Tennessean*, Jan. 28, 2016, https://www.tennessean.com/story/news/politics/2016/01/28/ramsey-durham-had-affair-lawmaker-forced-resignation/79464656.

23. Associated Press, "Rep. Leigh Wilburn Resigns from Tennessee General Assembly," *Tennessean*, Dec. 1, 2015, https://www.tennessean.com/story/news/politics/2015/12/01/rep-leigh-wilburn-resigns-tn-general-assembly/76634444.

24. Erik Schelzig and Associated Press, "Durham Takes Leave from State House Amid Allegations of Affair, Calls for Resignation," *Commercial Appeal*, Jan. 28, 2016, https://www.commercialappeal.com/story/news/government/state/2016/01/28/durham-takes-leave-from-state-house-amid-allegations-of-affair-calls-for-resignation/90387388.

25. Joel Ebert and Dave Boucher, "Harwell Committee to Lead Jeremy Durham Investigation," *Tennessean*, Feb. 2, 2016, https://www.tennessean.com/story/news/politics/2016/02/04/harwell-forms-committee-durham-probe/79840044.

26. Joel Ebert, Dave Boucher, and Jill Cowan, "Jeremy Durham Says AG Asked for His iPad, Emails," *Tennessean*, Feb. 16, 2016, https://www.tennessean.com/story/news/politics/2016/02/16/jeremy-durham-says-ag-asked-his-ipad-emails/80478924.

27. Dave Boucher and Joel Ebert, "Jeremy Durham Banished after AG Probe Finds 'Inappropriate Physical Contact," *Tennessean*, March 7, 2016,

https://www.tennessean.com/story/news/politics/2016/04/07/attorney-general-finds-inappropriate-physical-behavior-durham/82750152.

28. Boucher and Ebert, "Jeremy Durham Banished."

29. Joel Ebert, "Lawmaker: Durham Investigation Is a 'Witch Hunt' and Part of Harwell 'Hit List,'" *Tennessean*, May 20, 2016, https://www.tennessean.com/story/news/politics/2016/05/20/lawmaker-durham-investigation-witch-hunt-and-part-harwell-hit-list/84622204.

30. Joel Ebert, "Jeremy Durham Still Supported by Franklin GOP Lawmakers," *Tennessean*, May 27, 2016, https://www.tennessean.com/story/news/politics/2016/05/27/jeremy-durham-still-supported-franklin-gop-lawmakers/85057818.

31. "Jeremy Durham - Benton Smith Aff. – Attach. B," uploaded to Scribd by USA Today Network, June 8, 2016, https://www.scribd.com/doc/315190782/Jeremy-Durham-Benton-Smith-Aff-Attach-B.

32. Joel Ebert and Dave Boucher, "Casada: If New Allegations True, Durham Should Resign," *Tennessean*, June 9, 2016, https://www.tennessean.com/story/news/politics/2016/06/09/casada-if-new-allegations-true-durham-should-resign/85644346.

33. Jim Balloch and Tom Humphrey, "GOP Calls for Briley's Resignation after Arrests," *Knoxville News Sentinel*, Sept. 11, 2007, https://www.newspapers.com/image/777242409.

34. "Indictment Could Bring Loss of Leadership Post," *Tennessean*, Sept. 11, 2007, https://www.newspapers.com/image/278323401.

35. Ebert and Boucher, "Casada: If New Allegations True."

36. Joel Ebert, "Another Lawmaker Calls for End of Durham Investigation," *Tennessean*, June 16, 2016, https://www.tennessean.com/story/news/politics/2016/06/15/another-lawmaker-calls-end-durham-investigation/85953196.

37. Dave Boucher, "House Committee Investigating Jeremy Durham to Meet Wednesday," *Tennessean*, July 8, 2016, https://www.tennessean.com/story/news/politics/2016/07/08/house-committee-investigating-jeremy-durham-meet-wednesday/86866190.

38. Dave Boucher, Stacey Barchenger, and Joel Ebert, "Jeremy Durham Sues AG, Beth Harwell over Investigation," *Tennessean*, July 8, 2016, https://www.tennessean.com/story/news/politics/2016/07/08/durham-sues-ag-harwell-over-invwwwestigation/86876686.

39. Dave Boucher, "Attorney General: Jeremy Durham Investigation Should Be Public," *Tennessean*, July 11, 2016, https://www.tennessean.com/story/news/politics/2016/07/11/attorney-general-durham-investigation-should-public/86953028.

40. Boucher, "Attorney General: Jeremy Durham Investigation Should Be Public."

41. Dave Boucher, "AG Can Release Durham Investigation Report, Judge Rules," *Knoxville News Sentinel*, July 12, 2016, https://archive.knoxnews.com/news/politics/attorney-general-jeremy-durham-investigation-should-be-public-3772dc98-5ec5-192f-e053-0100007f3f00-386483911.html.

42. Article II, Section 12, Ad Hoc Select Committee, "Jeremy Durham Final Report into Inappropriate Conduct," available on Scribd, uploaded by USA

Today Network, July 13, 2016, https://www.scribd.com/document/318215789/Jeremy-Durham-final-report-into-inappropriate-conduct.

43. Dave Boucher and Joel Ebert, "Jeremy Durham Had Sexual 'Interactions' with 22 Women, Report Says," *Tennessean*, July 13, 2016, https://www.tennessean.com/story/news/politics/2016/07/13/jeremy-durham-investigative-committee-meet-wednesday/87010348.

44. Boucher and Ebert, "Jeremy Durham Had Sexual 'Interactions.'"

45. Boucher and Ebert, "Jeremy Durham had sexual 'interactions.'"

46. Kirk Bado, "Ron Ramsey Calls Jeremy Durham 'Despicable.'" *Tennessean*, July 14, 2016, https://www.tennessean.com/story/news/politics/2016/07/14/ramsey-durham-despicable-should-smacked-mouth/87084274.

47. Jordan Buie and Joel Ebert, "Williamson County Delegation, Franklin Mayor Call for Durham to Resign," *Tennessean*, July 14, 2016, https://www.tennessean.com/story/news/local/williamson/franklin/2016/07/14/franklin-mayor-says-jeremy-durham-should-resign/87083760.

48. Joel Ebert, "Read Jeremy Durham's Full July 14 Statement," *Tennessean*, July 14, 2016, https://www.tennessean.com/story/news/politics/2016/07/14/read-jeremy-durhams-july-14-full-july-14-statement/87106094.

49. Ebert, "Read Jeremy Durham's Full July 14 Statement."

50. Joel Ebert and Dave Boucher, "Rep. Jeremy Durham Suspends His Campaign, Doesn't Resign," *Tennessean*, July 14, 2016, https://www.tennessean.com/story/news/politics/2016/07/14/rep-jeremy-durham-holds-afternoon-news-conference/87097678.

51. Dave Boucher and Joel Ebert, "The Culture That Allowed Durham to Thrive," *Tennessean*, July 17, 2016, https://www.tennessean.com/story/news/politics/2016/07/17/exclusive-culture-allowed-durham- thrive/87156420.

52. Boucher and Ebert, "The Culture That Allowed Durham."

53. Dave Boucher, Joel Ebert, and Stacey Barchenger, "Woman in AG's Durham Report Harassed, Lawmaker Says," *Tennessean*, Aug. 4, 2016, https://www.tennessean.com/story/news/politics/2016/08/04/woman-ags-durham-report-harassed-lawamker-says/88273346.

54. Dave Boucher and Joel Ebert, "Emailer Tried to Out Victim in AG's Jeremy Durham Report," *Tennessean*, Aug. 5, 2016, https://www.tennessean.com/story/news/politics/2016/08/05/emailer-tried-out-victim-ags-jeremy-durham-report/88297506.

55. Lucas L. Johnson II, Erik Schelzig, and Associated Press "Feds Charge Tenn. Representative with Fraud, Tax Evasion," *Times News*, June 17, 2015, https://www.timesnews.net/news/local-news/feds-charge-tenn-representative-with-fraud-tax-evasion/article_9e6faf79-d536-5aeb-80d9-83d1f45ea3d3.htm.

56. Dave Boucher, "Trickle of Signatures for Jeremy Durham Ouster Session," *Tennessean*, Aug. 5, 2016, https://www.tennessean.com/story/news/politics/2016/08/05/jeremy-durham-special-session-signatures-grind-halt/88289296.

57. Stacey Barchenger, Dave Boucher, and Joel Ebert, "Feds Open Investigation of Rep. Jeremy Durham," *Tennessean*, Aug. 29, 2016, https://www.tennessean.com/story/news/2016/08/29/feds-open-investigation-rep-jeremy-durham/89554236.

58. Joel Ebert and Dave Boucher, "Durham Campaign Investigation Hints at 'Serious Violations.'" *Tennessean*, Aug. 29, 2016, https://www.tennessean.com/ story/news/politics/2016/08/16/durham-campaign-investigation-hints-serious-violations/88834620.

59. Dave Boucher and Joel Ebert, "Jeremy Durham's Campaign Invested in Company of GOP Donor," *Tennessean*, Aug. 30, 2016, https://www.tennessean.com/ story/news/politics/2016/08/30/jeremy-durhams-campaign-invested-company-gop-donor/89550968.

60. Dave Boucher and Joel Ebert, "Rep. Jeremy Durham Shutters Title Company," *Tennessean*, Sept. 2, 2016, https://www.tennessean.com/story/news/ politics/2016/09/02/jeremy-durham-shutters-title-company/89770114.

61. Joel Ebert and Dave Boucher, "Beth Harwell: Jeremy Durham Expulsion Vote Will Happen," *Tennessean*, Sept. 7, 2016, https://www.tennessean.com/ story/news/politics/2016/09/07/beth-harwell-jeremy-durham-expulsion-vote-happen/89971552.

62. Ebert and Boucher, "Beth Harwell: Jeremy Durham Expulsion."

63. Joel Ebert, "Jeremy Durham: Ouster Effort Similar to 'Medieval Beheading.'" *Tennessean*, Sept. 8, 2016, https://www.tennessean.com/story/news/politics/ 2016/09/08/jeremy-durham-ouster-effort-similar-medieval-beheading/ 90065766.

64. House Chamber, State of Tennessee, "Jeremy Durham September 2016 Letter," uploaded to Scribd by TNScandalsBook, April 16, 2023, https://www.scribd.com/ document/638680143/Jeremy-Durham-September-2016-Letter#.

65. Jill Cowan and Dave Boucher, "Tennessee Sexual Harassment Policy Mired in Secrecy, Experts Say," *Tennessean*, Jan. 24, 2016, https://www.tennessean.com/ story/news/politics/2016/01/24/tennessee-sexual-harassment-policy-mired-secrecy-experts-say/79130160.

66. House Chamber, State of Tennessee, "Durham Letter."

67. Joel Ebert and Dave Boucher, "Beth Harwell, Glen Casada Say Jeremy Durham Ouster Effort Will Pass," *Tennessean*, Sept. 12, 2016, https://www.tennessean.com/ story/news/politics/2016/09/12/beth-harwell-glen-casada-say-jeremy-durham-ouster-effort-pass/90261904.

68. Joel Ebert and Dave Boucher, "Jeremy Durham Expelled from Tennessee House in 70-2 Vote," *Tennessean*, Sept. 13, 2016, https://www.tennessean.com/story/news/ politics/2016/09/13/house-prepares-jeremy-durham-expulsion-vote/90127546.

69. Dave Boucher and Dessislava Yankova, "Few GOP Lawmakers Vote against Expelling Jeremy Durham," *Tennessean*, Sept. 13, 2016, https://www.tennessean.com/story/news/politics/2016/09/13/ few-gop-lawmakers-vote-against-expelling-jeremy-durham/90327352.

70. Joel Ebert and Dave Boucher, "Jeremy Durham Kicked Out of UT Football Game after Hitting Florida Fan," *Tennessean*, Sept. 26, 2016, https://www.tennessean.com/ story/news/politics/2016/09/26/jeremy-durham-kicked-out-ut-football-game-after-hitting-florida-fan/91113366.

71. "Durham Appeals to House but Is Expelled in Close Vote," *Tennessee Journal* 42, no. 35 (Sept. 16, 2016): 1.

72. Ebert and Boucher, "Jeremy Durham Kicked Out"; Joel Ebert and Dave Boucher, "Voucher Advocate Hosted Tennessee Lawmakers at Seaside Condo," *Tennessean*, Sept. 24, 2016, https://www.tennessean.com/story/news/politics/2016/09/24/ voucher-advocate-hosted-tennessee-lawmakers-seaside-condo/90781474.

73. Dave Boucher and Joel Ebert, "Jeremy Durham Gave Thousands in Campaign Funds to Pro Gambler," *Tennessean*, Feb. 7, 2017, https://www.tennessean.com/ story/news/politics/2017/02/07/jeremy-durham-gave-thousands-campaign-funds-pro-gambler/97586620.

74. Joel Ebert and Dave Boucher, "Read the Complete Jeremy Durham Campaign Finance Audit," *Tennessean*, Feb. 7, 2017, https://www.tennessean.com/story/news/politics/2017/02/08/ read-complete-jeremy-durham-campaign-finance-audit/97648882.

75. Erik Schelzig and Associated Press, "Campaign Audit: 100s of Potential Violations by Ex-Lawmaker," *Memphis Daily News*, Feb. 9, 2017, https://www.memphisdailynews.com/news/2017/feb/9/ campaign-audit-100s-of-potential-violations-by-ex-lawmaker.

76. "Registry on Trial? Durham Lawyer Hits 'Scorched Earth Treatment," *Tennessee Journal* 47, no. 36 (September 10, 2021) 1.

77. Joel Ebert and Dave Boucher, "Schmoozing, Boozing and a Quiet Resignation," *Tennessean*, Feb. 19, 2017, https://www.newspapers.com/image/273800396.

78. "Mark Lovell files," uploaded to Scribd by TNScandalsBook, April 18, 2023, https://www.scribd.com/document/639038734/Mark-Lovell-files.

79. Boucher and Ebert, "Jeremy Durham Banished."

## CHAPTER 6

1. Joel Ebert and Natalie Allison, "Casada Expands House Committee System, Names 2 Democratic Chairs," *Tennessean*, Jan. 11, 2019, https://www.newspapers. com/image/591274846; Natalie Allison, "Rep. David Byrd to Chair Education Subcommittee," *Tennessean*, Jan. 11, 2019, https://www.newspapers.com/image/ 591274846; Anita Wadhwani, "Women Dispute They Talked to Casada, Staff," *Tennessean*, Feb. 26, 2019, https://www.newspapers.com/image/591288853; Joel Ebert, "Dem Walkout, Chaos Mark Final Hours of Session," *Tennessean*, May 4, 2019, https://www.newspapers.com/image/559843378; Joel Ebert, "2 Claim Offers for Flipping Votes," *Tennessean*, April 28, 2019, https://www.newspapers.com/image /591306103; Joel Ebert, "Harwell, Casada Survive Contests over Speaker, Leader Posts," *Tennessean*, Nov. 18, 2016, https://www.newspapers.com/image/777551164.

2. Joel Ebert and Natalie Allison, "Casada to Resign," *Tennessean*, May 22, 2019, https://www.newspapers.com/image/566591520.

3. Joel Ebert and Natalie Allison, "GOP Joins Ouster Chorus," *Tennessean*, May 9, 2019, https://www.newspapers.com/image/591308391.

4.  John Swack, "4-H'ers Attend Dawson Springs Camp," *Park City (KY) Daily News*, July 25, 1972, https://www.newspapers.com/image/661465232; "Sholar-Casada," *Park City (KY) Daily News*, March 13, 1983, https://www.newspapers.com/image/662389551.

5.  Catherine Trevison, "Schools Meet Growth, but Trouble Is Ahead," *Tennessean*, March 11, 1996, https://www.newspapers.com/image/113496798; Jim East, "County Votes to Ask for Growth Plan Exemption," *Tennessean*, Feb. 17, 2000, https://www.newspapers.com/image/112052495.

6.  Nellann Young, "Hopefuls Jockey for Williams' Seat," *Tennessean*, Aug. 30, 2001, https://www.newspapers.com/image/112699612; "Rep. Williams Takes Job with Big Oil, Race for His Seat Already Under Way," *Tennessee Journal* 27, no. 36 (Sept. 3, 2001): 3.

7.  "Casada's Campaign Starts with Breakfast," *Tennessean*, Sept. 25, 2001, https://www.newspapers.com/image/113586290; Gary Pickett, "Casada Fiscally Tight, Thoughtful and Experienced," *Tennessean*, Oct. 10, 2001, https://www.newspapers.com/image/111961782; Jill Casada, "Political Mailer Contained Falsehoods," *Tennessean*, Oct. 17, 2001, https://www.newspapers.com/image/111833845; Nellann Mettee, "Growth Issue Rouses Franklin Voters," *Tennessean*, Oct. 24, 2001, https://www.newspapers.com/image/111843421.

8.  "A Look at Who the People Are on the House, Franklin Ballots," *Tennessean*, Oct. 22, 2001, https://www.newspapers.com/image/111841922; Nellann Mettee, "Casada, Cotton Take on Claus," *Tennessean*, Dec. 10, 2001, https://www.newspapers.com/image/112425408; "Political Roundup: Shelby GOP Hopes Shift to Scroggs," *Tennessee Journal* 27, no. 50 (Dec. 10, 2001).

9.  Nellann Mettee, "House Candidates Battle Apathy in December Election," *Tennessean*, Oct. 25, 2001, https://www.newspapers.com/image/111845489.

10. Nellann Mettee, "Voters Pick Casada to Fill House Seat," *Tennessean*, Dec. 12, 2001, https://www.newspapers.com/image/112431078; Nellann Mettee, "Strategists Dissect Lopsided Casada Win," *Tennessean*, Dec. 13, 2001, https://www.newspapers.com/image/112436943.

11. Mettee, "Strategists Dissect Lopsided Casada Win."

12. Nellann Mettee, "New Kid on the Hill," *Tennessean*, Jan. 2, 2002, https://www.newspapers.com/image/112671977.

13. Toby Sells, "'Choose Life' Plates Soon on Vehicles after Long Fight," *Tennessean*, Dec. 2, 2006, https://www.newspapers.com/image/776065284; Anita Wadhwani, "State GOP Rolls Out Plan for Crime, Safety Proposals," *Tennessean*, Dec. 19, 2003, https://www.newspapers.com/image/242689806; Tom Humphrey, "Younger Legislators Oust Top GOP Leaders in State House," *Knoxville News Sentinel*, Dec. 13, 2006, https://www.newspapers.com/image/777050924.

14. "Heft on the Hill," *Tennessean*, July 12, 2007, https://www.newspapers.com/image/278304054.

15. Tom Humphrey, "Knox Legislators Join Effort that Seeks Obama's Birth Certificate," *Knoxville News Sentinel*, Feb. 14, 2009, https://www.newspapers.com/image/777194489.

16. "It Happened One Night," *Tennessean*, Feb. 23, 2003, https://www.newspapers.com/image/113626702.

17. Dave Boucher, "Casada Wants Syrian Refugees Rounded Up," *Tennessean*, Nov. 18, 2015, https://www.newspapers.com/image/138092397.

18. Mike Morrow, "Income Tax Issue Will Not Die," *Tennessean*, Dec. 21, 2008, https://www.newspapers.com/image/278995884; Chas Sisk, "GOP Wants to Allow Corporate Donations," *Tennessean*, March 6, 2011, https://www.newspapers.com/image/283831538.

19. Tom Humphrey, "Senate Panel OKs Rule Requiring Voter Photo ID," *Knoxville News Sentinel*, Feb. 9, 2011, https://www.newspapers.com/image/777389037; Nate Rau, "Bill Would Block Extension of Metro Ordinance," *Tennessean*, Feb. 13, 2011, https://www.newspapers.com/image/283329714.

20. "Harwell, Casada Win Leadership Fights; McNally Coasts in Senate," *Tennessee Journal* 42, no. 44 (Nov. 18, 2016): 1.

21. Joel Ebert and Natalie Allison, "Casada Is Nominated for House Speaker," *Commercial Appeal*, Nov. 21, 2018, https://www.newspapers.com/image/777523092.

22. Joel Ebert, "Glen Casada Likens Himself to Conductor," *Tennessean*, Dec. 13, 2018, https://www.newspapers.com/image/512864039.

23. Alanna Autler, "House GOP Majority Leader Does Not Think Rep. David Byrd Should Resign," *Daily Herald*, April 4, 2018, https://www.columbiadailyherald.com/story/news/2018/04/04/house-gop-majority-leader-does/12826117007.

24. Jordan Buie, "Byrd, Accused of Sexual Assault, Seeks Re-election," *Tennessean*, April 4, 2018, https://www.newspapers.com/image/414364641.

25. "Casada Defends Byrd as National Group Takes Aim over Misconduct," *Tennessee Journal* 44, no. 37 (Sept. 28, 2018): 3.

26. Glen Casada, "Focus on Claims One-Sided," *Tennessean*, Feb. 24, 2019, https://www.newspapers.com/image/591288025.

27. Natalie Allison, "Women Escorted Out of Rep. Byrd's Meeting," *Jackson Sun*, March 1, 2019, https://www.newspapers.com/image/590995335.

28. Natalie Allison and Joel Ebert, "House Leadership under Scrutiny," *Tennessean*, May 12, 2019, https://www.newspapers.com/image/591310645; Joel Ebert, "With Casada, Cost of Running the House Rises," *Tennessean*, March 11, 2019, https://www.newspapers.com/image/591290743; Joel Ebert, "White Noise Machines, Eavesdropping on Hill," *Tennessean*, May 8, 2019, https://www.newspapers.com/image/591308508; Joel Ebert, "Records: Casada Used State Plane More Often Than His Predecessor," *Tennessean*, May 19, 2019, https://www.newspapers.com/image/591312056.

29. Joel Ebert, "Casada Warns Anti-LGBT-Bill Groups," *Tennessean*, May 5, 2019, https://www.newspapers.com/image/560554634.

30. "Ax Falls on Byrd's Chairmanship amid Regular Protests, Voucher Vote," *Tennessee Journal* 45, no. 13 (March 29, 2019): 3.

31. Jason Gonzales, "Voucher Backers See Opportunity with Lee," *Tennessean*, Jan 28, 2019, https://www.newspapers.com/image/526702948.

32. Jason Gonzales and Joel Ebert, "Gov. Lee's Voucher Plan Gets Panel OK," *Tennessean*, March 28, 2019, https://www.newspapers.com/image/847206842.

33. Ebert, "2 Claim Offers for Flipping Votes."

34. Joel Ebert, Jason Gonzales, and Natalie Allison, "Voucher-Style Bill Passes House," April 24, 2019, https://www.newspapers.com/image/557283392.

35. Joel Ebert, "2 Claim Offers for Flipping Votes."

36. Sam Stockard, "Calfee Links Casada, Governor to National Guard Promotion Offer," *Tennessee Lookout*, March 18, 2022, https://tennesseelookout.com/2022/03/18/stockard-on-the-stump-calfee-links-casada-governor-to-national-guard-promotion-offer.

37. Phil Williams, "Tennessee Lawmaker Says He Rejected House Speaker's Effort 'to Buy' His Vote on Vouchers Legislation," WTVF-TV, NewsChannel 5, July 21, 2019, https://www.newschannel5.com/news/newschannel-5-investigates/tennessee-lawmaker-says-he-rejected-speakers-effort-to-buy-his-vote-on-vouchers-legislation.

38. Tom Humphrey, "Dems Critical of Lobbyist Meetings," *Knoxville News Sentinel*, Sept. 6, 2010, https://www.newspapers.com/image/777423013.

39. Joel Ebert, "Dem Walkout, Chaos Mark Final Hours of Session," *Tennessean*, May 4, 2019, https://www.newspapers.com/image/559843378.

40. Joel Ebert, "Inside Casada's Fall," *Tennessean*, May 28, 2019, https://www.newspapers.com/image/591317065.

41. Phil Williams, "Did House Speaker's Office Attempt to Frame Activist? DA Asks for Special Prosecutor to Investigate," WTVF-TV, NewsChannel 5, May 2, 2019, https://www.newschannel5.com/news/newschannel-5-investigates/did-house-speakers-office-attempt-to-frame-activist-da-asks-for-special-prosecutor-to-investigate; end of legislative session press conference with Republican leadership with Gov. Bill Lee, Lt. Gov. Randy McNally, Senate Majority Leader Jack Johnson, House Speaker Glen Casada, and House Majority Leader William Lamberth, recorded by Joel Ebert, May 2, 2019.

42. Williams, "Did House Speaker's Office Attempt"; Phil Williams, "Speaker's Chief of Staff Says He Doesn't Recall Sending Racist Texts," WTVF-TV, NewsChannel 5, May 6, 2019, https://www.newschannel5.com/news/newschannel-5-investigates/speakers-chief-of-staff-says-he-doesnt-recall-sending-racist-texts.

43. Phil Williams, "TN House Speaker's Chief of Staff Admits Past Cocaine Use, Confirms Text Message," WTVF-TV, NewsChannel 5, May 6, 2019, https://www.newschannel5.com/news/newschannel-5-investigates/tn-house-speakers-chief-of-staff-admits-past-drug-use-confirms-text-messages.

44. Joel Ebert and Natalie Allison, "Casada's Top Aide Admits Past Cocaine Use," *Tennessean*, May 7, 2019, https://www.newspapers.com/image/561358860.

45. Joel Ebert and Natalie Allison, "Cothren Sex Texts Uncovered," *Tennessean*, May 7, 2019, https://www.newspapers.com/image/561358822.

46. "Cade Cothren Resigns as House Speaker's Chief of Staff," WTVF-TV, NewsChannel 5, May 6, 2019, https://www.newschannel5.com/news/newschannel-5-investigates/cade-cothren-resigns-as-house-speakers-chief-of-staff.

47. Joel Ebert, "Casada Tells Radio Station He's Not Resigning," *Tennessean*, May 8, 2019, https://www.newspapers.com/image/591308585; Natalie Allison, "Dems Calling on Casada to Step Down," *Tennessean*, May 8, 2019, https://www.newspapers.com/image/591308508.

48. Dave Boucher, "Butt's 'NAAWP' Comments Upset House Black Caucus," *Tennessean*, Feb. 27, 2015, https://www.newspapers.com/image/105335089.

49. Ebert, "White Noise Machines."

50. Phil Williams, "FBI Investigates Controversial Voucher Vote," WTVF-TV, NewsChannel 5, May 9, 2019, https://www.newschannel5.com/news/newschannel-5-investigates/fbi-investigates-controversial-voucher-vote.

51. Joel Ebert and Natalie Allison, "Legislative Culture Again in Spotlight," *Tennessean*, May 10, 2019, https://www.newspapers.com/image/591308713.

52. Natalie Allison, "Rep. Staples Facing Action after Violating Sexual Harassment Policy," *Tennessean*, April 11, 2019, https://www.newspapers.com/image/591300227; Joel Ebert and Natalie Allison, "Lawmaker Faces Allegations, Investigation of Sexual Misconduct," *Tennessean*, April 5, 2019, https://www.newspapers.com/image/591299973.

53. Natalie Allison, "What Gov. Lee Has Said So Far about Speaker Casada," *Tennessean*, May 10, 2019, https://www.newspapers.com/image/591308734; Natalie Allison, "Lt. Gov. McNally on Casada: 'If It Were Me . . . I'd Be Packing My Bags,'" *Tennessean*, May 10, 2019, https://www.newspapers.com/image/591308734; Natalie Allison, "Lee Comments on Scandal: If Casada Worked for Me, I'd Ask Him to Resign," *Tennessean*, May 11, 2019, https://www.newspapers.com/image/591309222; Natalie Allison, "McNally: Casada Should Vacate Office," *Tennessean*, May 11, 2019, https://www.newspapers.com/image/591309222.

54. Joel Ebert, "Inside Casada's Fall," *Tennessean*, May 28, 2019, https://www.newspapers.com/image/591317088.

55. Joel Ebert, "What the Audit Could Target," *Tennessean*, July 25, 2019, https://www.newspapers.com/image/587359860; Joel Ebert, "Who Paid for Party Fowl Visit?" *Tennessean*, May 16, 2019, https://www.newspapers.com/image/564303165.

56. Ebert and Allison, "Cothren Sex Texts Uncovered."

57. Ebert and Allison, "GOP Joins Ouster Chorus."

58. Natalie Allison, "Casada Supports Call for GOP Caucus Meeting," *Tennessean*, May 12, 2019, https://www.newspapers.com/image/591310639; Natalie Allison and Joel Ebert, "House Leadership under Scrutiny," *Tennessean*, May 12, 2019, https://www.newspapers.com/image/591310645.

59. Allison and Ebert, "House Leadership under Scrutiny."

60. Tom Humphrey, "Oops! Senate Raises Tax on Cigarette Packs by 80 Cents," *Knoxville News Sentinel*, June 2, 2007, https://www.newspapers.com/image/777066479; Tom Humphrey, "Sen. Norris Willing to Back Measure on Open Meetings," *Knoxville News Sentinel*, Jan. 10, 2013, https://www.newspapers.com/image/777355848.

61. Erik Schelzig, "Lawmakers Close Door for Meeting on Cuts," *Daily News Journal*, June 10, 2009, https://www.newspapers.com/image/291165093.

62. Joel Ebert and Natalie Allison, "Casada Loses Vote in GOP Caucus," *Tennessean*, May 21, 2019, https://www.newspapers.com/image/591312288.

63. Andy Sher, "Ethics Committee Member Mike Carter Calls on Tennessee House Speaker Casada to Resign amid Text Messaging Scandal," *Chattanooga Times Free Press*, May 16, 2019, https://www.timesfreepress.com/news/politics/state/story/2019/may/16/some-house-ethics-panel-balk-signing-draft-casada-legal-advisory-opinion/494833; Ebert and Allison, "Casada Loses Vote in GOP Caucus."

64. Ebert and Allison, "Casada Loses Vote in GOP Caucus"; Joel Ebert, "Inside Casada's Fall," *Tennessean*, May 28, 2019, https://www.newspapers.com/image/591317088; Joel Ebert and Natalie Allison, "Casada to Resign," *Tennessean*, May 22, 2019, https://www.newspapers.com/image/566591520.

65. Ebert and Allison, "Casada to Resign."

66. Joel Ebert, "Audit: Casada Failed to Report All Money," *Tennessean*, June 14, 2020, https://www.newspapers.com/image/667613662; "Durham a No-Show as Registry Turns Back Reduction of Record Penalty," *Tennessee Journal* 46, no 24 (June 12, 2020): 2.

67. "Embattled Casada Crashes Out of Williamson County Clerk's Race," *Tennessee Journal* 48, no 18 (May 6, 2022): 1.

## CHAPTER 7

1. Andy Sher, "FBI Searches Offices, Homes, of Tennessee Lawmakers, including Hixson Rep. Robin Smith," *Chattanooga Times Free Press*, Jan. 8, 2021, https://www.timesfreepress.com/news/local/story/2021/jan/08/fbi-searches-offices-homes-tennessee-lawmaker/539327.

2. Phil Williams, "FBI Executes Search Warrants on Former TN House Speaker Casada, Other Republicans," WTVF-TV, NewsChannel 5, Jan. 8, 2021, https://www.newschannel5.com/news/newschannel-5-investigates/fbi-executes-search-warrants-on-former-tn-house-speaker-casada-other-republicans.

3. "'Shhhhhhhhh': Ex-state GOP Chair Pleads Guilty to Kickback Plot," *Tennessee Journal* 48, no 10 (March 11, 2022): 1.

4. Andy Sher, "Republican Political Vendor Phoenix Solutions Worked in Bitter Tennessee Primary Battle Last Fall," *Chattanooga Times Free Press*, Feb. 27, 2021, https://www.timesfreepress.com/news/local/story/2021/feb/27/political-vendor-phoenix/542415.

5. Phil Williams, "Anonymous Campaign Attack Targets Republican Lawmaker," WTVF-TV, NewsChannel 5, July 14, 2020, https://www.newschannel5.com/news/newschannel-5-investigates/anonymous-campaign-attack-targets-republican-lawmaker; "Shadowy Campaign to Oust Tillis Presents Test Case for Registry," *Tennessee Journal* 46, no. 33 (Aug. 21, 2020): 1.

6. Natalie Allison, "Anonymous Tweets. A Peed-on Chair. Control of the Caucus Campaign Committee: The Latest House GOP Scuffle," *Tennessean*, Aug. 22, 2019, https://www.tennessean.com/story/news/politics/2019/08/22/

tennessee-house-gop-anonymous-twitter-account-pee-on-chair-andy-holt-rick-tillis-chbmole/2066321001.

7. Joel Ebert, "How Did $4 Million for Local Grants Make It into Tennessee's State Budget? Top Lawmakers Want Answers," *Tennessean*, Oct. 1, 2019.

8. Joel Ebert and Natalie Allison, "House Speaker Candidate's Christian Magic Supply Business Is Not Registered with the State," *Tennessean*, June 20, 2019, https://www.tennessean.com/story/news/politics/2019/06/20/matthew-hill-tennessee-house-speaker-christian-magic-supply-business-dock-haley-gospel-magic/1481310001.

9. "Tillis Saga Resonates as Capitol Crowd Awaits Details of FBI Raid," *Tennessee Journal* 47, no. 3 (Jan. 15, 2021): 1.

10. Schelzig, "Shadowy Campaign to Oust Tillis."

11. "Flight of the Phoenix: Campaign Cash Flows to Mystery Vendor," *Tennessee Journal* 47, no. 9 (Jan. 29, 2021): 1.

12. Andy Sher, "Tennessee Lawmakers in FBI Probe Spent Nearly $200,000 with New Campaign Vendors," *Chattanooga Times Free Press*, Jan. 23, 2021, https://www.timesfreepress.com/news/local/story/2021/jan/23/tennessee-lawmakers-fbi-probe/540253.

13. Sher, "Tennessee Lawmakers in FBI Probe."

14. "Campaign Finance Overhaul Posited under Specter of FBI Probe," *Tennessee Journal* 47, no. 7 (April 16, 2021): 1.

15. Erik Schelzig, "Ex-girlfriend Testifies Cothren Had Her Register PAC That Attacked Casada Foe Tillis," *TNJ: On the Hill*, Jan. 14, 2021, https://onthehill.tnjournal.net/ex-girlfriend-testifies-cothren-had-her-register-pac-that-attacked-casada-foe-tillis.

16. Erik Schelzig, "Casada Blasts Registry as 'Biased,' Ogles Threatens Legislative Action to Halt Subpoenas," *TNJ: On the Hill*, Jan. 21, 2022, https://onthehill.tnjournal.net/casada-blasts-Registry-as-biased-ogles-threatens-legislative-action-to-halt-subpoenas.

17. Erik Schelzig, "Registry Refers Casada, Cothren Probes to Williamson County Prosecutor," *TNJ: On the Hill*, March 17, 2022, https://onthehill.tnjournal.net/registry-refers-casada-cothren-probes-to-williamson-county-prosecutors.

18. "'Shhhhhhhhhh,'" *Tennessee Journal* 48, no 10 (March 11, 2022): 1.

19. Erik Schelzig, "Smith Strikes Plea Agreement with Feds," *TNJ: On the Hill*, March 7, 2022, https://onthehill.tnjournal.net/update-smith-strikes-plea-agreement-with-feds.

20. "Phoenix to the Ashes? Mystery Vendor Vanishes from Tennessee," *Tennessee Journal* 47, no. 29, (July 23, 2001): 1.

21. Schelzig, "Smith Strikes Plea."

22. Andy Sher, "Tennessee Legislative Leader Says He Was Targeted after Questioning Murky Vendor," *Chattanooga Times Free Press*, March 26, 2022, https://www.timesfreepress.com/news/local/story/2022/mar/26/grand-jury/565841.

23. "Feds Charge Former House Speaker, Aide with Bribery, Kickbacks," *Tennessee Journal* 48, no. 33 (Aug. 26, 2022): 1.

24. Adam Friedman, Melissa Brown, and Mariah Timms. "Three Legislative Informants Played Crucial Role in Casada, Cothren Arrests, Search Warrant Reveals," *Tennessean*, Aug. 29, 2022, https://www.tennessean.com/story/news/politics/2022/08/27/casada-cothren-search-warrant-feds-former-speakers-arrest-tennessee/7873047001.

25. Erik Schelzig, "'Make Sure No One Knows It's Me': Read the 20-Count Indictment of Former Speaker, Top Aide," *TNJ: On the Hill*, Aug. 23, 2022, https://onthehill.tnjournal.net/bribes-and-kickbacks-read-the-indictment-of-former-speaker-top-aide.

26. Schelzig, "Feds Charge Former House Speaker."

27. Adam Kleinheider, "Putting a Hogs Head in Bredesen's Front Yard," *Nashville Post*, May 21, 2008, https://www.nashvillepost.com/home/putting-a-hogs-head-in-bredesens-front-yard/article_6acc1979-a6bf-5468-b7d9-57ab629c6f0a.html; Lucas L. Johnson II and Associated Press, "Williams Critic Made Peace Offer for Chairmanship," *Jackson Sun*, Jan. 30, 2009, 2B, https://www.newspapers.com/image/284142130.

28. Michael Collins, "Congressman Says He Won't Run for Reelection," *Commercial Appeal*, Feb. 1, 2016, https://archive.commercialappeal.com/news/government/US-Rep-Fincher-says-he-wont-run-for-reelection-367249511.html.

29. Dave Boucher and Joel Ebert, "Private Club The Standard Has Food, Boxing and a PAC," *Tennessean*, April 3, 2017, https://www.newspapers.com/image/285431003.

30. Boucher and Ebert, "Private Club The Standard."

31. Boucher and Ebert, "Private Club The Standard."

32. Dave Boucher and Joel Ebert, "Expert: Money Trail Shows Possible Kelsey Violations," *Tennessean*, June 2, 2017, https://www.newspapers.com/image/307646923.

33. Dave Boucher and Joel Ebert, "Complaints: Kelsey, Others Broke Straw Donor Laws," *Tennessean*, June 22, 2017, https://www.newspapers.com/image/311561863.

34. Boucher and Ebert, "Complaints: Kelsey, Others."

35. Boucher and Ebert, "Complaints: Kelsey, Others."

36. Joel Ebert and Adam Tamburin, "Kelsey Faces Probe over Campaign Donations," *Tennessean*, Nov. 6, 2019, https://www.newspapers.com/image/619617593.

37. "Kelsey Indictment Features Familiar GOP Figures Durham, Miller," *Tennessee Journal* 47, no. 42 (Oct. 29, 2021): 1.

38. "Amanda Bunning Kelsey," Ingram Group, accessed on March 6, 2023, http://www.ingramgroup.com/amanda-bunning.

39. Schelzig, "Kelsey Indictment Features."

40. Schelzig, "Kelsey Indictment Features."

41. Brian Kelsey, "Debt, ISIS, Borders—I'm Your Congressman," *Jackson Sun*, July 13, 2016, https://www.newspapers.com/image/204800889.

42. "Notes & Quotes," *Tennessee Journal* 48, no. 1 (Jan. 7, 2022): 4.

43. Schelzig, "Kelsey Indictment Features."

44. Ebert and Boucher, "Jeremy Durham Kicked Out."

45. "From the Campaign Trail: Kelsey Successor." *Tennessee Journal* 48, no. 11 (March 18, 2022): 3.
46. "Feds: Contrition Key to Ex-Sen. Kelsey Avoiding Extra Prison Time," *Tennessee Journal* 48, no. 46 (Dec. 2, 2022): 1.
47. "The Kelsey Chronicles: Former Senator Tries to Pull About-Face on Guilty Plea in Federal Case," *Tennessee Journal* 49, no. 12 (March 24, 2023): 2.

**EPILOGUE**

1. "Convicted Sen. Robinson Laments 'Procedural Lynching' in GOP Ouster," *Tennessee Journal* 48, no 5 (Feb. 4, 2022): 2.
2. "Ketron Audits Reveal $241K Missing from Campaign and PAC Accounts," *Tennessee Journal* 46, no. 48 (Dec. 11, 2020): 3.

**APPENDIX**

1. United Press International, "2 Indicted in Interest Conflict," *Knoxville News Sentinel*, Aug. 14, 1970, https://www.newspapers.com/image/773775644; Associated Press, "Legislators Held Exempt from State Conflict Law," *Jackson Sun*, Oct. 6, 1970, https://www.newspapers.com/image/284268405; Larry Daughtrey, "High Court Won't Hear Elder Case," *Tennessean*, Oct. 19, 1971, https://www.newspapers.com/image/113154231.
2. "Sheriff, Legislator Trade Bribe Charges," *Kingsport Times*, May 10, 1979, https://www.newspapers.com/image/592940658; Gary Meyer, "Legislator Guilty of Bribe Attempt," *Kingsport Times*, Oct. 19, 1979, https://www.newspapers.com/image/595764651; Jeff Wilson, "House Chooses to Expel Fisher," *Jackson Sun*, Jan. 15, 1980, https://www.newspapers.com/image/282999010.
3. Associated Press, "Ford Resigns State Legislative Seat," *Jackson Sun*, Jan. 23, 1981, A5, https://www.newspapers.com/image/284346576.
4. Erik Schelzig and Associated Press, "Former Tenn. House Leader, Once Elected in Prison, Dies," *Memphis Daily News*, Sept. 18, 2009, https://www.memphisdailynews.com/news/2009/sep/18/former-tenn-house-leader-once-elected-in-prison-dies.
5. Duren Cheek and Larry Daughtrey, "Rep. Bell Accused of Harassment," *Tennessean*, June 21, 1995, https://www.newspapers.com/image/113186935; Rebecca Ferrar, "Lawmaker's Aide Probed in Missing Funds Case," *Knoxville News Sentinel*, Sept. 9, 1996, https://www.newspapers.com/image/775809763; "7 Seek Bell's Post," *Tennessean*, May 9, 1996, https://www.newspapers.com/image/113396923.
6. Associated Press, "Sen. Koella Listed 'Critical' Following Heart Surgery," *Leaf Chronicle*, Dec. 21, 1997, https://www.newspapers.com/image/467965239.
7. Associated Press, "Tennessee Legislator Charged with Exposure Kills Himself," *Commercial Appeal*, June 20, 2002, https://www.newspapers.com/image/774935953.

8. Tom Sharp and Associated Press, "Tenn. Lawmaker Faces Charges in Plot to Fake Passports," *Commercial Appeal*, Aug. 31, 2002, https://www.newspapers.com/image/775434243; "Indicted Lawmaker Loses," *Tennessean*, Nov. 6, 2002, https://www.newspapers.com/image/111927030; Rob Johnson, "Former State Lawmaker Gets 2-Year Prison Sentence," *Tennessean*, April 28, 2004, https://www.newspapers.com/image/244455497.

9. Tom Humphrey, "Can They Walk the Walk?" *Knoxville News Sentinel*, Jan. 11, 2006, https://www.newspapers.com/image/777038795.

10. Michael Cass, "Sen. Cooper Charged in Land Fraud," *Tennessean*, Aug. 23, 2006, https://www.newspapers.com/image/277522946; Associated Press, "Cooper Verdict: Not Guilty," *Daily News Journal*, June 9, 2007, https://www.newspapers.com/image/425426598; Jessica Fender, "State Sen. Cooper Fined for Campaign Fund Misuse," *Tennessean*, Nov. 15, 2007, https://www.newspapers.com/image/278557713.

11. Erik Schelzig and Associated Press, "Video Details Emotional Arrest," *Tennessean*, Sept. 13, 2007, B2, https://www.newspapers.com/image/278337977.

12. Erik Schelzig and Associated Press, "Affair Case Shakes Up Senate," *Tennessean*, July 23, 2009, https://www.newspapers.com/image/283406990; Erik Schelzig and Associated Press, "Tenn. State Senator Quits after Intern Affair," *Leaf Chronicle*, July 29, 2009, https://www.newspapers.com/image/294905975.

13. Richard Locker, "Veteran Legislator Indicted on Fraud, Tax Evasion Charges," *Commercial Appeal*, June 18, 2015, https://www.newspapers.com/image/777506657; Jamie Satterfield, "Ex-lawmaker Avoids Prison," *Knoxville News Sentinel*, Jan. 26, 2017, https://www.newspapers.com/image/778159956.

14. Clay Bailey, "State Rep Arrested after Removing Opponents' Signs," *Knoxville News Sentinel*, Aug. 3, 2016, https://www.newspapers.com/image/777805972; Clay Bailey, "Candidate Bails Out Rep Who Took Signs," *Knoxville News Sentinel*, Aug. 4, 2016, https://www.newspapers.com/image/777806770.

15. Alanna Autler, "3 Former Players Accuse Rep. David Byrd of Sexual Misconduct while They Were Teens," WSMV News, March 27, 2018, https://www.wsmv.com/news/3-former-players-accuse-rep-david-byrd-of-sexual-misconduct-while-they-were-teens/article_952160ab-da24-53bb-b5c6-3bf4e9d67591.html.

16. Natalie Allison, "Rep. Staples Facing Action after Violating Sexual Harassment Policy," *Tennessean*, April 11, 2019, https://www.newspapers.com/image/591300227; Joel Ebert and Natalie Allison, "Lawmaker Faces Allegations, Investigation of Sexual Misconduct," *Tennessean*, April 5, 2019, https://www.newspapers.com/image/591299973; Tyler Whetstone, "Rick Staples Slammed by State Election Board for Campaign Spending, Fined $26,640," *Knoxville News Sentinel*, Sept. 14, 2020, https://www.knoxnews.com/story/news/politics/2020/09/14/rick-staples-slammed-state-board-campaign-spending-fined-26-640/3471793001.

17. Erik Schelzig, "Democratic Rep. Torrey Harris Charged with Domestic Assault, Theft," *TNJ: On the Hill*, July 19, 2022, https://onthehill.tnjournal.net/democratic-rep-torrey-harris-charged-with-domestic-assault-theft.

18. Phil Williams, "Revealed: GOP Leader, Who Voted to Expel TN Three, Resigns; Found Guilty of Sexually Harassing Interns," WTVF-TV, NewsChannel 5, April 20, 2023, https://www.newschannel5.com/news/newschannel-5-investigates/ revealed/revealed-gop-leader-who-voted-to-expel-tennessee-three-found-guilty-of-sexually-harassing-interns.

# RESOURCES

**TENNESSEE PERIODICALS**

*Bristol Courier Herald*

*Chattanooga Daily Times*

*Chattanooga Times Free Press*

*Commercial Appeal* (Memphis)

*Daily Herald* (Columbia)

*Daily News Journal* (Murfreesboro)

*Jackson Sun*

*Johnson City Press*

*Johnson City Press-Chronicle*

*Journal and Tribune* (Knoxville)

*Kingsport Times*

*Knoxville Journal and Tribune*

*Knoxville News Sentinel*

*Leaf Chronicle* (Clarksville)

*Memphis Flyer*

*Memphis Press-Scimitar*

*Memphis: The City Magazine*

*Nashville Banner*

*Nashville Post*

*Tennessean* (Nashville)

*Times News* (Kingsport)

**A NOTE ON DOCUMENTS**

We have uploaded some of the documents we have used in our research, including the files we received in response to our Freedom of Information Act (FOIA) requests, to Scribd, at https://www.scribd.com/user/267295761/TNScandalsBook.

Printed in the USA
CPSIA information can be obtained
at www.ICGtesting.com
LVHW090326160923
758324LV00002B/212

9 780826 505859